Canadian Newspaper Ownership in the Era of Convergence
Rediscovering Social Responsibility

Canadian Newspaper Ownership in the Era of Convergence

Rediscovering Social Responsibility

Edited by Walter C. Soderlund and Kai Hildebrandt

The University of Alberta Press

Published by

The University of Alberta Press
Ring House 2
Edmonton, Alberta, Canada T6G 2E1

Library and Archives Canada Cataloguing in Publication

Canadian newspaper ownership in the era of convergence : rediscovering social responsibility / edited by Walter C. Soderlund and Kai Hildebrandt.

Includes bibliographical references and indexes.
ISBN 0-88864-439-6

1. Canadian newspapers—Ownership. 2. Press monopolies—Canada. 3. Newspaper publishing—Canada. 4. Social responsibility of business—Canada.
I. Soderlund, W. C. (Walter C.) II. Hildebrandt, Kai, 1946-

PN4914.O9C35 2005 071'.1
C2005-902030-X

Printed and bound in Canada by
Houghton Boston Printers, Saskatoon, Saskatchewan
First edition, first printing, 2005

Copyediting and Indexing by Brenda Belokrinicev

The University of Alberta Press is committed to protecting our natural environment. As part of our efforts, this book is printed on New Leaf paper: it contains 100% post-consumer recycled fibres and is acid- and chlorine-free.

The University of Alberta Press gratefully acknowledges the support received for its publishing program from The Canada Council for the Arts. The University of Alberta Press also gratefully acknowledges the financial support of the Government of Canada through the Book Publishing Industry Development Program (BPIDP) and from the Alberta Foundation for the Arts for its publishing activities.

Canada Council for the Arts | Conseil des Arts du Canada

Canadä

We gratefully dedicate the book to our families:
Nanci, David and Sheri, Eric and Joanna
SWH, Saskia, and Katia

Contents

List of Tables ix

Contributors xi

Preface xiii

Introduction **The Relationship between the Press and Democratic Politics | 1**
Walter C. Soderlund and Kai Hildebrandt

One **Failed Attempts at Regulation of Newspaper Ownership | 11**
The Davey Committee and the Kent Royal Commission
Walter C. Soderlund and Walter I. Romanow

PART ONE
Chain Ownership: Conrad Black and Hollinger

Two **Chain Ownership | 31**
Review and Analysis of Empirical Studies
Walter C. Soderlund and Kai Hildebrandt

Three **The Impact of Conrad Black's Ownership on Thomson, Armadale, and Southam Newspapers | 45**
Kai Hildebrandt and Walter C. Soderlund

Four **An Assessment of Conrad Black's Ownership | 75**
Walter C. Soderlund and Kai Hildebrandt

PART TWO
Convergence: The Aspers and CanWest Global

Five **Media Convergence and CanWest Global | 89**
Kai Hildebrandt, Walter C. Soderlund, and Walter I. Romanow

Six **CanWest Global's National Editorial Policy | 109**
Round One
Walter C. Soderlund, Ronald H. Wagenberg, and Walter I. Romanow

Seven **The Firing of Russell Mills, Round Two of National Editorials, and the CanWest News Service Initiative | 125**
Walter C. Soderlund and Walter I. Romanow

Conclusion **Ownership Rights Vs. Social Responsibility | 137**
Defining an Appropriate Role for Newspaper Owners
Walter C. Soderlund, Ronald H. Wagenberg, Kai Hildebrandt, and Walter I. Romanow

Notes | 151

Reference List | 167

Name Index | 183

Subject Index | 187

List of Tables

TABLE 1.1 Canadian average daily newspaper ownership as a percentage of total circulation (1994–2004) | 14

TABLE 1.2 Canadian daily newspapers, by ownership and circulation (2004) | 15

TABLE 3.1 Percent of local content, by ownership, pre- and post-acquisition | 50

TABLE 3.2 Percent of content written by local staff, by ownership, pre- and post-acquisition | 53

TABLE 3.3 Focus of content, by ownership, pre- and post-acquisition | 54

TABLE 3.4 Coverage and evaluation of free trade, by ownership, pre- and post-acquisition | 56

TABLE 3.5 Coverage and evaluation of business, by ownership, pre- and post-acquisition | 59

TABLE 3.6 Coverage and evaluation of unions, by ownership, pre- and post-acquisition | 60

TABLE 3.7A(i) Coverage and evaluation of federal political parties, by ownership, pre- and post-acquisition (ex-Thomson papers and control paper) | 62

TABLE 3.7A(ii) Coverage and evaluation of federal political parties, by ownership, pre- and post-acquisition (ex-Armadale papers and control paper) | 64

TABLE 3.7A(iii) Coverage and evaluation of federal political parties, by ownership, pre- and post-acquisition (ex-Southam and control papers) | 65

TABLE 3.7B(i) Coverage and evaluation of provincial political parties, by ownership, pre- and post-acquisition (ex-Thomson papers and control paper) | 67

TABLE 3.7B(ii) Coverage and evaluation of provincial political parties, by ownership, pre- and post-acquisition (ex-Armadale papers and control paper) | 68

TABLE 3.7B(iii) Coverage and evaluation of provincial political parties, by ownership, pre- and post-acquisition (ex-Southam papers and control papers) | 69

TABLE 3.7C Coverage of all political parties combined (federal and provincial), by ownership, pre- and post-acquisition | 70

TABLE 3.8 Left/right orientations of content, by ownership, pre- and post-acquisition | 71

TABLE 5.1 Sources consulted by Canadians for news, 1998 and 2002 | 95

TABLE 5.2 Cross-media ownership in Canada, by corporation | 97

TABLE 5.3 Market share and cross-ownership in nine local markets, 2002 | 98

Contributors

Kai Hildebrandt (PhD, University of Michigan, 1990) is Associate Professor of Communication Studies and Associate Dean in the Faculty of Arts and Social Sciences at the University of Windsor. He co-authored *Germany in Transition* (1981) and co-edited *Television Advertising in Canadian Elections* (1999). An expert in the use of quantitative and qualitative research methods, he recently completed a comparative study of legal education focused on issues of access to, and the success of, legal education. With Walter Soderlund, he is currently working on a project assessing the role of mass media in facilitating international intervention in third world crises.

Walter I. Romanow (PhD, Wayne State University, 1974) is Professor Emeritus in the Department of Communication Studies at the University of Windsor, the department he founded in 1968. He also served as Dean of the Faculty of Social Science and Dean of Students at the University of Windsor. He is the co-author of *Media Canada* (1992/1996) and co-editor of *Television Advertising in Canadian Elections* (1999). In 1990, he headed a research team that investigated negative political advertising in Canadian elections for the Royal Commission on Electoral Reform and Party Financing. The study appears in *Political Ethics: A Canadian Perspective* (1991), Vol. 12 of Research Reports done for the Royal Commission.

Walter C. Soderlund (PhD, University of Michigan, 1970) is Professor Emeritus in the Department of Political Science at the University of Windsor. Following his retirement in 2002, he served for a year as Acting Director of the University's newly created Centre for Social Justice and is currently Director of the Assumption University Centre for Religion and Culture. He is the author of *Media Definitions of Cold War Reality* (2001) and *Mass Media and Foreign Policy* (2003), as well as the co-editor of *Television Advertising in Canadian Elections* (1999) and *Profiles of Canada* (2003). In addition to research on mass media in Canada, he has an interest in international communication where his focus has been on the Caribbean, especially the manner in which events in Cuba and Haiti have been portrayed in North American media.

Ronald H. Wagenberg (PhD, London School of Economics, 1966) is Professor Emeritus in the Department of Political Science at the University of Windsor, where he taught for thirty-three years until his retirement in 1997. He is co-author of *Canadian Confederation* (1979) and co-editor of *Introductory Readings in Canadian Government and Politics* (1991) and *Leaders and Leadership in Canada* (1994). His introductory text on Canadian politics, *Introduction to Canadian Government and Politics*, co-written with Walter White and Ralph Nelson, was published in seven editions between 1972 and 1998 and has been translated for use in Japan and China. In addition to academics he enjoyed a political career, serving as an alderman in the City of Windsor from 1974 to 1982.

Beginning in the early 1970s and continuing into the 1980s, the effects of concentration of ownership among Canadian newspapers were examined in a number of studies by what at the time was referred to as the Windsor Group. The group was an informal association of scholars, the most regular participants being Walter I. Romanow (in Communications Studies), and Ronald H. Wagenberg, E. Donald Briggs, and Walter C. Soderlund (all in Political Science). Their work was presented in meetings of the Canadian Communication Association and the Canadian Political Science Association.

Through studies of newspaper coverage of the 1972 Canadian federal election (Wagenberg and Soderlund, 1975), the 1974 election (Wagenberg and Soderlund, 1976), the 1979 and 1980 elections (Soderlund, Romanow, Wagenberg, and Briggs, 1984), and the 1984 election (Wagenberg, Soderlund, Romanow, and Briggs, 1988), this group established how mass media functioned in the Canadian electoral process and demonstrated that, in the overall mix of factors contributing to campaign coverage, newspaper ownership was not a powerful influence.

At the same time, Romanow and Soderlund approached the question of the impact of chain ownership from a different perspective, through before and after studies of the content of individual newspapers, focusing on the point in time when each newspaper was acquired by chain owners. Research on changes in *The Windsor Star,* acquired by the Southam chain in 1971 (Romanow and Soderlund, 1978), and in *The Globe and Mail,* acquired by the Thomson chain in 1980 (Romanow and Soderlund, 1988), revealed that content changes did indeed accompany change of ownership; however, whether these changes were judged to be positive or negative depended in large part on individual value preferences. The question of the impact of media ownership was also a major focus of *Media Canada: An Introductory Analysis* (1992/1996), a text written by Romanow and Soderlund, from which Chapter 1 of this book draws heavily. In that all of the original group of researchers have reached the age of retirement and have begun the great sabbatical, this volume is no doubt their final contribution to the debate on the impact of ownership concentration on the health of Canadian democracy.

The introductory chapter of this book examines the question of the appropriate balance between the rights of media owners to control their property and the rights of society to have reasonable access to, and control over, its system of mass communication. It presents two seminal contributions to the debate: the *Report of the Commission on Freedom of the Press* (1947), prepared in the United States, and the widely influential book *Four Theories of the Press* (Siebert, Peterson, and Schramm, 1956), which formalized the concept of *social responsibility* introduced in the earlier commission report.

Chapter 1 reviews the history of the problem of concentration of media ownership in Canada, and efforts to deal with that problem, through an examination of two major investigations: the Davey Committee's *Special Senate Committee on Mass Media* (Canada, 1970), and the 1981 Kent Commission's report, the *Royal Commission on Newspapers* (Canada, 1981).

The *Interim Report on the Canadian News Media*, prepared by the Standing Senate Committee on Transport and Communication in 2004, points out that since these seminal studies were published "the world has changed in ways that almost no one could predict in 1970 or even 1981, and few elements of western society have been more profoundly affected by change than the news business" (Canada, 2004, p. 2).

To examine these changes, two case studies are used, and they comprise the core of this book. The first case study deals with the ongoing issue of *ownership concentration*, in the form of traditional newspaper chains, while the second addresses the immediate consequences of the newer concept of *convergence*, which intensifies conventional concentration by consolidating different types of media under one corporate owner.

The study of the impact of Hollinger ownership[1] under the control of Conrad Black (Lord Black of Crossharbour since October 2001), focuses attention on the high-water mark in conventional ownership concentration: by midsummer of 1996, a single corporate owner controlled over half of the daily newspapers in Canada. Indeed in the mid-1990s, when the extent of Mr. Black's ownership aspirations became apparent, a groundswell of concern and criticism was heard across the nation. The extent of Hollinger influence is addressed through the before and after research strategy used by Romanow and Soderlund in their earlier studies of *The Windsor Star* and *The Globe and Mail*.

When, in the summer of 2000, Mr. Black sold the bulk of his Canadian newspaper holdings to CanWest Global Communications—controlled by the Asper family, who were already the owners of a major television network—the issue of convergence (previously known as *cross-media ownership*) entered the Canadian media scene in a significant way. Convergence involving the ownership of television *and* newspaper holdings was a strategy also pursued in 2000 by both Bell Canada Enterprises (BCE) and Quebecor, with business success to date judged to be mixed at best.

In Chapter 5, beginning with a discussion of the motivations underlying, as well as the economic consequences associated with, convergence strategies, the CanWest Global case study focuses on three controversial policy initiatives implemented by the Aspers in the years immediately following their entry into the newspaper industry: the "national editorial/no contradiction policy" introduced in late 2001; the firing of Russell Mills, publisher of *The Ottawa Citizen*, in June 2002 over an editorial calling for the resignation of the prime minister; and the implications arising from the establishment of a new Winnipeg-based CanWest News Service in early 2003.

The past half-century has clearly established the overwhelming importance of mass media ownership in the process of democratic governance, so compellingly identified in 1947 by the Commission on Freedom of the Press. And, as we are reminded by Robert Hackett and Yuezhi Zhao writing fifty years later, while the concept of freedom of the press may have had its historical origins in "freedom from government censorship," over time its meaning has been expanded to include "freedom from undue influence by hidden interests or by excessive concentrations of private power" (1998, p. 2).

Studies investigating concepts such as gatekeeping (White, 1950), agenda setting (McCombs and Shaw, 1972), parameter setting (Stairs, 1977–78), priming (Iyengar and Kinder, 1987; Mendelsohn, 1994), indexing (Bennett, 1990), and framing (Entman, 1993; Iorio and Huxman, 1996; Iyengar, 1991) have done much to elaborate on the various ways in which mass media influence politics. Taken as a whole, these studies point to the pervasive impact of mass media on democratic practices.

Radio and television, cable and satellite distribution, and the Internet are obviously important, perhaps dominant, political media of the twenty-first century. However, with these media the principle of government regulation has long been established and the current debate is centred not on *whether* they should be regulated but to what extent, for what purposes, and how such regulation should be accomplished. Furthermore, as Romanow and Soderlund have argued, government regulation of electronic media was premised on a concept of societal benefit. Government regulations served as the bulwark of a defensive strategy to protect Canadian culture from pressures arising primarily from the popularity of U.S. television programming (see 1996, chaps. 7, 10).

The Canadian Radio-television and Telecommunications Commission (CRTC) exists to address questions of criteria and performance standards for those holding broadcast licences. In the late 1980s, the Progressive Conservative government of Brian Mulroney tied the Canadian economy to the American economic engine, first under the *Free Trade Agreement* (FTA, 1988) and later under the *North American Free Trade Agreement* (NAFTA, 1994). The Liberal government of Jean Chrétien, elected in 1993, did not challenge this strategy in any fundamental way. Until the Mulroney government's changes, the CRTC had administered a web of regulations designed to ensure that content, as well as ownership, of Canadian broadcast media remained Canadian. Media were granted an exemption from the free trade rules of NAFTA on grounds of cultural protection but, under constant pressure from the United States as well as pressure from Canadian media conglomerates arguing the need for growth to compete with the American media giants (Jack, 2003; Tuck, 2003), the CRTC's regulatory resolve steadily eroded during the 1990s with respect to cross-media ownership. As Hackett and Zhao have argued, "consolidation of media power has been abetted by general governmental retreat from even nominal efforts to regulate media behemoths in the public interest" (1998, p. 4). This, however, is the subject for a different book.

The case of newspapers is different. As Chris Dornan notes, "none of this applies to the newspaper industry. Like the domestic advertising industry on which they depend, ...newspapers are not licensed by the state nor do they solicit state support" (1996, p. 62). Consequently, until now, newspapers have largely escaped government regulation except for controls over foreign ownership through the *Income Tax Act*, which set a 25% limit for advertising claimed against taxes. Moreover, since 1982, the *Charter of Rights and Freedoms* constitutionally enshrines "freedom of thought, belief, opinion and expression including freedom of the press and other media of communication," making any form of government intervention far more difficult than it had been. Thus the debate over government regulation of newspapers involves a new set of factors, and the concerns reflected in this debate interest us here. While perhaps not the dominant force they once were, newspapers do tend to drive the agendas of other media, especially of television news (see Canada, 2004; Fletcher, 1981), and continue to be important sources of information for political and business elites—if not in the traditional hard copy format, increasingly through on-line editions designed to meet readers' varying needs.

The book ends with our reflections on how the country might deal, in terms of realistic public policy responses, with the problems of ownership concentration in the newspaper industry, problems which at the beginning of the twenty-first century are significantly intensified by strategies of multimedia convergence. The suggestions we offer are based not only on an appraisal of the values underlying Canada's democratic society, but also on an understanding, gained from over three decades of empirical research, of the role of mass media in that society combined with an appreciation of the art of the possible with respect to balancing the economic rights of ownership against the informational needs of a democratic society.

In preparing this book, we have many institutions and persons to thank, some for recent help and some for contributions that go back decades.

Unfortunately, some deserving of mention may be inadvertently omitted, but we would like to specifically acknowledge the following for their assistance over the years: the University of Windsor, first for employing us and second for providing a long-term atmosphere conducive to research; the Social Sciences and Humanities Research Council, for grants that enabled us to carry out and publish studies of media coverage of the 1979 election (Soderlund, Romanow, Briggs, and Wagenberg, 1984), of political advertising in the 1993 election (Romanow, de Repentigny, Cunningham, Soderlund, and Hildebrandt, 1999), and of the impact of Conrad Black's ownership beginning in 1996; as well as the publishers of these books—Holt Rinehart and Winston; Wilfrid Laurier University Press; and the University of Alberta Press, the publisher of this volume. Editors along the way to whom we owe thanks include Anthony Luengo, Brian Henderson, Jeff Miller, Sandra Wollfrey, and Michael Luski, as well as Brenda Belokrinicev, who helped us on this project.

Fred Fletcher and Arthur Siegel at York University, and Peter Desbarat and the late Andrew Osler at the University of Western Ontario, provided both support and constructive criticism of our work over many years, as did colleagues at the University of Windsor: Hugh Edmunds, Stuart Surlin, Tom Carney, Stanley Cunningham, Stuart Selby, Lawrence LeDuc, Robert Krause, and Richard Price. Special thanks go to Don Briggs, our collaborator on the study of the 1979, 1980, and 1984 elections, as well as to students Karen Spierkel and Alex Gill, who contributed far more to our work than one could reasonably expect. Barry Cooper and Chris Dornan offered valuable comments on this manuscript, as did Kenneth Goldstein. We would also like to express our appreciation to the media executives who consented to be interviewed by us in 2002, and whose views on a number of issues, ranging from Conrad Black's ownership style to convergence to the Aspers' national editorial policy, are reported in Chapters 4, 5, and 7 of the book.

Since the report of the Davey Committee in 1970, much has been written regarding concentration of media ownership in Canada. Over thirty years ago, Senator Keith Davey asked whether freedom of the press is "enhanced or diminished by corporate control of news" (Canada, 1970, p. 8). Perhaps the only thing we can say without fear of contradiction is that the question is still with us. For example, in the keynote address given at the February 2003 conference *Who Controls Canada's Media?* sponsored by the McGill Institute for the Study of Canada, Governor General Adrienne Clarkson pointed to the confusion over media ownership that is created by the failure to distinguish between the economic and legal side of concentration and "its cultural and political aspects" (Clarkson, 2003). While recognizing the validity of this distinction, we must point out that the two are not unrelated. In the age of convergence more than ever before, policies leading to the melding of newspaper and television newsrooms to create economies of scale have a direct effect, not only on the number of interpretations available for a particular story, but on what news gets reported, as well as on how that news is reported (Canada, 2004). Plainly, given the added implications of convergence strategies to the health of Canada's democratic governance, we believe that arriving at an answer to Senator Davey's question is even more important today than it was when he first posed it.

Walter C. Soderlund
Kai Hildebrandt
Windsor, Ontario
December 2004

Introduction

The Relationship Between the Press and Democratic Politics

Walter C. Soderlund and Kai Hildebrandt

In the mid-1950s at the height of the cold war, Fred Siebert, Theodore Peterson, and Wilbur Schramm published their highly influential book *Four Theories of the Press,* which outlined the operating principles of what they felt were four distinct mass media systems. These they identified as *authoritarian, Soviet Communist, libertarian,* and *social responsibility.* The thread connecting what were essentially four separately written essays was the concept "that the press always takes on the form and colouration of the social and political structures within which it operates. Especially, it reflects the system of social control whereby the relations of individuals and institutions are adjusted" (1956, pp. 1–2).

Arguing that the Soviet Communist system was essentially an offshoot of the older authoritarian tradition and that social responsibility was derived from the libertarian tradition, the authors maintained that there are basically two fundamental operating principles underlying media systems. The first, the authoritarian tradition, is based on the principle of top-down rule, whereby

> truth was conceived to be, not the product of the great mass of people, but of a few wise men who were in a position to guide and direct their fellows. Thus truth was thought to be centered near the center of power. (Siebert, Peterson, and Schramm, 1956, p. 2)

The consequence for mass media was that "publishing was…a sort of agreement between power source and publisher, in which the former granted a monopoly right and the latter gave support" (1956, p. 3); in effect a system existed wherein rulers informed the public and the press functioned as a handmaiden of the state.

The second, the libertarian tradition, reverses the relative emphasis of state and society just described:

> Man is no longer conceived as a dependent being to be led and directed, but rather as a rational being able to discern between truth and falsehood, between a better and worse alternative, when faced with conflicting evidence and alternative choices. Truth is no longer conceived of as the property of power. Rather, the right to search for truth is one of the inalienable

> natural rights of man. And, where does the press fit into the scheme? The press is conceived of as *a partner in the search for truth*. (Siebert, Peterson, and Schramm, 1956, p. 3; italics in original)

While much of the discussion in *Four Theories of the Press* focuses on differences between the Soviet Communist model and its democratic alternatives, of particular interest here is the discussion of differences within what are essentially two democratic models. These are the classic libertarian approach and the new concept of social responsibility, premised on the realities emerging from the twentieth-century communications revolution and the perceived failures of the older tradition to deal with these.

> The power and near monopoly positions of the media impose [on owners and managers] an obligation to be socially responsible, to see that all sides are fairly presented and that the public has enough information to decide; and that if the media do not take on themselves such responsibility it may be necessary for some other agency of the public to enforce it. (Siebert, Peterson, and Schramm, 1956, p. 5)

While acknowledging that the concept had earlier roots, Theodore Peterson, author of the *Four Theories* chapter dealing with social responsibility theory, relied heavily on the 1947 report of the Commission on Freedom of the Press (often referred to as the Hutchins Commission after its Chairman, University of Chicago President Robert M. Hutchins). This commission, privately funded by Henry Luce's Time Inc. and Encyclopaedia Britannica Inc., began its work in 1942. The commission defined as its mandate "to study the role of agencies of mass communication [radio, newspapers, motion pictures, magazines, and books] in the education of the people in public affairs" (Commission on Freedom of the Press, 1947, p. vi).

Ross Eaman has pointed out that Mr. Luce "wanted the commissioners to make a statement about the dangers of governmental news management to freedom of the press" (Eaman, 1987, p. 83). Instead, what the commission's corporate sponsors received for their money ($215,000) was a report dealing "with the responsibilities of the owners and managers of the press to their consciences and the common good for the formation of public opinion" (Commission on Freedom of the Press, 1947, p. vi). The sponsors' money was well spent, however, as for their investment they received a consummate exploration into the nature of a free press and the problems facing it in a society undergoing revolutionary changes with respect to mass media—an analysis that continues to have significance well over a half-century after it was written. The commission's conclusion was that the nature of the society within which media functioned, one that had supported libertarian theory, had fundamentally changed. As a consequence, media owners needed to adopt a *social responsibility* framework as the motivating concept for their behaviour. This change would come about, the commission hoped, because of the owners' self-interest and public pressure; if not, the change would have to be imposed, reluctantly, by government.

Even before the popularization of television, the commission understood the profound impact mass communication was having on modern society: "The Commission is aware that the agencies of mass communication are only one of the influences forming American culture and American public opinion. They are, taken together, however, probably the most powerful single influence today" (Commission on Freedom of the Press, 1947, p. vii). The commission also perceived that "people make decisions in large part in terms of favorable and unfavorable images. They relate fact and opinion to stereotypes " (1947, p. 26). This led the commission to conclude that "the tremendous influence of the modern press makes it imperative that the great agencies of mass communication show hospitality to ideas which their owners do not share. Otherwise, these ideas will not have a fair chance" (1947, p. viii). The commission related the dangers facing freedom of the press to three principal factors:

> First, the importance of the press to the people has greatly increased with the development of the press as an instrument of mass communication. At the same time [this development] has greatly decreased the proportion of the people who can express their opinions and ideas through the press.
>
> Second, the few who are able to use the machinery of the press as an instrument of mass communication have not provided a service adequate to the needs of the society.
>
> Third, those who direct the machinery of the press have engaged from time to time in practices which the society condemns and which, if continued, it will inevitably undertake to regulate or control. (1947, p. 1)

It is superfluous to point out that, with respect to Canadian mass media, these words could have been written yesterday.

The commission was well aware of the conflicts between the imperatives of a modern communication system, which on the one hand demand the concentration of economic resources and power to provide adequate services and on the other must serve the needs of a free democratic society for open channels of communication. In the resolution of these conflicts, the commission unerringly sided with the needs of society:

> Freedom of the press is essential to political liberty. Where men cannot freely convey their thoughts to one another, no freedom is secure.... [Civilized society] must guarantee freedom of expression, to the end that all adventitious hindrances to the flow of ideas shall be removed. (1947, p. 6)

The commission also pointed to the dangers inherent in the chief concern giving rise to this book: the trend toward concentration of media ownership was already apparent in the mid-twentieth century. The consequences of ownership concentration were seen to be limiting "the variety of sources of news and opinion" (Commission on Freedom of the Press, 1947, p. 17), as "the owners and managers of the press determine which persons, which facts, which versions of the facts, and which ideas reach the public" (1947, p. 16). Clearly, the commission concluded, a media system totally in the control of owners and managers was inadequate to meet the needs of a modern society.

Government regulation was not, however, the commission's preferred solution to this dilemma. The commission was well aware of the reality (much more apparent now than it had been in the mid-1940s) that abuses of power through attempts to control the press were not limited to authoritarian governments:

> Any power capable of protecting freedom is also capable of endangering it. Every modern government, liberal or otherwise, has a specific position in the field of ideas; its stability is vulnerable to critics in proportion to their ability and persuasiveness. A government resting on popular suffrage is no exception to this rule. It also may be tempted—just because public opinion is a factor in official livelihood—to manage the ideas and images entering public debate. (1947, pp. 8–9)

The solution to this problem offered by the commission has come to be known as the social responsibility theory of the press.[1] Social responsibility theory adds to the rights inherent in media ownership under a libertarian system a concomitant set of duties or responsibilities, as well as the notion of media being held accountable to society. The principles of social responsibility are perhaps most clearly stated in the following passage from the report: "Freedom of the press can remain a right of those who publish only if it incorporates into itself the right of the citizen and the public interest" (Commission on Freedom of the Press, 1947, p. 18).

On this point, Theodore Peterson explained the ways in which social responsibility theory differed from the libertarian tradition from which it evolved:

> [According to social responsibility theory] freedom of expression is a moral right with an aspect of duty about it.... The theory thus differs from libertarian theory on the nature of the right. For under libertarian theory, freedom of expression was a natural right, a right which man was born with, a right which no one could take away, although its exercise might temporarily be prevented. No duty was attached to the right.... It was justified because free speech and a free press would promote the victory of truth over falsehood in the market place of ideas.
>
> Under social responsibility theory, freedom of expression is grounded on the duty of the individual to his thought, to his conscience. It is a moral right.... It has a value both for the individual and for the society.... It is society's sole source of intelligence, the seeds from which progress springs. (Siebert, Peterson, and Schramm,1956, p. 96)

Peterson also points out that social responsibility theory differs from its libertarian antecedent not only in its views regarding a changing and increasingly complex society, but also in changing perceptions of the rationality of man's behaviour:

> Under traditional theory, man was regarded as primarily a moral and rational being who was inclined to hunt for truth and to be guided by it.... There was no need to remind publishers of their public responsibilities; they would assume them without exhortation because of the moral sense which gave them their dignity. Nor need one worry about the occasional publisher who, because of human frailty, lied or distorted. Other publishers would find it profitable to expose him. His lies and distortions would be recognized, for the public would put his utterances to the powerful test of reason....
>
> [Social responsibility theory] does not deny the rationality of man, although it puts far less confidence in it than libertarian theory, but it does seem to deny that man is innately motivated to search for truth and to accept it as his guide. Under the social responsibility theory, man is viewed not so much irrational as lethargic. He is capable of using his reason, but he is loath to do so. Consequently, he is easy prey for demagogues, advertising pitchmen, and others who would manipulate him for their selfish ends. (Siebert, Peterson, and Schramm, 1956, p. 100)

The combination of societal changes and a narrowing media ownership base (the commission spoke in terms of "media empires"), along with a sense of pessimism regarding man's dedication to searching out the truth, placed in jeopardy two major tenets of libertarian theory: the "free market place of ideas" and the societal "self-righting" principle. With these called into question, the commission challenged media owners and managers to adopt a posture of social responsibility. The theory was formally outlined by Peterson as follows:

> Freedom carries concomitant obligations; and the press, which enjoys a privileged position under our government, is obliged to be responsible to society for carrying out certain essential functions of mass communication in contemporary society. To the extent that the press recognizes its responsibilities and makes them the basis of operational policies, the libertarian system will satisfy the needs of society. To the extent that the press does not assume its responsibilities, some other agency must see that the essential functions of mass communication are carried out. (Siebert, Peterson, and Schramm, 1956, p. 74)

Four Theories of the Press not only gave form and substance to the theory of social responsibility, the fundamental notion of congruence between media and political systems that it introduced has led to the formulation of other types of media systems. In most cases, the original four presented have survived (with some alteration and renaming), and these have been augmented by discussions of "developmental" and "revolutionary" media systems as well (see Hatchen, 1992; Lowenstein and Merrill, 1990; Mowlana, 1986; Romanow and Soderlund, 1996). It is, however, the book's contribution to social responsibility theory that we will pursue here.

Two scholars, John Merrill and Robert Picard, have gone furthest in exploring the consequences of social responsibility. Merrill's work is critical of the concept because he sees it as opening the door to government control of the press. Picard is also critical of the new approach, but on the grounds that it does not go far enough in encouraging government intervention.

It is safe to say John Merrill is an uncompromising individualist and libertarian. In the introduction to *The Imperative of Freedom* (1974), Merrill states the theme of his book clearly and unequivocally:

> American journalism is becoming so institutionalized and professionalized and so immured with the nascent concept of "social responsibility," that it is voluntarily giving up the sacred tenet of libertarianism—"editorial self determinism"—and is in grave danger of becoming one vast, gray, bland, monotonous, conformist spokesman for some collectivity of society. (1974, p. 3)

> [American journalists] are escaping from freedom and self-responsibility into the comfortable sanctuary of social ethics and fuzzy altruism. [They,]

> like most journalists in the Western world, while still chanting the tenets of libertarianism, are marching into an authoritarian sunset under the banners of "social responsibility." (1974, p. 4)

While critical of social responsibility theory on a number of philosophical grounds, Merrill is skeptical of claims that it will not inevitably lead to government regulation, and hence to creeping authoritarianism. His argument is an interesting one:

> [Under social responsibility theory,] with one voice, the press of the nation would be responsible to its society; and the definition of "responsible" would be functional in a monolithic way—defined and carried out by government or by some non-journalistic power.
>
> Many persons will object to this line of analysis and will say that "social responsibility" of the press of a nation does not necessarily imply government control. I contend that it does, since if left to be defined by various publishers or journalistic groups the term is quite relative and nebulous; and it is quite obvious that in the traditional context of American libertarianism no "solution" that would be widely agreed upon or practiced could ever be reached by non-governmental groups or individuals.
>
> The only way a "theory" of social responsibility could have any significance in any country is for the governmental power elite to be definer and enforcer of this type of press. (1974, pp. 91–92)

Merrill concludes his argument by pointing out that, in the final analysis, the notion of social responsibility of the press is relative to the values of the society within which it functions. This leads to the following anomaly:

> A capitalist press, operating in a pluralist and autonomous context, would be diametrically opposite to what the Soviets consider a socially responsible press. It would be to the Soviets the most irresponsible press system imaginable, since "social responsibility" is roughly synonymous in Marxist theory to "party/government support." The Communist press *is* government, *is* reflective of the society, *is* an instrument for social harmony, conformity and support. As such it is "socially responsible." (1974, p. 92; italics in original)

For Merrill, for a press to be free, such freedom has to be based on autonomy, not on regulation:

> All press systems can claim to be responsible to their societies, but the idea of autonomous media injecting a variety of opinions and ideas into the

> social fabric is one which only the libertarian system can reasonably claim. Libertarianism, or press autonomy, then, if it is to be considered as a separate theory must embrace the right of, or at least the possibility for, some press units to deviate from others to the degree that they will be considered "irresponsible." When the term and concept of "irresponsible journalism" disappears...or even comes close to disappearing—then will be the time when journalistic freedom and autonomy are dead. (1974, p. 95)

In his book *The Press and the Decline of Democracy* (1985), Robert Picard views the problems facing journalism quite differently and argues for a radically different solution—that of greater government intervention. As Merrill does, Picard states his position early in the book; it is reminiscent of concerns voiced by the Hutchins Commission:

> This study accepts the premise that democracy has declined in the Western democratic world in recent decades because public participation in originating policy proposals and deciding public policy has been eroded. This erosion has occurred because of the growth of bureaucracy and technocracy in the decision-making apparatuses and because of increasing elite control and manipulation of the vehicles of public opinion and political expression. (Picard, 1985, p. 5)

Picard appears to agree with Merrill on the importance of preserving the liberties of individual citizens: "The instruments through which true democracy is made possible are those rights and privileges that protect individual liberty and individuals' ability to seek self-realization" (1985, p. 11). However, Picard goes on to bring the common good of society into the equation: "The goal of democracies should be to alleviate all encroachments on individual rights *that are not necessary for the greater societal good*" (1985, p. 12; italics added).

It is on this point that Picard and Merrill part company. Picard feels that the role of the press as provider of information in the libertarian market is fundamentally changed by the growth of advertising as the financial base of newspaper profitability: "The needs of the mass audience in democracies were submerged..., and the marketplace of ideas no longer functioned by allowing the public to make considered judgments about the worth of ideas" (1985, p. 14). It also "created a situation in which monopolization and concentration of ownership was inevitable," leading to a reduction in the number of viewpoints reaching society (1985, p. 15). For Picard, "because the number of newspapers has declined to the point where the individual cannot easily receive diverse views and opinions, and thus cannot easily be an informed, active participant in democratic society," government intervention had become necessary (1985, p. 17).

As a solution to the problem, Picard offered an additional theory to those presented in *Four Theories of the Press,* that of a *democratic socialist* model of press behaviour. Democratic socialist theory, unlike the libertarian and social responsibility models, is premised on a view that does not see the state as a negative force, as "an enemy of the people," but rather "as a more respected institution, pursuing policies on behalf of its citizens" (1985, p. 26). Thus, it is "a theory that takes a very different—and much less suspicious—view of state involvement in communications than existing Western theories" (1985, p. 27).

Based on Western European experience after World War II rather than on North American practice, the *democratic socialist* theory sees state intervention as necessary to the maintenance of a communications system that is open to all societal participants, particularly those who are economically disadvantaged.

> Under the democratic socialist view, media can be truly democratic only if they are removed from the private sector, spared the effects of economic competition, freed from undue restraints and pressures—whatever the source—and induced to provide the capacity for citizens to communicate effectively with other citizens. These conditions include the requirements of the traditional Western liberal view of press freedom: the absence of governmental restraints and undue interference with communication of opinion and viewpoints. But the democratic socialist model also combines [the above] negative liberty characteristics...with positive liberty characteristics (i.e., action taken to promote a free exchange of ideas among all citizens...). (Picard, 1985, p. 35)

Picard goes on to describe the philosophy of *positive press freedom*:

> Media owners will be asked to give up some control over their "property" in the name of social advancement and the common good; the state will compel them to do so if they do not do so voluntarily. Although concern about asking the state to protect individual liberty and the democratic process is understandable, the state is the only institution capable of bringing private control of the means of expression into check. Short of complete social revolution, there is no instrument but the state to control the competitive forces that are rapidly diminishing the units of media—units necessary to carry the views and ideas of the public if the democratic process is to survive and flourish. (1985, p. 50)

In his analysis of the contemporary situation in the United States, Robert McChesney charges that "the notion of public service—that there should be some motive for media other than profit—is in rapid retreat if not total collapse" (2000, p. 51). It is the thesis of the present book that, with respect to

Canada, the concept of voluntary recognition on the part of media owners of their *duties* to society as well as their *rights* as property owners—as described by the Hutchins Commission and embedded in social responsibility theory by Peterson—deserves renewed consideration.

In matters of public policy there are no perfect solutions, and we do not maintain that we have found a perfect solution in social responsibility theory. This said, however, two things are clear. First, the problems involved in reconciling the economic viability of a mass media system with the political needs of a modern democratic society, so persuasively reviewed by the Hutchins Commission, are still with us—and in this era of convergence these problems take a more obvious and troubling form. Second, we see neither the libertarian alternative favoured by John Merrill nor the democratic socialist model advanced by Robert Picard as likely to provide the answers for Canadian society as it enters the twenty-first century. In searching for solutions, we believe that it is time to look afresh at the concept of social responsibility. We will present our arguments supporting this position in the book's conclusion.

One

Failed Attempts at Regulation of Newspaper Ownership

The Davey Committee and the Kent Royal Commission

Walter C. Soderlund and Walter I. Romanow

In the preface to his influential book *Rich Media, Poor Democracy*, Robert McChesney points to the underlying contradiction "between a for-profit, highly concentrated, advertising-saturated, corporate media system and the communication requirements of a democratic society" (2000, p. ix). While McChesney's critique is focused primarily on the United States, one is hard pressed to find words to better describe the relationship between Canada's newspapers and its democratic political system. In 1998, John Miller claimed "that concentration of ownership is a bigger issue now than it was when Tom Kent measured it nearly twenty years ago" (1998, p. 63). According to Robert Hackett, in the mid-1990s Canada held the dubious distinction of having "the highest degree of press concentration in the advanced industrial world" (as quoted in Green, 1998, p. 8; see also Nesbitt-Larking, 2001, p. 110). In comparative terms, the concentration of chain and conglomerate ownership in Canada during the late 1990s (about 95% of newspapers were controlled by six chains) was far in excess of the concentration in the United States, where, "in 1998, no newspaper or chain dominated the nation's news dissemination" and the largest fifteen chains owned 25% of daily newspapers (Compaine, 2000, pp. 13–14, 53; also see Cohen-Almagor, 2002; Lorimer and Gasher, 2001, pp. 210–14).

Christopher Dornan frames the problem of ownership concentration in Canada as follows:

> Bluntly, the fear is that when members of a local demographic market have no alternative but to depend on a single title as a source of social intelligence, and when a small number of corporations owns these agencies of public address, corporate owners may be in a position to use their holdings to promote a particular view of political and economic affairs at the expense of alternative perspectives. The worry is that proprietors might restrict the range of debate within newspapers and skew news coverage so as to favour select interests, thus propagandizing the population.... Partisan control over public expression would amount to control over public opinion, and therefore to control over the political process itself. (2003b, p. 98)

While most of the criticism of ownership concentration comes from those viewing Canadian and American societies from the left of the political spectrum, such criticism has also been voiced from the political right. For example, Diane Francis offered the following commentary on the problem:

> Most Canadians live in one newspaper towns.... Their window on the world is narrow, their information fed through a biased, cost-effective focus.... The iron grip held by a handful of magnates is a problem in a country where balance, impartiality and independence from other tycoons such as big powerful advertisers is sorely needed. (1986, p. 317)

Francis suggested the following remedies:

> Ottawa should immediately adopt the suggestions of the Kent Commission into concentration of ownership in the newspaper industry, which include a freeze of the size of newspaper chains retroactive to the year the commission sat; a directive to the [CRTC] ordering it to refuse to renew licenses of broadcasters also owning newspapers in the same market areas, unless they divest one or the other; and the separation, in terms of ownership of the Globe and Mail and Thomson newspaper chain, because Thomson-owned newspapers dominate forty communities in Canada. (Francis, 1986, p. 335)

The 2004 *Interim Report* of the Standing Senate Committee on Transport and Communication begins with the following observation:

> News matters. Journalism matters. No real democracy can function without healthy, diverse and independent news media to inform people about the way their society works, what is going well and, perhaps most important, what is not going well or needs to be improved. (Canada, 2004, p. 1)

Given the importance of newspapers' role in providing information that citizens need to make intelligent decisions regarding their democratic governance, no one should remain comfortable with the current level of ownership concentration in Canada's newspaper industry. Let us be clear on this issue: there is simply too much power concentrated in too few hands, and to believe that all is well would be foolhardy in the extreme. (See Canada, 1970; Cohen-Almagor, 2002; Dornan, 2003b; Hackett and Zhao, 1998; Lorimer and Gasher, 2001; McPhail and McPhail, 1990; Romanow and Soderlund, 1996; Wagenberg and Soderlund, 1975.)

Background

While the trend toward consolidation in the North American newspaper industry began in the late nineteenth and early twentieth centuries (Bennett, 2001; Desbarats, 1996; Kesterton, 1967), in Canada, since the publication in 1970 of the *Report of the Special Senate Committee on Mass Media* (the Davey Committee) which first focused Canadian attention on the problem, the past thirty-plus years have seen an acceleration in that process. This trend toward consolidated ownership has been viewed with increasing apprehension by those concerned with Canada's democratic governance.

These concerns are not without foundation: in 1970, the Davey Committee reported that chains owned 66% of the country's daily newspapers, controlling 77% of total circulation. It reported further that only five cities in the country could be categorized as having "genuine competition" between newspapers and that in seven of the country's eleven largest cities "chains enjoy monopolies" (Canada, 1970, p. 5). Recommendations put forward by the Davey Committee were unfortunately not enacted into legislation and, by 1995, chains owned 88% of Canadian dailies, accounting for 83.5% of circulation (Romanow and Soderlund, 1996). In 1999, chains controlled approximately 95% of dailies, accounting for over 99% of daily circulation. Only a handful of newspapers in Canada were categorized as independently owned (Lorimer and Gasher, 2001, p. 212).

Table 1.1, which adds 2004 data received directly from the Canadian Newspaper Association (personal communication, Dec. 6, 2004) to data taken from the 2004 Standing Senate Committee on Transport and Communication's *Interim Report on the Canadian News Media* (Canada, 2004, Table 1), shows the evolution in ownership of Canadian newspapers over the eleven-year period 1994 to 2004. It shows that the composition of corporate owners has changed dramatically since 1994, with long-term major players such as Thomson, Southam, and Hollinger moving largely out of the picture. Moreover, the data show clearly that the concentration of ownership peaked in 1999, reflecting Conrad Black's ownership dominance—42% of daily circulation. Following the sale of his newspapers to CanWest Global in 2000, the percentage of total daily circulation controlled by both the top three and the top five owners decreased by almost 15%. However, circulation controlled by the major chain owners remained higher than had been the case in the pre-Black era (Canada, 2004, pp.7–9).

Table 1.2 shows our own count of newspapers, indicating their average daily circulation (as of March 2004, supplied by the Canadian Newspaper Association); and grouped by ownership (as of October 2004). Chris Dornan

TABLE 1.1 Canadian newspaper ownership as a percentage of total average daily circulation (1994–2004)

Company	1994	1996	1999	2000	2004	2004
	Percent of total circulation					No. of papers
Total	100.0%	99.9%	99.9%	100.1%	99.9%	100
Southam	27.0	31.5				
Hollinger/Southam			42.0			
Hollinger	3.8	9.0			1.2	10
Hollinger/HCI				5.6		
CanWest/Southam				28.2		
CanWest Global /CanWest MediaWorks					28.6	13
CanWest/Hollinger (National Post)				5.2		
Sun Media (Quebecor)	8.8	9.3	21.3	21.3	20.3	17
Toronto Sun	11.0	11.3				
Power Corp					9.2	7
Gesca	6.0	5.8	5.7	8.9		
Bell Globemedia				6.0	6.6	1
Thomson	20.6	12.3	10.5	3.2		
Torstar	*	*	13.7	14.0	13.4	4
Osprey					7.1	21
Médias Transcontinental					3.1	11
FP Canadian LP					2.8	2
Brunswick News (Irving)	2.3	2.3	2.0	2.0	2.1	3
Halifax Herald			2.3	2.2	2.2	1
Horizon			.5	2.0	1.8	5
Black Press			.4	.3	0.4	1
Annex			.3	.3		
Armadale	2.3					
Newfoundland Capital		1.0				
Burgoyne	.8					
Independent	17.4	17.4	1.2	.9	1.1	4

* The Toronto Star was included in the Independent category in 1994 and 1996.
Adapted from the 2004 Standing Senate Committee on Transport and Communication's *Interim Report on the Canadian News Media*, with 2004 data from the Canadian Newspaper Association.

reported that in 1993 "an average of 5,491,150 daily newspapers were sold in Canada on any given day, down from a peak of 5,824,736 in 1989" (1996, p. 64). Our calculations show that, in 2004, that average had fallen to 4,938,029, indicating a drop of just over half a million in copies sold per day over a twelve-year period and a loss of almost one million daily circulation since 1989.

Table 1.2 indicates a more balanced ownership situation, especially with respect to the number of newspapers owned by any one chain. New players have emerged. For example, the Osprey Media Group owns twenty-one papers in Ontario, while Médias Transcontinental owns eleven papers, primarily in Atlantic Canada. However, although there are more major owners, the total percentage

TABLE 1.2 Canadian daily newspapers, by ownership and circulation (2004)

Ownership	No. of papers	Average daily circulation (ADC)	% of ADC
Total	100	4,938,029	100.00
Osprey Media Group	21	350,767	7.10
St. Catharines Standard		31,872	
The Kingston Whig-Standard		28,273	
The Expositor, Brantford		24,126	
The Peterborough Examiner		22,752	
The Observer, Sarnia		20,591	
The Sault Star, Sault Ste. Marie		19,236	
The Sudbury Star		18,658	
Niagara Falls Review		17,555	
The Sun Times, Owen Sound		17,222	
The North Bay Nugget		16,161	
The Intelligencer, Belleville		15,545	
Standard-Freeholder, Cornwall		14,545	
The Tribune, Welland		14,495	
The Chatham Daily News		13,408	
The Daily Press, Timmins		9,763	
The Barrie Examiner		9,680	
The Packet & Times, Orillia		8,276	
The Daily Observer, Pembroke		5,937	
Lindsay Daily Post		4,849	
Cobourg Daily Star		4,404	
Port Hope Evening Guide		2,395	
Sun Media (Quebecor)	17	1,003,496	20.31
Le Journal de Montréal		279,333	
The Toronto Sun		224,093	
Le Journal de Québec		103,111	
The London Free Press		91,948	
The Edmonton Sun		74,477	
The Calgary Sun		69,929	
The Ottawa Sun		50,837	
Winnipeg Sun		43,987	
The Brockville Recorder and Times		12,200	
The Beacon-Herald, Stratford		10,698	
Daily Herald-Tribune, Grande Prairie		8,269	
The Simcoe Reformer		8,433	
St. Thomas Times-Journal		7,830	
The Woodstock Sentinel-Review		7,097	
Fort McMurray Today		4,696	
Daily Miner and News, Kenora		3,391	
The Daily Graphic, Portage La Prairie		3,166	
CanWest MediaWorks	13	1,413,508	28.60
National Post		258,068	
The Vancouver Sun		186,794	
The Province, Vancouver		161,241	
The Gazette, Montreal		143,154	
The Ottawa Citizen		140,365	

TABLE 1.2 (*continued*)

Ownership	No. of papers	Average daily circulation (ADC)	% of ADC
Edmonton Journal		132,924	
Calgary Herald		119,478	
The Windsor Star		75,202	
Times-Colonist, Victoria		73,407	
The StarPhoenix, Saskatoon		56,419	
The Leader-Post, Regina		51,291	
Nanaimo Daily News		9,416	
Alberni Valley Times, Port Alberni		5,750	
Médias Transcontinental	11	155,771	3.15
The Telegram, St. John's		33,344	
Cape Breton Post, Sydney		26,265	
The Daily News, Halifax		23,528	
The Guardian, Charlottetown		20,897	
The Journal Pioneer, Summerside		9,408	
The Times-Herald, Moose Jaw		8,900	
The Evening News, New Glasgow		8,015	
The Western Star, Corner Brook		7,638	
Prince Albert Daily Herald		7,147	
The Daily News, Truro		7,113	
Amherst Daily News		3,517	
Hollinger Canadian Newspapers LP	10	57,553	1.16
The Prince George Citizen		16,479	
The Kamloops Daily News		14,180	
The Record, Sherbrooke		4,898	
The Trail Times		4,558	
Alaska Highway News, Fort St. John		3,790	
Cranbrook Daily Townsman		3,735	
Nelson Daily News		3,176	
The Daily News, Prince Rupert		3,070	
Peace River Block Daily News, Dawson Creek		1,889	
The Daily Bulletin, Kimberley		1,778	
Power Corp. (Desmarais)	7	459,067	9.29
La Presse, Montréal		216,263	
Le Soleil, Québec City		86,750	
Le Nouvelliste, Trois-Riviéres		43,072	
Le Droit, Ottawa		36,228	
La Tribune, Sherbrooke		31,969	
Le Quotidien, Chicoutimi		28,528	
La Voix de l'Este, Granby		16,257	
Horizon Operations (BC) Ltd.	5	90,130	1.82
The Chronicle-Journal, Thunder Bay		30,124	
Lethbridge Herald		21,354	
The Daily Courier, Kelowna		16,597	
Medicine Hat News		14,078	
Penticton Herald		7,977	
Torstar	4	661,716	13.39
Toronto Star		472,478	
The Hamilton Spectator		107,371	

TABLE 1.2 *(continued)*

Ownership	No. of papers	Average daily circulation (ADC)	% of ADC
The Record, Kitchener-Waterloo		67,470	
Guelph Mercury		14,398	
Brunswick News (Irving)	3	103,132	2.09
New Brunswick Telegraph Journal, Saint John		40,305	
Times and Transcript, Moncton		37,959	
The Daily Gleaner, Fredericton		24,896	
FP Canadian Newspapers LP	2	138,924	2.81
Winnipeg Free Press		123,565	
Brandon Sun		15,360	
Halifax Herald Ltd.	1	108,216	2.19
The Chronicle-Herald, Halifax		108,216	
Bell Globemedia	1	324,167	6.56
The Globe and Mail		324,167	
Black Press (David Black)	1	19,272	0.39
Red Deer Advocate		19,272	
Independents	4	55,474	1.12
Le Devoir		28,908	
L'Acadie Nouvelle		20,296	
Flin Flon Reminder		3,900	
White Horse Star		2,368	

of newspapers operating under chain ownership remains extraordinarily high at 96%, and those newspapers account for 98.9% of total daily circulation. Only four of one hundred daily newspapers are classified by the Canadian Newspaper Association as Independent, and of these only one, *Le Devoir,* is considered to be a major newspaper.[1] According to our calculations, in 2004, the five largest chains (measured by number of newspapers owned) controlled 72% of all daily newspapers, while the five largest chains (measured by circulation) accounted for 78.6% of total average daily circulation.

For many years ownership was consolidated when chains acquired family owned newspapers as they came on the market. By the 1970s, with fewer and fewer individually owned papers remaining, Ben Bagdikian predicted that, in a logical culmination of the trend towards ownership consolidation, chains would acquire other chains, in a process of bigger fish devouring smaller fish (1977, p. 11; see also Blevens, 1997).

This is precisely what happened in Canada. In 1980, Thomson newspapers took over the FP Publication's chain of newspapers, bringing under Thomson's control, among other papers, *The Globe and Mail,* arguably the country's most influential newspaper (see Romanow and Soderlund, 1988). The subsequent simultaneous closing, also in 1980, of rival newspapers in Winnipeg and Ottawa by the Thomson and Southam chains, which left each chain in a monopoly position in the respective cities, led to the almost immediate appointment of the (Kent) Royal Commission on Newspapers. The Kent Commission proposed a Canada Newspaper Act, aimed at limiting further ownership concentration and reducing concentration through a process of divestment. However, as had been the case with the Davey Committee's recommendations a decade earlier, the Kent Commission's recommendations for restrictions on newspaper ownership failed to find their way into legislation, and the process of ownership consolidation continued through the 1980s and 1990s.

The reports of the Davey Committee and the Kent Commission are extremely important documents. Not only do they provide an understanding of the evolving problem of ownership concentration in Canada over the second half of the twentieth century; they also serve as a repository of possible public policy responses to the problem. The various measures of government regulation proposed in their recommendations, taken singly or combined, cover what might be seen as the bounds of permissible government intervention into the workings of the newspaper industry in capitalist market economies.

The Davey Committee

Ross Eaman places the Davey Committee within the series of investigations into the effects of concentration of ownership in the newspaper industry that began with the U.S. Hutchins Commission on Freedom of the Press (1947; see Introduction, this volume) and was followed by the British Royal Commission on the Press (Great Britain, 1949). Calling the Davey Committee "the first serious investigation of newspapers in Canada," Eaman traces its origins to then-Prime Minister Trudeau's response to New Democratic Party (NDP) calls for a royal commission to report on the problem (Eaman,1987, p. 92). In language that invokes the concept of press responsibility, Liberal Senator Keith Davey explains the creation of the committee:

> The question I have been asked most frequently is what prompted me to propose such a Committee in the first place. I have, of course, had a lifelong interest in the media; and then too anyone who has been active in public life soon becomes aware of the all-pervasive influence of the mass media. It occurred to me that there had never been a national accounting for the media. Most people agreed that freedom of the press assumes responsibility, but few had really stopped to assess that responsibility. It also occurred to me that Parliament might be the ideal instrument through which the people of Canada could determine whether they have the press they need or simply the press they deserve. (Canada, 1970, p. vii)

Whatever the factors behind its creation, the Davey Committee recognized the conflicts between society's need for a diversity of voices and what it referred to as "the media's tendency towards monopoly" (1970, p. 4). As it was phrased in the report, "many voices may be healthier, but fewer voices are cheaper" (1970, p, 3), an argument still heard in support of strategies of convergence.

It is important to recognize that the Davey Committee did not regard chain ownership as necessarily evil. The committee pointed to positive contributions chains had made to the newspaper industry and acknowledged that "there is simply no correlation between chain ownership and editorial performance." For the committee, public policy was the central issue and

> [in terms of public policy] what matters is the fact that control of the media is passing into fewer and fewer hands, and that experts agree this trend is likely to continue and perhaps accelerate. The logical (but wholly improbable) outcome of this process is that one man or corporation could own every media outlet in the country except the CBC. The Committee believes that at *some* point before this hypothetical extreme is reached, a line must be drawn.... The prudent state must recognize that, at some point, enough becomes enough. If the trend towards ownership concentration is allowed to continue unabated, sooner or later it must reach the point where it collides with the public interest. The Committee believes it to be in the public interest to ensure that that point is not reached. (1970, p. 6; italics in the original)[2]

In *Media Canada*, Romanow and Soderlund place the recommendations of the Davey Committee in four categories: the establishment of regional and national press councils; the initiation of a publications development loan fund; measures to protect the magazine industry[3]; and the proposal to create a press ownership review board (1996, pp. 99–103).

The Davey Committee felt that press councils offered the best opportunity to foster press accountability to the wider community, as they "would function as a watchdog on behalf of press freedom in the country" (Romanow and Soderlund, 1996, p. 100). While a number of voluntary press councils were created in the wake of the report's release, a National Press Council as envisioned in the report has never materialized.

In an attempt to open the country's mass media to wider ownership, the committee recognized that the costs of entry into the industry were becoming prohibitive. Thus it proposed a fund that "would make money available to potential newspaper and magazine publishers to permit them to publish, on a minimal level, alternative editorial positions in communities where newspaper competition did not exist" (Romanow and Soderlund 1996, p. 101). While some government money was made available to develop a so-called Volkswagen Press, the recommendation made no impact on the structure of the mainstream newspaper industry. To deal with the problem of ownership concentration, the Davey Committee boldly proposed "to establish a press ownership review board with powers to approve or disapprove mergers between, or acquisitions of, newspapers and periodicals." Given the level of chain domination existing at the time, the committee concluded that the guiding framework for the board's operations should be that "*all* transactions that increase concentration of ownership in the mass media are undesirable and contrary to the public interest—unless shown to be otherwise" (1970, p. 7; italics in original). In offering this recommendation, the committee made it clear that it was not proposing measures to dismantle existing levels of ownership concentration. Rather, what the committee envisioned was a board that would examine new proposals for mergers and acquisitions, keeping the principles of "undesirability" and "contrary to the public interest" as guides to its decisions.

The Davey Committee was aware that its recommendations regarding both the creation of a press ownership review board and a publications development loan fund would be controversial in that "they will be seen...as the thin edge of the wedge towards a system of government licencing of the press." The committee, while recognizing these concerns, pointed out that government intervention was not the only threat to press freedom; there was another threat, and that was "the power of the corporation in modern society" (1970, p. 103). The committee felt strongly that it was necessary to address the possibility that both government and corporate owners might abuse their powers, and that the time was at hand to deal with the threat of abuse by concentrated corporate ownership before it mushroomed out of control.

If a press ownership review board had been created in response to the Davey Committee recommendations (which was not the case), it is difficult to say to what extent the trend toward greater concentration of ownership would have been slowed. However, the operation of even a weak press ownership review board would no doubt have resulted in a less concentrated pattern of newspaper ownership than the one that confronted the Kent Royal Commission in 1980. That commission was to propose far stronger remedies than those proposed by the Davey Committee.

The Royal Commission on Newspapers (The Kent Commission)

In contrast to the Davey Committee, the Royal Commission on Newspapers, commonly referred to as the Kent Commission after Commissioner Tom Kent, was "born out of shock and trauma." As explained in obituary-like language by the commission:

> Simultaneously, in Ottawa and in Winnipeg, two old and respected newspapers died. The Winnipeg Tribune was 90 years old; the Ottawa Journal was almost 95. Both had striven valiantly for some years before their abrupt closing to survive by excelling in what they offered to the public; both died while optimism within their staffs was high. Journalists and other employees of the two papers were stunned. Readers were angry. Thoughtful people throughout the country became seriously concerned, for the demise of the Journal and the Tribune was merely the culmination of a series of takeovers and "rationalizations" that have changed the face and nature of the press in Canada. (Canada, 1981, p. XI)

As noted earlier, the Winnipeg and Ottawa papers were closed by their respective owners, Southam Press and Thomson Newspapers. The result was that each company was left in a monopoly position in the two cities with the remaining papers, the *Winnipeg Free Press* (Thomson) and *The Ottawa Citizen* (Southam). Consequent to what appeared to be a clear case of collusion, the mandate of the Kent Commission was "to inquire generally into the newspaper industry in Canada [as well as] to study specific aspects of the situation, and to suggest remedies" (Canada, 1981, p. xi).

Perhaps owing to the circumstances of its birth, the Kent Commission's attitude towards ownership concentration was a good deal more confrontational than that of the earlier Davey Committee. This position is clearly stated in the often quoted opening paragraph of its report:

> Freedom of the press is not a property right of owners. It is a right of the people. It is part of their right to free expression, inseparable from their right to inform themselves. The Commission believes that the key problem posed by its terms of reference is the limitation of those rights by undue concentration of ownership and control of the Canadian newspaper industry. (Canada, 1981, p. 1)

Terence Corcoran, Editor-in-Chief of the *Financial Post,* maintains that this "opening sentence should have been seen as outrageous in 1981. It was not.

And it still is not seen as a basic affront to principles I think all Canadians should hold dear." Echoing the argument advanced by John Merrill (discussed in the Introduction to this book), Corcoran claims that the logical implication of the commission's statement is that "freedom of the press belongs to the government" (2003, Feb. 13–15).

Confronted with a far more concentrated pattern of newspaper ownership and employing a less than neutral framework in approaching the problem, the Kent Commission put forward recommendations to remedy the situation that far exceeded the scope of those proposed by the Senate Committee a decade earlier. Even more clearly than had been the case with the earlier Davey Committee, the concept of social responsibility permeated the report of the Kent Commission:

> It is generally agreed that the press has a responsibility to the public, although there is little agreement on how to define it and even less on how to put it into practice. The existence of such a responsibility is, however, the cornerstone of the Commission. Without social responsibilities, the press would be but a business like others and the market its only law. There would be no special reason for the prime representative of the citizen, the State, to become involved....
>
> [Thus, the commission saw as falling within its purview the need to] examine all that constitutes the motivating force and moral framework of journalism. (Canada,1981, p. 21)

As with the Davey Committee, Romanow and Soderlund categorized the recommendations of the Kent Commission under four headings: rules of ownership; concentration of ownership; freedom of editorial expression; and quality of journalism (1996, pp. 104–107). Rules of ownership and concentration of ownership were dealt with in the form of the proposed Canada Newspaper Act, designed "to prevent any further increase in concentration and to reduce the worst features of concentration that has hitherto been allowed" (Canada 1981, p. 238). While not outlawing all further newspaper acquisitions by chains, the so-called *rule of five* was proposed as a guideline, whereby such acquisitions could take place only if:

1. The total number of daily newspapers owned thereby does not exceed five.

2. The circulation of daily newspapers thereby owned does not exceed five per cent of the circulation...of all daily newspapers in Canada.

3. The point of publication of any acquired newspaper is not less than 500 kilometers distant from any other paper in the same ownership. (Canada, 1981, p. 239)

The commission anticipated what has since become known as convergence as it addressed the issue of cross-media ownership; its solution, however, ran counter to what ultimately developed. While the commission agreed that "the economic reality of daily newspaper monopoly in most communities has to be recognized, ...[it saw] no economic necessity for the same ownership of other media in the same community." Thus it proposed:

> a reasonable guideline...would be that the proprietor of a newspaper may not own or control a television or radio station or a cable system if 50 per cent or more of the population within good reception reach of the electronic medium live in the areas where the newspaper is generally available by home delivery or by box or newsstand sales. (Canada,1981, p. 239)

Beyond establishing rules for further expansion of chain ownership, the commission proposed a strategy of divestment for situations where it felt existing levels of ownership concentration had already exceeded reasonable limits. Thus,

> specific recommendations for divestiture to break up what the commission considered to be monopolies were introduced for publishers in the provinces of New Brunswick [Irving], Saskatchewan [Armadale], and Newfoundland [Thomson] where concentration of ownership was especially prominent.... A choice...would be offered to Thomson for reducing its share of ownership by selling off either the forty newspapers it held across the country or selling The Globe and Mail, a newspaper that was rapidly gaining national circulation through satellite printing. (Romanow and Soderlund, 1996, pp. 104–105)

Issues of editorial freedom and quality of journalism generally were also linked to chain ownership, which was seen as a negative influence on both. In light of the editorial policies initiated by CanWest Global for the Southam newspapers purchased from Conrad Black (see Chapters 6 and 7, this volume), the recommendations offered by the Kent Commission in the area of editorial freedom take on special contemporary significance. The commission was specifically concerned with ownership interference in the news operations of chain-owned papers and that such interference would be incompatible with a social responsibility orientation of the press:

> The reader of the newspaper is buying a product for the mind, and little can properly be done by regulation to ensure that he gets the quality product to which a citizen of a democracy is entitled. The social responsibility of the newspaper in any case extends far beyond its own customers. There is a responsibility to the people and institutions the paper writes about, a responsibility to be accurate and fair. There is a responsibility to the community generally, which will be influenced indirectly by what the readers get directly from the paper; good newspapers are essential to the democratic process in a free society. This is the root of the special kind of social responsibility which makes the newspaper more than a business. (Canada, 1981, pp. 245–246)

Romanow and Soderlund explained the intent of the Kent Commission's stance on the issue of editorial freedom as follows:

> The commission introduced several measures to offer journalists freedom from interference on the part of vested ownership interests. In the situation of chain-ownership, the editor-in-chief would be obliged to submit an annual report on the question of editorial independence. This report would then be published in his or her newspaper. In communities in which a chain newspaper was published, there would also be an Editorial Advisory Committee, which would function in two ways. First, it would review the annual report by the editor; second, it would itself report annually to a National Press Rights Panel (that panel would be appointed by the federal cabinet). Finally, in such a chain of command, the Press Rights Panel would report on the behaviour of newspapers across the country to Parliament through the Minister of Justice. (1996, p. 105)

The quality of journalistic products of Canadian newspapers was also a concern of the Kent Commission, as it had been of the earlier Davey Committee. Focusing on the ratio between editorial expenses and revenues, the commission proposed "that the tendency of some newspapers to skimp on their editorial services to their communities should be counteracted by a system of tax credits and surtax" (Canada, 1981, p. 253). Specifically, the commission recommended "that where newspapers assumed an initiative to spend more than the industry average on editorial expenses, tax credits should be offered to that newspapers as an incentive." The commission also recommended that Canadian Press (CP) should receive a tax incentive to improve its international reporting (Romanow and Soderlund, 1996, p. 105).

In the spring of 1982, the Liberal government introduced a bill that was somewhat less restrictive than proposals advanced by the Kent Commission but that called for a 20% limit on the newspaper holdings of any owner

(Eaman, 1987, p. 109). Its provisions were controversial, and it was not voted upon prior to the dissolution of parliament before the 1984 election. The result of that election was Brian Mulroney's Progressive Conservative government. Eaman suggests that "had it been enacted, the proposed legislation would not have gone nearly as far as the Kent Commission had recommended. However, it would have meant an unprecedented degree of government regulation over the Canadian newspaper industry" (1987, p. 110). Rowland Lorimer and Mike Gasher point out that "the Canadian government largely ignored Davey and Kent and has consistently refused to regulate the newspaper industry" (2001, p. 10). In any case, no legislation to regulate newspaper ownership has since been introduced.

Evaluation

Ross Eaman outlined four possible strategies to deal with ownership concentration—Laissez Faire, Limited Controls, Preventive Measures, and Strong Counter-measures—and argues that one's position as to which to embrace is determined by how one evaluates the scientific evidence on negative effects of chain ownership and by whether one perceives government action as a threat to freedom of the press (1987, p. 100, Figure 4).[4] The recommendations of the Davey Committee fall under Preventive Measures, while those of the Kent Commission can be categorized as Strong Counter–measures (1987, pp. 115–140).

While most academic commentators generally saw the recommendations of the Davey Committee as reasonable and necessary, those of the Kent Commission were greeted far more circumspectly. Even as strong a critic of ownership concentration as John Miller acknowledged that "Kent's recommendations seem draconian and unthinkable by today's standards" (1998, p. 82, note 11). Among the most thorough and thoughtful critiques of the commission's work is that offered by Arthur Siegel in *Politics and the Media in Canada* (1983). Siegel takes issue with the Kent Commission recommendations, on the grounds that they are not supported by evidence and that they involve the government too closely in the running of newspapers. In light of the current trend toward convergence, in which we see new patterns of ownership concentration emerging, Siegel's arguments are worthy of re–examination.

Siegel refers to the Kent Commission report as "one of the most controversial...ever presented by a Canadian Royal Commission" and notes that it "was produced in haste at the request of the government" (1983, p. 146). He argues further, saying that it failed to offer evidence to back up two major assertions: "specifically, that concentration of newspaper ownership and press ownership by conglomerates had resulted in a decline in the quality of Canadian newspapers or that it had resulted in restraints on the free flow of information." Moreover, he goes on to criticize the commission for not "conducting research on the most critical issue of central editorial direction and abuse of power that may have its roots in the extraneous interests of the owners" (1983, pp. 146–147).

On the first issue, Siegel notes that the commission's negative evaluation regarding the quality of Canadian journalism was not backed up by research conducted for it, which indicated that two-thirds of those surveyed reported the press was doing either a good or an excellent job. This failure to acknowledge the research findings he attributes to the commission's use of standards for the editorial quality of newspapers that were "based on an élitist perception of what the press should be like" (1983, p. 148).

The second criticism Siegel makes, and the one directly related to chain ownership, is the commission's differential perception of the negative consequences of concentrated ownership in Quebec and in English-speaking Canada: it was presented as less significant in the former than in the latter. Siegel claims (rightly so, as far as we can determine) that this presentation was not substantiated by the research carried out by the commission. His conclusion on this point bears repeating:

> If the principle of extensive concentration is bad, then concentration is as undesirable in the French as in the English press. Further, there can be no distinction between "good" chains and "bad" chains, a distinction made by the Commission in its evaluation of the English press. (1983, p. 149)

Siegel's overall evaluation of the Kent Commission's recommendations is mixed. He supports the recommendation for the creation of press councils and compliments the commission for performing "a laudable service in focusing public attention on the extent of concentration of ownership, cross-media ownership, the involvement of conglomerates in media operations and the possible societal implications of this pattern of ownership in the mass communication industry" (1983, p. 150).

In the end, however, Siegel is skeptical as to whether the recommendations might not do as much harm as they would do good:

> The control and supervisory process recommended by the Kent Commission could become a restraining influence. The idea of committees at both the local and national levels second guessing journalistic decisions in hindsight of later developments is likely to lead to a pallid product in which avoidance of controversy

> could become a major consideration in the information presentation process. This situation carries the dangers of psychological self-censorship. (Siegel, 1983, p. 150)

A similar set of concerns has been raised regarding "chilling effects" leading to self-censorship stemming from the CanWest Global "national editorial/no contradiction" policy, which will be discussed in Chapters 6 and 7 of this volume. On the matter of possible government responses to this controversial policy, Terence Corcoran revisits the Kent Commission's findings, arguing that "this new attempt to get governments into the newsroom of the nation's newspapers is a dangerous extension of the Kent Commission's Marxist conclusion that the owners of the means of production should not be allowed to act as owners" (2003, Feb. 13–15). Clearly, as evidenced by the discussion in the *Interim Report on the Canadian News Media*, both the problems identified by the Kent Commission and the question of whether its recommendations suggest the appropriate way to deal with those problems are still very much a part of public policy debate.

PART ONE

Chain Ownership: Conrad Black and Hollinger

Two

Chain Ownership
Review and Analysis of Empirical Studies

Walter C. Soderlund and Kai Hildebrandt

The empirical question regarding the extent to which newspaper owners *use* the power that they have to shape both the *editorial positions* and the *news coverage* in the newspapers they control has been one of continuing interest to media researchers (see Demers, 1996a, 1996b, 1999). In the context of the research reported in this book, the editorial function will be referred to as "evaluation-providing" and the news function will be referred to as "information-providing" roles of the press.

Interestingly but not surprisingly, extensive previous research into the question of ownership impact has yielded differing conclusions. This is due, at least in part, to conflicting pressures on newspaper owners. Do owners wish to maximize profits by tailoring their newspapers' content to appeal to the broadest possible audience (often referred to as finding and appealing to the centre of mass opinion)? Or do they wish to use their newspapers as vehicles for the dissemination of partisan political commentary, thereby running the risk of alienating some portion of their readership, lowering their circulation, and ultimately their advertising revenues and corporate profits? (See Bennett, 2001; Demers, 1999; Fletcher and Taras, 1995.)

Should Newspaper Ownership Be Regulated?

Based solely on numbers of newspapers owned and percentages of total circulation controlled as discussed in Chapter 1, a convincing case could be made for the regulation of newspaper ownership in Canada. However, let us look at the arguments advanced for and against chain ownership and examine further what the empirical evidence tells us about actual owner influence on newspaper content.

It is beyond dispute that, on a number of dimensions, both the information provided by newspapers and the evaluation they place on that information are important for democratic governance. If one takes at all seriously the role of the mass public in democratic decision-making, it is immediately apparent that information—"democracy's oxygen," as it is termed by James Winter in the title of his book (1997)—is crucial to citizens who wish to provide rational input on issues that affect them (see Altschull, 1984; Canada, 2004; Chew, 1994).

Indeed, over the years, research in areas such as gatekeeping, agenda setting, priming, and framing[1] has firmly established the key role played by mass media in selecting, amplifying, shaping, and interpreting events and issues for mass publics (see for example Entman, 1991; Fletcher and Taras, 1995; Fridkin, Khan, and Kenny, 2002; Gamson, 1989; Gans, 1979; McCombs and Shaw, 1972; Mendelsohn, 1994; Rogers and Dearing, 1988; White, 1950). This body of research makes it clear that the information and evaluation that appear in mass media (print and electronic) are not the result of chance or accident. Rather, there are identifiable patterns, not only in the selection of the news we read, hear, and see, but in the degree of amplification a particular issue or event will receive, as well as the spin that the media will place on it (Bennett, 2001; Herman and Chomsky, 1988; McChesney, 2000; Nimmo and Combs, 1990; Soderlund, 1994).

Press ownership is one of the factors that has been prominently identified as a determinant of news content. Current patterns of ownership contribute to problems of democratic governance. Not only are we witnessing a trend toward the consolidation of media ownership in fewer and fewer hands, it has been noted that within the narrow composition of this group of owners there appears to be a decided advantage accruing to those who hold positions of wealth, and social and corporate power (Curry and Dassin, 1982; Desbarats, 1996; Parenti, 1997). Linda McQuaig frames this issue as follows:

> We must always remember that virtually all media outlets are owned by rich, powerful members of the elite. To assume that this fact has no impact on the ideas they present would be the equivalent to assuming that, should the entire media be owned by say labour unions, women's groups or social workers, this would have no impact on the editorial content. (1995, p. 12)

Tycoons with left-of-centre political orientations are remarkably few, and the kinds of groups mentioned by McQuaig tend not to own media outlets. It is argued that, as a consequence, left-of-centre points of view are not adequately represented in the nation's press (McChesney, 2000; Taras, 2001).

The issue of whether newspaper ownership should be regulated falls within the classic debate between those who hold a *libertarian* (free marketplace of ideas) philosophy and those with a *social democratic* (governmental regulation for the public good) orientation (see Introduction, this volume). The issue is further complicated by the apparent paradox that, if left to free market devices, libertarian press systems tend to end up as oligopolies or monopolies—exactly the outcome that restricts the number of diverse opinions voiced in the media and maximizes the power of a small number of owners

(Canada, 1970; Romanow and Soderlund, 1996; see also Lacy and Picard, 1990). Yet, the perception remains that libertarianism (that is, a system with no government interference) is a necessary condition for the existence of a free press.

A number of diverse elements enter into this debate:

1. In addition to providing information to mass publics, newspapers exist first and foremost as businesses, and as such, need to make a profit for their owners to remain in operation (Atkinson, 1997; Bennett, 2001; Blevens, 1997; Compaine, 2000; Demers, 1996a, 1999; Hallman, Oliphant, and White, 1981; Picard and Brody, 1997; Underwood, 1998):

> Newspaper publishing is a business. In order to improve the results of the business, revenues must increase; there is a limit to what can be achieved through cost-cutting. To increase revenues we will have to improve our newspapers. If we do that, circulation will increase and, more importantly, we will become more attractive to advertisers. (Atkinson, 1997, p. 28)

> Newspapers, of course, *are* businesses, but they are businesses that must perform a public service for their customers. The more profitable the business, in theory, the better it is to invest in the gathering of the news, which in turn delivers readers, which in turn attracts advertisers. (Miller, 1998, p. 13)

> [Black would] publish a communist newspaper if he thought he could make money with it. (Unidentified Canadian journalist, as quoted in Jones, 1998, p. 41)

> Whatever the public wants in commercially significant numbers, since the public is always right, we as an industry will provide. As I have said many times before, if readers want our contents towed around the skies of our cities behind blimps, we'll provide that too. (Black, 1998, p. 92)

2. Historically, newspaper owners in Canada did indeed influence the content of their newspapers in a partisan manner, a tendency curtailed only in the twentieth century due to the rise of the mass circulation daily (as publishers realized that overt partisanship tended to reduce their readership base) (Kesterton, 1967; Waite, 1962). Even in modern times, however, owners and publishers have set the editorial direction of their newspapers (Newman, 1996).[2]

> Your article in the *Gazette* was on the whole favourable, but I wish you had come out a little stronger.... We expect from our friends a generous

confidence and hope that when you have anything to our disadvantage you will communicate with us, and hear our answers and explanations before committing yourself or your paper against us. In fact we want you to "Be to our faults a little blind/And to our virtues always kind".... We are making arrangements about the government patronage in the way of advertisements, which will be complete in a few days, and will advise you thereof. (Sir John A. Macdonald, as quoted in Hill, 1968, p. 47)

3. Some things are done better or more cheaply, or both, under chain ownership. For instance, high quality reporting (especially from foreign bureaus) is expensive, and tends to be beyond the reach of small independent owners. Most raw materials needed to run a newspaper are less expensive when bought in large volume. As well, their purchase by a chain owner has no doubt saved a number of newspapers from closing (Atkinson, 1997; Compaine, 2000).

But suppose there *are* fewer and fewer owners: is this necessarily a bad thing? There is a lot of evidence to suggest exactly the opposite. Chain ownership has rescued more than one newspaper from extinction. Chain ownership has turned a number of weeklies into dailies. Chain ownership has financially strengthened some newspapers, so they're better able to serve their employees and communities. Chain ownership may in some cases have resulted in a decline in editorial quality; but there are also instances where chain ownership has upgraded it. In other words, there is simply no correlation between chain ownership and editorial performance. (Canada, 1970, pp. 5–6)

Lynn Haddrall has argued that the quality of *The Kingston Whig-Standard* improved under Southam ownership: "According to Haddrall, the newspaper used to be an uneven and bizarre entity. Since the takeover, professional consistency was introduced and the newspaper began to offer comprehensive and predictable local coverage." (as cited in Nesbitt-Larking, 2001, p. 128)

Most of the criticism against the corporate newspaper is more myth than fact. Although structurally organized to maximize profits, the corporate newspaper actually places much more emphasis on quality journalism and much less emphasis on profits than its entrepreneurial counterpart.... Also...the corporate newspaper is more, not less vigorous editorially, which suggests it has a greater capacity to effect social change that lessens inequalities and injustices. (Demers, 1999, p. 84)

4. Because their economic base is spread over a wide area, chains have more resources to stand up against advertisers who threaten to pull advertising because of coverage that offends them. Economic strength is also important in exposing wrongdoing by governments. In the Watergate scandal, *The Washington Post*, a cross-media owned paper, took on the Nixon White House even when economic threats were made against television licences also held by its owner (Romanow and Soderlund, 1996).

5. Even if scientific studies do not conclusively demonstrate editorial control, the current extraordinary level of concentrated corporate ownership of the nation's newspapers is unhealthy for democracy (Barlow and Winter, 1997; Dornan, 2003b; Francis, 1986; Romanow and Soderlund, 1996; Taras, 2001; Winter, 1997):

    > I hold that concentration of ownership impinges pluralism and increases the likelihood that the economic interests of publishers would overshadow public interests. (Cohen-Almagor, 2002, p. 36)

    > I accept that the fact that Hollinger owns a little more than 40 percent of the daily circulation of Canada is, on its face, a fact that justifies legitimate public interest. (Black, 1998, p. 94)

6. Newspaper owners, publishers and editors do in fact have enormous control over the newspapers that they run:

    > The most important mechanism of ownership control is the power to hire, promote and fire. (Chomsky, 1999, p. 592)

    > I am ultimately the publisher of all these pages and if editors disagree with me, they should disagree with me when they are no longer in my employ. I am responsible for meeting the payroll, therefore I will ultimately determine what the papers say and how they're going to run. (David Radler, as quoted in Green, 1998, p. 8)

7. Newspaper owners, either directly or indirectly through the publishers and editors they hire, will to some extent influence the content of the newspapers they own. Even if an owner does not take a hands-on position in running a newspaper, reporters tend to develop a keen sense of the newspaper owner's positions and expectations; they tend to self-censor

so as not to provoke the ire of those who control the trajectories of their careers (Chomsky, 1999; Fox, 1988):

> When Neil Reynolds left *The Telegraph-Journal* (Saint John) in 1995 after a stormy reign as editor, he told reporters that the paper's owner, J. K. Irving, called him every day, telling him what he liked and did not like in the paper. (Steuter, 1999, p. 631)

> They [the Aspers] wanted to see it [the editorial calling for Jean Chrétien's resignation] in advance and they felt I should have submitted it to them for approval. I had no way of knowing that was their expectation. (Russell Mills, as quoted in Southam Newspapers, 2002, June 18, p. A5)

> Some journalists feel if they push the envelope too far, that is consistently advocate positions that Black and his managers feel irksome, then their careers will languish. They will be cut off at the knees, banished to newspaper obscurity, into professional oblivion. (Taras, 2001, p. 19)

> Will it be possible for journalists to think for themselves, or simply more profitable [for them] to think like Black? (Dalton Camp, as quoted in Miller, 1998, p. 63)

8. In order to sell advertising at prime rates (and thus maximize profits), owners must sell more, not fewer, newspapers. Therefore, they tend to avoid ideas and content that are demonstrably out of synch with the values and belief systems of the majority of the population (Bennett, 2001; Demers, 1996a; 1996b; 1999; Fletcher and Taras, 1995):

> Something I am prepared to assume is that he [Black] has not made himself the owner of more newspapers in Canada than anyone else for the purpose of running them into the ground. (Bain, 1996, p. 48)

> Let me assure those of you who need it, I am comfortably within the political mainstream in this country and a good deal closer to the centre of it than many of the myth-makers who have been active on this subject. (Conrad Black, as quoted in Green, 1998, p. 80)

> It is clear from the history of the newspaper industry that using newspapers for systematic propaganda or vendettas leads directly to the evaporation of the franchise. Hollinger saw that in London with the

> Observer when it was owned by Lonrho. It was a flying carpet for its proprietor's capricious likes and hates and lost 40 percent of its circulation in 10 years to the Sunday Times and Sunday Telegraph. (Black, 1998, p. 95)

9. Conrad Black's reputation as a ruthless manager and unabashed ideologue (Barlow and Winter, 1997; Driedger, 1996; Flavelle, 1996; McCarthy, 1997; Newman, 1996; Winter, 1995, 1997) is balanced by the fact that he is interested in newspapers and quality journalism. That is, he is first and foremost a "newspaper man" (Bain, 1996; Jones, 1998; Wells, 1996).

10. Finally, and most importantly, a significant body of research examining the effects of ownership on newspapers on a number of dimensions can best be described as inconclusive. Depending on the questions asked and the methods used to answer them, different results have emerged. A recent review of the American literature[3] summarized such research results as follows:

> Of 17 studies examined, three generally supported the critical model [that advanced by Barlow and Winter, Herman and Chomsky, and McChesney], seven show no relationship or have mixed findings, and seven suggest that chain organizations are more vigorous or create conditions conducive to greater diversity. (Demers, 1996a, p. 857)

The Canadian Literature

Canadian studies[4] dealing with questions of the effects of monopoly generally and of chain ownership specifically are few enough in number that they can be reviewed in at least some detail. *Monopoly* deals with the phenomenon of the one-newspaper city, specifically with what happens when there is no competition, and is usually studied when a rival newspaper ceases publication. Theoretically, monopoly may or may not be linked to chain ownership but, given the trend in Canada toward chain ownership of newspapers, the two tend to overlap to a considerable extent in this country.

In their study of the coverage of local government by the *Winnipeg Free Press* and *The Ottawa Citizen* following the closings of their competitors in 1980, Katherine Trim, Gary Pizante, and James Yaraskavich noted that, even though the Kent Commission felt monopoly conditions adversely affected newspaper quality, the commission did not make recommendations that would restore competition to one-newspaper cities (1983, p. 34). While Trim et al. pointed out that news about local governments received "little attention" in *any* of the newspapers they studied, they concluded that, in Winnipeg and Ottawa, there clearly was a decline in coverage of local affairs in the surviving paper following the demise of the competition. The *Winnipeg Free Press* saw a decline from 141 stories to 47—a drop of nearly 100 stories—between a six-month period in 1979 and the same six-month period in 1981. For *The Ottawa Citizen,* the decline was less dramatic, with the number of stories dropping from 99 to 79. Although the authors acknowledge that the *Free Press* also experienced a change of ownership in 1980 (from FP Publications to Thomson Newspapers), which makes it difficult to establish links of causality, they cite "the less competitive environment" following the closure of the rival newspaper as key to the reduced interest in local government affairs.

Doris Candussi and James Winter also studied the *Winnipeg Free Press,* but with a broader focus: "specifically, whether a particular monopoly led to an inferior editorial product and advertisement price gouging" (1988, p. 141). As with the previous study, Candussi and Winter found changes they regarded as negative. However, they observed that from 1979 to 1983, while the entire newspaper became smaller and advertising declined by 27%, "in fact, newshole [that part of the newspaper devoted to news, i.e., non-advertising] as a percentage of total space [the usual measure of newshole] increased from 33% to 38%" (1988, p. 142).

Monopoly effects on advertising appeared clearer: despite an actual decline in the amount of advertising in the paper, "advertising revenue in 1983 represented a 5% increase over 1979" (1988, p. 143). The authors concluded their study with the observation: "The 5% increase in advertising revenue, especially when coupled with the 67% increase in circulation revenue, indicates that—in the true monopolistic tradition—the Winnipeg market is being put through the wringer in pursuit of profit maximization" (1988, p. 145).

In their pursuit of the effects of chain ownership on advertising rates over the period 1966 to 1981, Michael Charette, Lloyd Brown-John, Walter Soderlund, and Walter Romanow (1984) studied both the impact of the acquisition of a previously independent newspaper by chain owners (nine cases) and the closure of a chain-owned newspaper in a previously competitive market (three cases, including the previously studied cases of the *Winnipeg Free Press* and *The Ottawa Citizen*). Counting the control papers used in the study, advertising rates for thirty-three newspapers were included in the multivariate analysis used to explain advertising rates.

Conflicting trends were found for the two situations. Chain acquisition of newspapers had no statistically significant impact on the rates charged to advertisers, while the creation of a monopoly situation through closure did result in higher advertising rates charged by the remaining paper. The authors concluded that, although competition from alternative media functions as a protective barrier, "should the competition be diminished, especially as we have seen by the withdrawal from the market of a newspaper, the potential or classic monopoly behaviour by newspapers is evident" (Charette et al., 1984, p. 61).

Romanow and Soderlund (1978, 1988) also investigated the impact of chain acquisitions on the content of *The Windsor Star*, acquired by Southam Press in 1971, and of *The Globe and Mail*, acquired by Thomson Newspapers in 1980. In both cases there were substantial changes in the newspapers, as evidenced by an examination of content appearing in the four-year period prior to the ownership transfers against content during the four-year period following the transfers.

In the case of *The Windsor Star*, the change was from independent ownership to chain ownership and most, although not all, changes could be expected.[5] The increased use of Southam News Service Wire material was predictable. As well, there were more Canadian sources used overall after the change in ownership, which offered readers a greater Canadian perspective on events. Most significantly, the study found that *The Windsor Star* became a more politically involved paper under Southam ownership, one much more willing to criticize the political parties in power (the Liberals federally and the Progressive Conservatives provincially). The study's conclusions bear repeating:

> Clearly...we see that the chain ownership question cannot be dealt with adequately by the divergent hypotheses (that is socially desirable and undesirable) which are evident in the literature. Changes in *The Windsor Star* coincident with ownership change have occurred. These changes may be evaluated positively or negatively, depending on one's view of the role of a newspaper in its community. (Romanow and Soderlund, 1978, p. 270)

With *The Globe and Mail*, the change in ownership that occurred in 1980 was from one chain owner to another (FP Publications to Thomson Newspapers). Using the same method as had been used in *The Windsor Star* study, examining content for a period of four years prior to and four years after the ownership change, Romanow and Soderlund's research was designed to test assurances by Kenneth Thomson, that there would be no changes made to *The Globe and Mail*, against the concerns raised by Royal Commission Chair Tom Kent with respect to the continued editorial independence of the paper.

The results of the study showed that percentages of content in the categories of front page stories, editorials, feature columns, editorial cartoons, and letters to the editor remained virtually unchanged over the two periods of the study. However, there was a dramatic, statistically significant change in the *focus* of content, most notably a drop in Toronto-related material from 10.2% to 4.8%. The strategy behind these changes, which made *The Globe and Mail* truly "Canada's National Newspaper," depended on "the infusion of funds from the new corporate ownership [that] allowed the newspaper to expand its domestic and international bureau coverage" (Romanow and Soderlund, 1988, p. 11).[6]

Unlike *The Windsor Star*, *The Globe and Mail* showed no increase in political partisanship although, like *The Windsor Star*, it criticized the party in power, both federally and provincially. The authors concluded that "using an even more detailed research instrument than in the previous research, even fewer changes were discovered coincident with the Thomson takeover of *The Globe and Mail* than was the case with the Southam takeover of *The Windsor Star*" (Romanow and Soderlund, 1988, p. 15).

To examine the effects of chain ownership on content, Wagenberg and Soderlund (1975) compared editorials dealing with the 1972 Canadian federal election in newspapers belonging to the Free Press (FP) chain with those in non-Free Press papers. With respect to themes covered, the authors concluded that *region*, rather than ownership, was more likely to influence thematic coverage. They found no apparent pattern of interest in, or evaluation of, political leaders or parties; however, the study did show a contradiction between the pattern of formal editorial endorsement—three of the four FP papers formally endorsed the Liberal party—and the consistently negative evaluation of the Liberal party in editorials of both FP and non-FP papers. While not finding any evidence of "collusion between editorialists within the Free Press chain to stress any particular issue or promote the fortunes of any political party," the authors pointed out that this finding "does not forestall the possibility that there could have been in some previous elections and may be in some future ones" (1975, p. 98).

To further investigate the influence of chain ownership, the same authors (Wagenberg and Soderlund, 1976) also studied editorials dealing with the 1974 election in sixteen newspapers, adding four newspapers from each of the Thomson and Southam chains to the previously studied Free Press and independent papers. In coverage of political, economic, and socio-cultural issues, on only two of twelve issues compared were there statistically significant differences by chain ownership. Southam newspapers commented heavily on the issue of size and cost of government, while independents were relatively silent on that topic. Independent papers, on the other hand, stressed bilingualism, which received below-average coverage in Thomson papers. All groups of newspapers were consistently anti-Liberal in their partisan commentary, while partisan commentary on the Progressive Conservatives (PC) tended to be balanced between positive and negative evaluations.

The only other statistically significant finding related to chain ownership was an overall negative evaluation of PC leader Robert Stanfield by Thomson newspapers. Wagenberg and Soderlund ascribed this negative evaluation to Mr. Stanfield's rejection of a controversial Tory candidate Leonard Jones (for his negative views on bilingualism) in Atlantic Canada, where two of the four Thomson papers were published. While pointing out that there were "some indicators that chain ownership would foster within the chain a community of attitudes on social issues and political philosophy," the authors concluded that "this does not take the form of central direction of editorial policies" (1976, p. 689).

In 1979, with the support of a Canada Council grant, Walter Soderlund, Walter Romanow, E. Donald Briggs, and Ronald Wagenberg studied television and radio coverage, as well as newspaper coverage, of that year's Canadian federal election—the first comprehensive, bilingual study of media coverage of an election in Canada. Twenty-three newspapers in total (seventeen published in English and six in French) were included in the print media part of the study.

Their conclusions regarding the impact of newspaper ownership on campaign coverage are stated in *Media and Elections in Canada*:

> The rank ordering of percentage of stories devoted to the political parties and major electoral issues are quite consistent from chain-owned to independent papers within each language group. On the French side, two items appear "out of step" between independent and chain papers. (Soderlund et al., 1984, p. 90)

Stories dealing with the Progressive Conservative party appeared more often in independent papers, and Quebec separatism appeared more frequently in chain-owned papers. "On the English side, there is even less variation, ...with unemployment being the only issue on which the difference in coverage was over 7%. Independent papers touched on this issue more frequently than did chain-owned ones" (1984, p. 90). The authors concluded that chain ownership had no appreciable effect on campaign reporting with respect to the issue agenda of the election.

On the dimension of evaluation of political parties and their leaders, the study did find differences, but these ran in different directions depending on language of publication. While evaluations of Pierre Trudeau and Joe Clark were negative for chain- and non-chain-owned papers in both languages (and in all regions of the country), among the French-language papers, independent papers were more negative toward both the Liberal and PC parties and their leaders. Among the English-language papers, it was the chain-owned papers that were more negative toward these parties and leaders.[7]

Michael Clow's 1989 doctoral dissertation on newspaper coverage of issues concerning nuclear power during the 1970s and 1980s was not specifically designed to test for the influence of chain ownership. However, Clow's findings have relevance to the ownership concentration debate. Two of the papers he examined, Fredericton's *The Daily Gleaner* and Saint John's *Telegraph-Journal* were owned by the Irvings; *The Globe and Mail* was owned first by FP Publications and then by Thomson Newspapers; and the *Toronto Star* was at the time, although huge in terms of circulation, not part of any newspaper chain. Specifically, Clow discovered a common pattern of coverage for all the papers in his study, regardless of ownership: all types of papers "prevented the [anti-nuclear] movement from communicating its position or case to the public in any coherent way.... On the contrary, the nuclear industry has been much more able to communicate its position coherently and routinely to the public" (1989, p. 387).

The last Canadian study that we were able to find dealing with the impact of chain ownership on newspaper content was Erin Steuter's investigation of how four Irving-owned newspapers (all in New Brunswick) covered the strike at the Irving Oil refinery in Saint John, which lasted from 1994 to 1996. In terms of finding ownership effects, this appears to be very close to what Harry Eckstein referred to as a "crucial case" (1974). Indeed, Steuter reported that a consistent anti-strike position was displayed by the Irving papers, and that "media coverage [by Irving papers] reinforced an ideology of defeatism and aided in the increased legitimization of a 'roll back' orientation" (1999, p. 629). Interestingly, Steuter reported that *The Globe and Mail*'s coverage was closer to that in the Irving papers (in not characterizing Irving Oil as a bully) than it was to coverage in other Canadian papers included in the study (1999, pp. 641–642).

Steuter also examined sources used by reporters. Somewhat surprisingly, given that Irving owned both the struck oil refinery and the newspapers reporting on the strike, the study found that "the union was either the defining source in a story or the responding source in 70% of the articles, while the company was the definer or responder only 54% of the time." This apparent anomaly, whereby "the union had more opportunities to put forward their version of events to journalists and the readership" (1999, p. 642), is interpreted in terms of the "power of silence." As Steuter interprets it, "likely the reason we heard from the unions and not from the company was that the company was not interested in speaking to their own or anyone else's reporters" (1999, p. 644). Steuter explains the Irvings' strategy as follows: "When the public's expectation of an explanation of the Irving company's position on a more than two-year-long strike is met with silence, an attribution of meaning is developed which, in this particular context, becomes one of fear and foreboding" (1999, p. 644). Assessing the coverage of the strike, not only by four Irving-owned papers, but by fourteen other Canadian papers published from Newfoundland to British Columbia, Steuter's overall conclusion is that, although newspaper coverage of the strike extended over three hundred pages, "a comprehensive, balanced, detailed account of the central issues and events of the strike was never presented to readers" (1999, p. 645).

How are we to evaluate these disparate findings? In his research report to the Kent Commission, Fred Fletcher summarized the literature as follows:

> As we have seen, the negative effects of chain ownership on public affairs coverage, if any, are subtle and difficult to measure. The case against chains rests on a few examples, and some circumstantial evidence, and the obvious *potential* for abuse. (1981, p. 46; italics added)

With the benefit of over twenty years of added research, we can confirm that this conclusion still holds true. For example, in his presentation to the Standing Senate Committee on Transport and Communications, when asked specifically if there was evidence that cross-ownership reduced "the diversity of information generally available to the Canadian public" (Canada, 2004, p. 65), Vince Carlin indicated that to his knowledge "there is no academic study to prove this, although there is anecdotal evidence" (as quoted in Canada, 2004, p. 65).

In Canada, as in the United States, different studies have reached different conclusions regarding the impact of chain ownership, some finding negative effects, some finding positive effects, but most often finding *no* apparent effects. This disparity is, we suggest, due to a number of factors. It could be an effect of the questions asked or the research designs employed, or it could perhaps be an effect of the different chains or newspapers being investigated, as not all chains behave identically. As well, the time period and/or type of event (for example, an election versus a strike) studied is very likely to influence findings. Central to the issue, however, is that newspaper content is the outcome of a very complex set of factors, of which ownership is but one component (see Shoemaker and Reese, 1996).

Although as we have seen the empirical evidence regarding the impact of chain ownership is mixed, the cautionary advice offered by Wagenberg and

Soderlund in their first report on research into the effects of chain ownership bears repeating, as the situation has grown increasingly worrisome over time:

> That the over-concentration of power in any sector of society is cause for concern is a well-worn maxim for those who value democratic norms. At present, there is no way of ensuring that those who own large segments of the Canadian newspaper industry will not use that power to mould Canadian opinion to their own advantage. (1975, p. 98)

Three

The Impact of Conrad Black's Ownership on Thomson, Armadale, and Southam Newspapers

Kai Hildebrandt and Walter C. Soderlund

The question as to which ownership motivation—profit or control of content—is ultimately the stronger prompted the research reported in this chapter. Conrad Black, as Chairman and Chief Executive Officer of Hollinger, was a newspaper owner with a clearly identified conservative ideology and a reputation for using his newspapers to promote that ideology. As Peter Newman reported at the time of the Hollinger takeovers, "There isn't the slightest doubt that he intends to use his newspapers to influence public opinion to back his conservative view of life" (Newman, 1996, p. 34; see also Barlow and Winter, 1997; Winter, 1997). Therefore, in Hollinger's acquisitions of early 1996, we had a strong case with which to test the impact of ownership on newspaper content. Shoemaker and Reese have noted that content serves as the basis for media impact (1996). Thus, if there was any truth to the charge of owners using their power to control content, a content analysis of Black's papers should provide the evidence to support the charge.

The context for the research reported in this chapter is as follows: beginning in late 1995 and culminating in May 1996, Hollinger, headed by Conrad Black, entered into a period of major expansion of its Canadian newspaper holdings. In this expansion, over a relatively brief period of time, Hollinger acquired eighteen newspapers from the Thomson chain, two newspapers from the Armadale chain in Saskatchewan (controlled by the Sifton family), and finally, all twenty newspapers owned by Southam, the latter through a buyout of Paul Desmarais' shares of Southam stock. Thus, in a period of less than a year, Hollinger grew from a small chain of primarily low-circulation newspapers to a chain that owned 58 of the country's 104 daily newspapers (56%), which in turn controlled 41% of daily newspaper circulation (Saunders, Mahood, and Waldie, 1996).[1]

This degree of control by one corporate owner led to the voicing of renewed fears of the consequences for open democratic expression in Canada (see for example Barlow and Winter, 1997; Driedger, 1996; Flavelle, 1996; Goldberg, 1998; McCarthy, 1997; Winter, 1997). An editorial in *Canadian Dimension* illustrates a typical concern raised: "The effect [of the acquisition] is to viciously narrow the range of public debate, advancing corporatist ideals while suffocating dissenting voices" (*Canadian Dimension*, 1996, p. 4).

While Hollinger's sale of its Southam newspaper holdings to CanWest Global Communications Corp. in the summer of 2000 may have ended Conrad Black's tenure as the country's premier newspaper owner, it did not lay to rest the question of concentration of media ownership.[2] On the contrary, the purchase by CanWest (controlled by the Aspers) opened a new chapter on conglomerate ownership in Canada's mass media. Specifically, it initiated a process of *convergence*, characterized by the merging of the functions of content acquisition and editing, and the delivery of that content through multiple media channels—all this combined with cross-promotion and cross-media advertising sales (see Chapter 5 of this book) (Goldstein, 2002, June 14; also see Gerbner et al., 1996; McChesney, 2000; Wendland, 2001). Thus, while Mr. Black's ownership is no longer the central focus of the debate, the problem of concentrated press ownership remains as salient as ever. In fact, with the addition of the feature of cross-media ownership, inherent in convergence, this new style of conglomerate ownership is arguably even more problematic for Canadian democracy than the old horizontal style of integration characteristic of conventional newspaper chains.

Hypotheses and Methods

Hollinger's acquisition of a large number of newspapers from the Armadale, Thomson, and Southam chains over a brief period of time in late 1995 and early 1996 offered a unique opportunity to study the effects of ownership change on newspaper content. As James Winter argues, Conrad Black, Hollinger's CEO, was no ordinary corporate owner. Black appeared to be intensely committed to newspaper downsizing: "We must never underestimate Black's ability to go where no man has gone before when it come to 'demanning' in the interests of profits" (Winter, 1997, p. 26). In addition, Black had well-known conservative views and there was "a feeling that he will use his views to influence content" (Winter, p. 40). In our opinion, if ownership did make a difference with respect to newspaper content, the extent and direction of such differences should be evident in the content of newspapers transferred from previous owners to Mr. Black's control.

Specifically, we intended to test seven hypotheses (H) related to changes in newspaper content that underlay what we have refered to as the "critical model":

H1 Under Hollinger ownership, newspapers will run a smaller proportion of content dealing with local issues as a consequence of staff reductions (Winter, 1997).

H2 Under Hollinger ownership, a smaller proportion of content will be written by local staff, again as a consequence of staff reductions at individual newspapers (Winter, 1997).

H3 Under Hollinger ownership, newspapers will show an increased focus on economic issues (business and free trade) and a decreased focus on social and political issues (McChesney, 2000).

H4 Under Hollinger ownership, newspapers will present more material containing positive evaluations of business and free trade (Grenier, 1992; McChesney, 2000).

H5 Under Hollinger ownership, newspapers will show both less interest in, and a more negative evaluation of, organized labour (Briarpatch, 1997; McCarthy, 1997).

H6 Under Hollinger ownership, newspapers will present more material on, and a more favourable evaluation of, conservative political parties (the Progressive Conservatives and especially Reform) and less material on, and a more unfavourable evaluation of, social democratic parties (the New Democrats) at both the federal and provincial levels (Winter, 1997).

H7 Under Hollinger ownership, in terms of overall political, social, and economic positions, newspapers will move to a more right-wing, conservative orientation (Winter, 1997; see also Parenti, 1997).

To test the above hypotheses, our study used a classic "before and after" research design, employing content analysis as the primary research tool (Romanow and Soderlund, 1978, 1988). Twelve newspapers in total (two Thomson, two Armadale, four Southam, along with four control papers for which ownership did not change during the study period) were examined for periods of three years prior to and three years following their acquisition by Hollinger. The two Armadale papers were the Regina *Leader-Post* and the Saskatoon *StarPhoenix* (studied from January 1993 through the end of 1998); the two Thomson papers were the St. John's *Evening Telegram* and the Charlottetown *Guardian* (studied from May 1993 through April 1999); and the four Southam papers were the Montreal *Gazette, The Ottawa Citizen,* the *Calgary Herald,* and the *Vancouver Sun* (studied from June 1993 through May 1999). Because general trends in the newspaper industry, as well as regional idiosyncrasies, may have contributed to changes in newspaper content over the six years of the study irrespective of ownership change, the Halifax *Chronicle-Herald* served as the control paper for the Thomson acquisitions in Atlantic Canada, the *Winnipeg Free Press* for the Armadale acquisitions in the Prairies, and both *The Globe and Mail* and the *Toronto Star* were used as controls for the Southam acquisitions that extended across the country from Quebec to British Columbia.[3]

Using a table of random numbers, composite Monday through Saturday weeks were constructed for each of the six years in the study; thus all newspapers were read and coded on the same dates. This method yielded a sample of 36 issues per newspaper—432 newspaper issues in total. For those newspapers acquired by Hollinger during the study period, half the dates sampled fell under the previous ownership and half under Hollinger ownership. Control newspapers were divided on the same basis as the papers of the chain to which they were attached. Front-page news stories, editorials, feature columns (commentary), and letters to the editor were read and coded by six coders working over a period of nearly two years.[4] Coding assignments were allocated over both ownership periods so as to distribute any coding idiosyncrasies that might have remained after training.

Information-providing and evaluation-providing dimensions of content were coded as follows:

Information-providing variables:

Type of content: local, provincial, national, international (with a subcategory of United States-specific), human interest, and other

Source of content: local staff, CP, AP, other wire services, chain columnists, national columnists, international columnists, academics, freelancers, and other

Focus of content: economic (business, free trade, labour), political, social, human interest, and other.

Evaluation-providing variables:

For *labour unions, business, and free trade*: favourable and unfavourable evaluations

For *political parties:* pro- and anti-evaluations of all major political parties at both federal and provincial levels

Left/right orientation: measured on a 5-point scale where 1=far left, 3=centre, and 5=far right.

Prior to the beginning of production coding, intercoder reliability of 87% was achieved for a sample of stories on the information-providing variables, while 82% reliability was established on the evaluation-providing variables (Holsti, 1969, p. 140). These levels were checked at various times during the study and any evident problems were dealt with. Finally, when all the coding was complete, the authors rechecked approximately 20% of the coding done by students and made appropriate changes if deemed necessary.[5]

The Canadian newspaper landscape of the 1990s presented a unique opportunity to assess the impact of an ownership change that would, it was widely predicted, affect the content of the acquired newspapers in foreseeable ways. Mr. Black acquired newspapers from three different owners (more or less at the same time), and control papers were available to indicate whether industry trends or regional peculiarities may have influenced change in newspaper content independent of the change in ownership. From this research, then, we anticipated being able to determine what kind of newspaper owner Conrad Black would be: a committed ideologue or a shrewd businessman.

Findings and Analysis

Tables 3.1, 3.2, and 3.3 relate to the first three hypotheses and deal with fundamental aspects of newspapers' informational content: (1) what percentage deals with local issues, (2) how much of the content is written by local staff, and (3) what is the primary focus of the content? Following the arguments of our critical model regarding corporate media in general and Conrad Black specifically, in newspapers under Hollinger ownership we expected to find less local material featured, less material generated by local writers, less attention devoted to political and social issues, and more attention devoted to economic issues. The data are presented in tables constructed to highlight differences between the papers that changed ownership and those that did not, for each of the three chains, for the pre- and post-acquisition periods of three years each.

Information-providing Functions

Data in Table 3.1 show the percentage of local content appearing in front-page stories, editorials, feature columns, photos, and letters to the editor in the aquired papers and their control paper for three years before and three years after the sale of the Hollinger-acquired papers, beginning in January of 1996.

TABLE 3.1 Percent of local content, by ownership, pre- and post-acquisition

i)	Ex-Thomson Papers		Control (Halifax CH)	
	Pre-acquisition	Post-acquisition	Pre-acquisition	Post-acquisition
Front page	24.5%	23.0%	35.1%	31.1%
Editorials	19.2%	22.2%	14.9%	16.9%
Features	3.3%	3.9%	24.0%†	9.5%†
Letters	24.0%	26.7%	19.1%	23.6%
Photos	39.1%	35.2%	32.4%*	13.1%*
Avg. no. of pgs.	31.3	34.3	40.8*	49.9*
ii)	**Ex-Armadale Papers**		**Control (Winnipeg FP)**	
	Pre-acquisition	Post-acquisition	Pre-acquisition	Post-acquisition
Front page	21.1%	24.2%	31.5%	36.0%
Editorials	11.4%	16.2%	13.9%	13.9%
Features	1.1%	0.0%	7.4%*	0.0%*
Letters	27.5%	28.4%	29.7%	32.6%
Photos	28.2%	22.5%	50.0%	43.5%
Avg. no. of pgs.	45.3	45.4	50.1	50.6
iii)	**Ex-Southam Papers**		**Controls**	
	Pre-acquisition	Post-acquisition	Pre-acquisition	Post-acquisition
Front page	16.7%	17.7%	18.7%	11.7%
Editorials	8.7%†	15.2%†	15.3%*	6.5%*
Features	5.1%	7.5%	5.6%	6.0%
Letters	26.4%	25.8%	9.3%	10.9%
Photos	19.3%	21.6%	14.8%	17.6%
Avg. no. of pgs.	65.1	75.0	78.2	85.4

* Pre- and post-acquisition differences significant at the .05 level chi^2 tests
† Pre- and post-acquisition differences significant at the .10 level (suggestive of trends)

Findings for two of the Thomson newspapers (the St. John's *Evening Telegram* and the Charlottetown *Guardian*), as well as for their control paper (the Halifax *Chronicle-Herald*), can best be described as mixed. For example, while the percentage of local stories appearing on the front page decreased marginally in the ex-Thomson papers, their control paper experienced an even greater decline. It is important to note that this finding runs counter to long-term trends in Canadian newspapers (Romanow and Love, 1989), as well as to survey data which point to local news as the one sector in which newspapers hold a competitive advantage over other media (Soderlund, Lee, and Gecelovsky, 2002). For editorials, both the ex-Thomson papers and the control paper registered small increases in local content. For features, while local material in the ex-Thomson papers remained virtually unchanged, the control paper showed a sharp decline (14.5%). For letters to the editor, both types of papers showed small increases in locally oriented material. For photos, both categories of papers moved in the direction hypothesized. However, while local photos in the ex-Thomson papers dropped by nearly 4%, in the control paper they dropped more sharply, by nearly 20%. On the question of newspaper size, both the ex-Thomson papers and the control paper ran more pages after the date of acquisition of the former, with a 10% increase for the ex-Thomson papers and a 20% increase for *The Chronicle-Herald.*

Data for the ex-Armadale papers (the Regina *Leader-Post* and the Saskatoon *StarPhoenix)* and their control paper, the *Winnipeg Free Press*, show that the percentage of local news on the front page increased slightly for both categories of papers. For editorials, an increase of nearly 5% was seen only in the ex-Armadale papers. While consistent with newspaper trends, this increase ran contrary to our hypothesis H1. For both categories of papers, the percentage of locally oriented features declined, but this decline was statistically significant only for the *Winnipeg Free Press.* Local photos on the front page also registered a decline of about 6% for both categories of papers, while letters to the editor on topics of local interest showed a modest increase. The size of both ex-Armadale papers and of the *Winnipeg Free Press* remained unchanged over the study period.

With respect to local content, the comparison of the four ex-Southam papers (the Montreal *Gazette, The Ottawa Citizen,* the *Calgary Herald,* and the *Vancouver Sun*) with their control papers (*The Globe and Mail* and the *Toronto Star*) was not supportive of our hypothesis H1. In the ex-Southam papers, local material either increased (by 6.5% in editorials) or remained essentially at the same levels. This was in contrast to a drop in the control papers of 7% in front-page stories and a statistically significant drop of nearly 9% in editorials. Only in the category of photos did the control papers register a modest increase in local material. As was the case with the ex-Thomson papers and their control, both sets of papers in this comparison increased in size during the second three-year period of the study.[6]

The reduced percentage of local news on the front page and in local photos found in the ex-Thomson papers was the only evidence that appeared consistent with the diminution of local content hypothesis (H1). However, even in this instance, the trend for the control paper moved in the same direction as the ex-Thomson papers, and the control paper moved more dramatically for both types of content. For editorials and letters to the editor, changes observed ran counter to the hypothesis, with the ex-Thomson papers and the control paper experiencing similar trends. For the ex-Armadale papers, the percentage of local news increased on front pages and in editorials, and decreased in features and photos. For the ex-Southam papers as well, increases in local content far outstripped declines. The percentage of local content found in a newspaper appeared to be directly related to the salience of local issues in a particular community, factors that are difficult to predict or control for either newspaper owners or editors. Finally, of all the changes discussed above, the only statistically significant changes (at the .05 level), which all showed declines in local material, were found in the control papers, where no ownership change had occurred.

Data in Table 3.2 show the percentage changes in the use of local staff to write front-page stories and feature columns for the Hollinger-acquired papers and their various control papers. For the ex-Thomson papers, findings with respect to our second hypothesis (H2) were again mixed. The percentage of locally generated content on the front page actually increased for both categories of papers, and in this case the change (of 12%) was statistically significant only for the ex-Thomson papers. This is exactly the opposite of what we had hypothesized would be the case. On the other hand, supporting the hypothesis, the percentage of features written by local staff did decline for both categories of papers, and the percentages were higher in the control paper than in the ex-Thomson papers. In this case, the decline (of 22%) was statistically significant only for the control paper.

When we examined the ex-Armadale papers, we found that the percentage of locally written material on the front page increased significantly (11.2%), while there was a decrease of about 6% for the control paper—the opposite of what we had hypothesized. However, trends reversed for feature material, where the ex-Armadale papers registered a 9.5% decline, while the control paper experienced a statistically significant 22% increase in locally written material.

An analysis of ex-Southam papers revealed a trend similar to that seen in other Hollinger-purchased papers—in this case, an increase in locally written material on the front pages, combined with a statistically significant decline of 10.3% in locally written feature material. Also mirroring trends observed in the ex-Armadale comparison, the control papers moved in the opposite direction, showing a slight decline in locally written front-page stories and an increase of nearly 10% in locally written features.

Interestingly, the changes seen in the Hollinger-purchased papers appeared to support hypothesis H2 with respect to feature material, but to run counter to the hypothesis in the area of front-page stories. That the trends in both front page and feature material were consistent in all Hollinger-purchased papers, can be seen as evidence of a uniform corporate strategy with respect to content; however, the strategy is only partially consistent with the predictions of Mr. Black's critics.

Data in Table 3.3 show trends in the focus of content for Hollinger acquisitions and their control papers. Findings for the ex-Thomson papers were for

TABLE 3.2 Percent of content written by local staff, by ownership, pre- and post-acquisition

i)	Ex-Thomson Papers		Control (Halifax CH)	
Type	Pre-acquisition	Post-acquisition	Pre-acquisition	Post-acquisition
Front page	49.5%*	61.5%*	58.1%	66.2%
Features	14.1%	9.1%	43.0%*	22.8%*
ii)	**Ex-Armadale Papers**		**Control (Winnipeg FP)**	
Type	Pre-acquisition	Post-acquisition	Pre-acquisition	Post-acquisition
Front page	56.0%*	67.2%*	85.9%	79.7%
Features	16.7%†	7.2%†	34.6%*	56.8%*
iii)	**Ex-Southam Papers**		**Control**	
Type	Pre-acquisition	Post-acquisition	Pre-acquisition	Post-acquisition
Front page	65.6%	72.4%	87.2%	81.4%
Features	43.1%*	32.8%*	34.4%†	43.6%†

* Pre- and post-acquisition differences significant at the .05 level
† Pre- and post-acquisition differences significant at the .10 level (suggestive of trends)

the most part consistent with the focus of content hypothesis (H3); however, the patterns tended to be shared with the control paper. Most significant is the predicted trend away from items dealing with political issues (down just over 13% on the front pages and in features, and down nearly 16% for letters to the editor, in the ex-Thomson papers). These changes go hand in hand with the hypothesized increase in attention given to economic issues in the ex-Thomson papers (up just over 20% on the front pages, 10% in editorials, 8% in features, and 6% in letters to the editor). However, there do not appear to be consistent trends with respect to decreased coverage of social issues over the different types of content.

At the same time, the control paper exhibited behaviour similar to that of the ex-Thomson papers: declines in political issues appeared in front-page news, editorials, and letters to the editor. As well, there were consistent increases in the focus on economic issues in the control paper, *The Chronicle-Herald*, for all categories of content. Again, as with the ex-Thomson papers, no consistent pattern emerged in the control paper with respect to increased or decreased attention paid to social issues.

Data for the ex-Armadale papers were generally consistent with the trends shown above for the ex-Thomson papers. Interest in political issues declined for every type of content, except for letters to the editor, with a statistically significant decline of 11% on front pages. For the *Winnipeg Free Press*, while an increase in interest in politics was shown on the front page, declines were seen for all other types of content. It is in the focus on economic issues that we see strong confirmation of the hypothesized relationship. For the ex-Armadale

TABLE 3.3 Focus of content, by ownership, pre- and post-acquisition*

i)		Ex-Thomson papers				Control (Halifax CH)			
	Period	Pol	Soc	Econ	Other	Pol	Soc	Econ	Other
Front page	Pre	55.9†	34.0	18.1†	25.0	50.0	37.8	12.2	31.1
	Post	42.6†	28.4	38.5†	21.6	43.2	33.8	21.6	35.1
Editorials	Pre	73.1	25.0	38.5	9.4	67.2	23.9	19.4	17.9
	Post	73.2	24.4	48.8	12.2	53.6	36.6	26.8	19.7
Features	Pre	72.2†	21.7	21.7	5.4†	50.0	32.0	10.0	22.0
	Post	58.4†	28.6	29.9	14.3†	52.4	35.7	19.0	23.8
Letters	Pre	40.3‡	49.6	25.6	18.6	46.3	39.8	21.6	22.8
	Post	24.8‡	44.6	31.7	13.9	40.0	47.3	25.5	22.4
ii)		Ex-Armadale Papers				Control (Winnipeg FP)			
Front page	Pre	33.6†	31.3	13.4†	44.8‡	28.1	46.9	29.7	18.8
	Post	22.7†	26.1	27.7†	54.6‡	39.1	39.1	28.1	18.8
Editorials	Pre	72.7	25.8	25.8†	13.6‡	74.4	20.5	35.9†	5.1
	Post	61.0	30.5	40.7†	25.4‡	64.7	35.3	23.5†	2.9
Features	Pre	77.4	19.0†	20.2	14.3	65.4	42.3	19.3	25.0‡
	Post	69.6	34.8†	27.5	18.8	56.8	36.4	13.6	11.4‡
Letters	Pre	29.9	47.7†	30.2	31.5†	32.1	47.2	26.4‡	19.8
	Post	31.3	34.4†	24.2	49.2†	28.0	51.5	17.4‡	16.7
iii)		Ex-Southam Papers				Control papers			
Front page	Pre	46.2	29.5	20.3	27.2	50.3	14.0†	16.2†	34.6
	Post	43.1	27.9	19.1	31.7	48.3	22.7†	24.4†	33.7
Editorials	Pre	75.6†	24.4†	17.3	16.1	72.9‡	16.5‡	23.5	21.2
	Post	58.8†	36.8†	17.6	20.3	61.0‡	25.6‡	23.2	26.8
Features	Pre	69.3†	26.5†	20.1	15.0	69.5	16.9	16.9	24.0
	Post	61.5†	36.1†	17.5	16.9	66.1	21.8	22.4	23.6
Letters	Pre	37.4	40.8	20.9†	31.3	40.5	22.9†	17.2†	49.9†
	Post	34.4	39.9	12.0†	36.0	39.5	30.0†	25.3†	39.5†

* Multiple foci were coded for each story where appropriate; consequently row percentages for paper groups sum to more than 100%

† Pre- and post-acquisition differences significant at the .05 level

‡ Pre- and post-acquisition differences significant at the .10 level (suggestive of trends)

papers, interest in economic topics increased for all types of content, except for letters to the editor, with increases for front page and editorial content being statistically significant. Curiously, and counter to other papers, the control paper moved in the opposite direction, showing declines in interest in economic issues in all types of content, with the decline statistically significant for editorials.

As with the ex-Thomson papers discussed above, coverage of social issues tended not to follow the trend established by coverage of political issues. For the ex-Armadale papers, while attention to social topics decreased in front-page material and in letters to the editor, it increased in editorials and features, with statistically significant changes for both increases in features and decreases in letters to the editor. The pattern for the *Winnipeg Free Press* was also mixed: while social issues decreased as a proportion of front-page material (consistent with the ex-Armadale papers), all other types of content increased.

The ex-Southam papers were also consistent with hypothesis H3 with respect to trends in attention given to political issues, which was down for all categories of content except letters to the editor, where there was no change. What is more, the decline in attention to political issues (nearly 17% in editorials) was statistically significant. On the other hand, the change in attention paid to economic issues was neither consistent with hypothesis H3 nor with the trends seen in the other Hollinger-purchased papers; there were either declines or there was no change from the pre- to the post-acquisition period. Also out of step with other Hollinger-acquired papers was attention to social issues, which clearly increased in the ex-Southam papers, with statistically significant increases of 12.4% in editorials and 9.6% in features.

In the control papers, *The Globe and Mail* and the *Toronto Star*, trends with respect to attention to political issues tended to follow those seen in nearly all papers—interest declined. For the control papers, there was also an increase in attention given to economic issues, a trend seen in nearly all papers except, as noted above, in the ex-Southam papers. In the two control papers, a dramatic increase in attention to social issues was apparent, with statistically significant increases of 8.7% in front-page coverage and 7.1% in letters to the editor.

Trends for all Hollinger-purchased papers appeared generally consistent with one part of hypothesis H3 (diminished attention paid to politics), data for both the ex-Thomson and ex-Armadale papers (but not for the ex-Southam papers) also confirmed the hypothesized increase in attention to economic issues. While these trends were also characteristic of most control papers, the *Winnipeg Free Press* emerged as somewhat unique among the papers—it registered a decreased interest in economic issues in all content categories, combined with increased attention to political issues of over 10% in front-page content. There appeared to be no clear trend with respect to social issues, either in the Hollinger-purchased papers or their various control papers.

Evaluation-providing Functions

Beginning with Table 3.4, and continuing with Tables 3.5, 3.6, 3.7A, 3.7B, 3.7C, and 3.8, we examined additional specific hypothesized changes in both content and evaluation found in the newly acquired Hollinger papers, contrasted with those found in their control papers. Specifically, in the Hollinger-acquired papers we expected to find *more* items dealing with free trade, along with *a more positive* evaluation of free trade (H4); *more* items dealing with

TABLE 3.4 Coverage and evaluation of free trade, by ownership, pre- and post-acquisition (evaluation coded -1=negative evaluation; 0=neutral; +1=positive evaluation)

i)	Ex-Thomson Papers				Control (Halifax CH)			
	Pre	Post	Pre	Post	Pre	Post	Pre	Post
	Mentions		Evaluation		Mentions		Evaluation	
Front page	3.7%	.7%	-0.3	+1.0	2.7%	1.4%	+0.5	+1.0
Editorials	1.9%	4.9%	+1.0	+1.0	3.0%	0%	+0.5	—
Features	5.4%	7.8%	-0.4	-0.2	0%	0%	—	—
Letters	.8%	1.0%	*+1.0*	*-1.0*	.6%	0%	*-1.0*	—
ii)	Ex-Armadale Papers				Control (Winnipeg Free Press)			
Front page	2.2%	2.5%	*0*	*0*	3.1%	4.7%	+.5*	*-1.0**
Editorials	4.5%	0%	*0*	—	2.6%	8.8%	0.0	+0.7
Features	7.1%	2.9%	-0.17	1	5.8%	11.4%	-1.0	+0.6
Letters	1.3%	0.8%	*0*	*1*	2.8%	0.8%	-0.7	*-1.0*
iii)	Ex-Southam Papers				Control			
Front page	1.6%	1.2%	-.2	.0	4.5%	6.4%	+.1	+.0
Editorials	3.0%	1.0%	.6	.5	4.7%	3.7%	+.0	+.7
Features	4.8%*	1.8%*	0	.33	3.2%	7.3%	+.4	+.1
Letters	0%	0.4%	—	.0	1.5%	1.9%	+.2	+.1

* Pre- and post-acquisition differences significant at.05
† Pre- and post-acquisition differences significant at.10 (indicative of trend)
Italics: fewer than 10 cases

business, along with *a more positive* evaluation of business (H4); *fewer* items dealing with organized labour, along with *a more negative* evaluation of unions (H5); more items dealing with federal and provincial conservative political parties (the PCs and Reform), along with *a more positive* evaluation of their positions and policies (H6); *fewer* items dealing with the one political party on the left of the political spectrum (the NDP), along with *a more negative* evaluation of its positions and policies (H6); and finally, a shift to *a more right-wing*, conservative ideological orientation in newspaper content generally (H7).

Data in Table 3.4 address the issue of free trade, and show both the level of interest in (as measured by percentage of mentions) and the direction and strength of evaluation (with a negative evaluation coded -1 and a positive evaluation coded +1). For ex-Thomson papers, findings with respect to interest in free trade were mixed. For the Hollinger as well as the control papers, front-page interest declined following their acquisition by Hollinger in 1996, casting doubt on hypothesis H4. On the other hand, data for both editorials and features, which may be more open to ownership influence, appear to confirm the hypothesis. The ex-Thomson papers ran increased percentages of editorials and features dealing with free trade, while

The Chronicle-Herald showed declining interest in its editorials, and no interest and no change in features. Finally, free trade received little attention in letters to the editor in Atlantic Canada.

Data on evaluations were based on small numbers. This is often the case with respect to analyses of evaluations in newspaper articles, as many stories report facts without judgments being obvious to the reader, or in our case to the coders. Generally, these data pointed in the direction of support for the hypothesis. This was especially true in front-page treatment, where, although coverage declined, evaluations of free trade became dramatically more positive, moving from -0.29 under Thomson ownership to +1.0 under Hollinger ownership. In this case, the change for the control paper, while it moved in the same direction, was not as dramatic, moving from +0.5 to +1.0. Editorial evaluations of free trade remained consistently positive for Thomson papers: +1.0 in both ownership periods. With respect to feature material, the findings were less clear. While the direction of change was in the hypothesized direction (rising from -0.40 to -0.17), the overall evaluation remained negative under Hollinger ownership. Thus, while the percentage of feature columns dealing with the free trade issue increased, the balance of their evaluations on the issue had not shifted to the positive side of the ledger. Letters to the editor dealing with free trade were so few as to preclude any meaningful analysis, although it is noted that the letters in the ex-Thomson papers did not reflect increased approval.

In the Prairies, the issue of free trade played out somewhat differently. Contrary to coverage in Atlantic Canada, attention to the issue increased slightly in front-page coverage in both ex-Armadale papers and in their control paper, the *Winnipeg Free Press*. In the *Free Press*, this trend of increased attention to free trade was seen for all types of content except letters to the editor. However, contrary to our hypothesis, with the exception of their front pages, the ex-Armadale papers showed less interest in free trade than did their control paper.

Firm trends with respect to evaluation were even harder to discern in the Prairies than had been the case for Atlantic Canada. While greater approval was registered in feature material (rising from -0.17 to +1.0), approval fell for letters to the editor (dropping from 0.0 to -1.0) in the ex-Armadale papers. The control paper recorded a statistically significant drop in approval in front-page content (+0.5 to -1.0), as well as a decline in support in letters to the editor. However, these declines were balanced by increases in approval for editorials and features (0.0 to +0.67 and -1.0 to +0.60, respectively).

The analysis of coverage of the free trade issue in the ex-Southam papers was also not supportive of hypothesis H4. Interest in the issue declined in three of the four types of content, with a statistically significant decrease of 3% for features. Evaluations of free trade became somewhat more positive in front-page stories and features, while in editorials evaluations became slightly more negative. Not only was free trade initially given greater attention in the two control papers, this attention increased on the front pages and in features during the second three-year period of the study. Evaluation in the control papers tended to be more negative, except for editorials, which saw an increase in positive evaluation from 0.0 to +0.67.

Table 3.5, which examines attention to and evaluation of business issues, presents data that once again do not speak with a clear voice in support of our hypothesis (H4.). With the ex-Thomson papers in Atlantic Canada, attention to business on the front pages and in features did in fact increase, but the control paper actually showed greater increases for both categories of content. Editorials presented strong evidence of counter trends, as the percentage of editorials mentioning business issues declined by 19% for ex-Thomson papers and by 12% for the control paper; both of these changes were statistically significant. Letters to the editor dealing with business decreased slightly in the ex-Thomson papers and increased moderately in the control paper.

With respect to evaluations, the data were even less supportive of hypothesis (H4). For the ex-Thomson papers, no change in evaluation was seen in front-page stories, while a move in the negative direction was evident in editorials (from +0.13 to -0.57) and in features (from -0.02 to -0.53), the latter change being statistically significant. These same evaluative trends were seen as well for the control paper. With respect to letters to the editor, evaluations became less negative in the ex-Thomson papers, while the trend ran in the opposite direction for the control paper.

For the ex-Armadale papers, attention to business issues on front pages increased by a statistically significant 13%. Business issues also received increased attention in letters to the editor. However, contradicting our hypothesis H4, attention to business fell in editorial and feature content. In contrast, for the control paper, there was increased attention to business issues in all types of content.

With respect to evaluation (H4), in the ex-Armadale papers, every type of content, except letters to the editor, showed increases in positive evaluations of business. In the control paper, two types of content (front page and features) showed increased positive evaluations, while the other two types of content (editorials and letters to the editor) were more critical of business during the final three years of the study.

Our examination of the ex-Southam papers presented another situation where the findings were mixed with respect to support for our hypotheses. While front pages and editorials showed increased attention to business issues,

TABLE 3.5 Coverage and evaluation of business, by ownership, pre- and post-acquisition (evaluation coded -1=negative evaluation; 0=neutral; +1=positive evaluation)

i)	Ex-Thomson Papers				Control (Halifax CH)			
	Pre	Post	Pre	Post	Pre	Post	Pre	Post
	Mentions		Evaluation		Mentions		Evaluation	
Front page	19.7%	23.0%	-.2	-.2	9.5%	14.9%	-.6	+.1
Editorials	28.8%*	9.8%*	+.1	-.5	11.9%*	23.9%*	+.4	+.3
Features	19.6%	22.1%	-.0*	-.5*	8.0%	16.7%	.0	-.4
Letters	20.9%	18.8%	-.5	-.2	9.9%	14.5%	-.3	-.6
ii)	Ex-Armadale Papers				Control (Winnipeg Free Press)			
Front page	23.1%*	36.1%*	+.2	+.2	18.8%	28.1%	.0	+.3
Editorials	22.7%	18.6%	+.2	+.4	12.8%	17.6%	+.6	-.3
Features	42.9%	30.4%	+.2	+.5	11.5%†	25.0%†	-.5	.0
Letters	24.8%	28.9%	-.2	-.6	14.2%	18.9%	-.1	-.4
iii)	Ex-Southam Papers				Control			
Front page	20.0%†	25.2%†	+.1	+.1	34.1%*	57.6%*	-.03	.05
Editorials	15.5%	21.4%	-.1†	+.2†	58.8%	54.9%	.0	-.02
Features	19.8%	15.1%	-.3*	+.4*	33.1%*	47.9%*	-.12	-.07
Letters	10.7%	10.2%	-.1	-.2	58.7%*	51.5%*	-.08	-.07

* Pre- and post-acquisition differences significant at the .05 level
† Pre- and post-acquisition differences significant at the .10 level (suggestive of trends)
Italics: : fewer than 10 cases

features showed less attention and there was no change in letters to the editor. On the evaluative dimension, trends with respect to editorials and features ran strongly in the positive direction, with a statistically significant increase (from -0.26 to +0.41) seen in features. Evaluations in front-page stories and in letters to the editor either remained the same or became slightly more negative.

Data for the two control papers, *The Globe and Mail* and the *Toronto Star*, not only showed an extraordinary interest in business issues, but showed as well that this interest increased significantly for front-page stories (34.1% to 57.6%) and features (33.1% to 47.9%), while it decreased significantly for letters to the editor (58.7% to 51.5%). Evaluations of business were mainly flat across the two periods and were characterized by a hardly perceptible negative orientation.

A reduced focus on labour unions combined with a more negative evaluation of their activities under Hollinger ownership was the change hypothesized (H5) based on the literature. Data in Table 3.6 are again inconclusive with respect to ex-Thomson papers. One category of content (editorials) moved in the expected direction, another (front-page stories) moved in the opposite direction; features showed a combination of less attention with less negative evaluation, and letters to the editor showed a combination of less interest and more positive evaluation.

TABLE 3.6 Coverage and evaluation of unions, by ownership, pre- and post-acquisition (evaluation coded -1=negative evaluation; 0=neutral; +1=positive evaluation)

i)	Ex-Thomson Papers				Control (Halifax CH)			
	Pre	Post	Pre	Post	Pre	Post	Pre	Post
	Mentions		Evaluation		Mentions		Evaluation	
Front page	16.0%	20.3%	-.03	+.17	8.1%	12.2%	+.33	+.11
Editorials	23.1%	12.2%	+.13	-.50	7.5%*	27.5%*	+.38	+.29
Features	17.4%	14.3%	-.50	-.36	6.0%	11.9%	+.67	-.20
Letters	20.2%	13.9%	-.08	.07	6.8%	7.9%	+.09	-.08
ii)	Ex-Armadale Papers				Control (Winnipeg Free Press)			
Front page	23.1%	21.8%	+.03	+.04	6.3%*	23.4%*	-.25	0.0
Editorials	22.7%	13.6%	+.07	0.0	6.1%	8.8%	0.0	0.0
Features	41.7%*	18.8%*	-.03	0.0	9.6%	13.6%	0.0	+.17
Letters	24.8%†	16.4%†	+.05	-.05	6.6%*	15.9%*	+.14	+.19
iii)	Ex-Southam Papers				Control			
Front page	17.4%	19.6%	+.07	-.03	27.4%*	50.6%*	+.08	-.05
Editorials	11.3%	16.5%	-.05	+.06	54.1%	53.2%	+.02†	-.04†
Features	16.9%	13.6%	-.09	+.02	63.6%*	49.1%*	-.01	+.01
Letters	9.3%	8.6%	0.0	-.06	56.3%*	48.2%*	.02*	-.01*

*Pre- and post-acquisition differences significant at the .05 level
†Pre- and post-acquisition differences significant at the .10 level (suggestive of trends)
Italics: fewer than 10 cases

In the case of front-page stories, mentions of organized labour increased by about 4% in both ex-Thomson papers and their control paper, and for the ex-Thomson papers evaluations became more positive, moving from -0.03 to +0.17. In the case of the control paper, however, evaluations became more negative, dropping from +0.33 to +0.11 over the two periods of the study. Editorials provide strong evidence confirming the hypothesis. Not only did attention drop from 23.1% to 12.2% in the ex-Thomson papers, editorial evaluations also became more negative from +0.13 to -0.50. With respect to attention, the control paper moved in the opposite direction, increasing a statistically significant amount, from 7.5% to 27.5%, while its evaluation of unions remained positive but dropped from +0.38 to +0.29. With respect to features, attention dropped by about 3% in the ex-Thomson papers and increased by about 6% in their control paper. In this case, however, a negative evaluation of -0.50 under Thomson ownership actually improved slightly to -0.36 under Hollinger ownership. For the control paper, a positive evaluation of +0.67 in the first three years of the study fell to -0.20 in the second three years. For letters to the editor, there was a decrease in reader input on labour issues (20.2% to 13.9%) in the ex-Thomson papers, however, the evaluation of unions contained in the letters to the editor turned slightly more positive

(-0.08 to +0.07). For the control paper, attention to labour issues increased marginally in letters to the editor, and the evaluation of labour issues became slightly more positive. Only for editorials did the hypothesized relationship (less attention and more negative evaluation) materialize in the ex-Thomson papers. Even here, we found that the control paper also moved in the same direction with respect to evaluations, albeit still ending up on the positive side of the ledger while the ex-Thomson papers shifted from a positive to a negative evaluation.

In the Prairie comparison, the issues surrounding organized labour offered the strongest support yet seen in our analysis for confirmation of a critical school hypothesis. For ex-Armadale papers, attention to labour issues declined for all types of newspaper content, with a statistically significant drop from 41.7% to 18.8% recorded for feature material. Moreover, and significant for our hypothesis, the control paper registered increases in attention to labour issues for all types of content; changes were statistically significant for both front-page coverage and letters to the editor.

These clear trends, however, did not carry over into the realm of evaluation where, for the ex-Armadale papers, we see a change from a supportive to a critical posture (from +0.05 to -0.05) only in letters to the editor. The control paper registered modest increases in positive evaluation of unions in all categories of content except for editorials, which hovered at the neutral point.

While the trends dealing with attention to labour unions confirmed the hypothesis rather strongly, it must be pointed out that evaluations of labour unions were neither strongly positive nor strongly negative on the part of either ex-Armadale papers or their control paper, either before or after the sale of the former to Hollinger. At most, we can confirm that less attention was paid to labour unions in Armadale papers following their purchase by Hollinger and that their control paper moved in the opposite direction. However, the data do not suggest that the decrease in attention given to unions by the ex-Armadale papers was accompanied by a more negative evaluation of their activities.

Breaking the consensus established by the ex-Thomson and ex-Armadale papers, the ex-Southam papers, although showing decreased interest in organized labour in two categories of content (features and letters to the editor), recorded increased attention in front-page stories and editorials. In addition to these countervailing trends, there was no marked movement in either direction with respect to evaluation of union activity and policies, which overall tended to be neither strongly positive nor strongly negative.

As they had for business issues, the control papers for the ex-Southam papers focused a great deal of attention on issues related to organized labour

TABLE 3.7A(i) Coverage and evaluation of federal political parties, by ownership, pre- and post-acquisition (ex-Thomson papers and control paper)
(evaluation coded -1=negative evaluation; 0=neutral; +1=positive evaluation)

		% mentioned		eval (-1.0 to +1.0)		% mentioned		eval (-1.0 to +1.0)	
Federal Party	Pre/ Post	Ex-Thomson	Control	Ex-Thomson	Control	Ex-Thomson	Control	Ex-Thomson	Control
		Front Page				Editorials			
Liberals	Pre	4.3	0	0.0†	—	11.5	3.0	0.0	+1.0
	Post	3.4	1.4	-1.0†	-1.0	12.2	1.4	+.60	-1.0
Reform	Pre	0	2.7	—	-1.0	1.9	3.0	-1.0	-1.0
	Post	1.4	4.1	1.0	-.33	0	1.4	—	-1.0
PC	Pre	1.6	0	-1.0	—	3.8	4.5	0	-1.0
	Post	.7	0	1.0	—	2.4	1.4	-1.0	-1.0
Bloc Quebecois	Pre	2.7	0	-.6	—	1.9	1.5	-1.0	-1.0
	Post	0	1.4	—	-1.0	4.9	1.4	0	-1.0
NDP	Pre	.5	0	-1.0	—	1.9	1.5	+1.0	-1.0
	Post	0	0	—	—	0	1.4	—	-1.0
All fed. parties	**Pre**	**5.9**	**2.7**	**-.18**	**-1.0**	**17.3**	**9.0**	**0**	**-.33**
	Post	**4.1**	**6.8**	**-.33**	**-.60**	**14.6**	**2.8**	**+.33**	**-1.0**
		Features				Letters			
Liberals	Pre	20.7†	2.0	-.37	-1.0	5.4	1.9	-.14	-.33
	Post	27.3†	2.4	-.81	+1.0	6.9	4.2	+.43	-1.0
Reform	Pre	6.5	2.0	-1.0	-1.0	.8	.6	+1.0	-1.0
	Post	2.6	0	0	—	1.0	2.4	+1.0	+.50
PC	Pre	7.6	4.0	-1.0	-1.0	2.3	2.5	-.33	-1.0
	Post	5.2	2.4	-1.0	-1.0	1.0	1.8	1.0	-1.0
Bloc Quebecois	Pre	8.7	4.0	-1.0	-1.0	0	.6	—	-1.0
	Post	3.9	2.4	-1.0	-1.0	0	2.4	—	-1.0
NDP	Pre	1.1	0	-1.0	—	0	0	—	—
	Post	0	0	—	—	0	.6	—	-1.0
All fed.parties	**Pre**	**31.5**	**6.0**	**-.73**	**-1.0**	**7.8**	**4.9**	**-.20**	**-.75**
	Post	**32.5**	**7.1**	**-.76**	**-.33**	**7.9**	**7.3**	**-.33**	**-.83**

* Pre- and post-acquisition differences significant at the .05 level
† Pre- and post-acquisition differences significant at the .10 level (suggestive of trends)
Italics: fewer than 10 cases

and, although this interest declined significantly for features and letters to the editor, a statistically significant increase in attention of just over 23% was recorded in front-page stories. Also, evaluations of organized labour tended to group around the neutral point in the control papers, with not much movement in either direction. This was also the case with the ex-Southam papers.

Tables in the 3.7A series show the extent to which all federal political parties were mentioned in front-page stories, editorials, features, and letters to the editor, as well as indicate their evaluation (negative coded -1 and positive coded +1), as contained in the commentary on those parties. Tables in the 3.7B series offer the same information for all provincial political parties.

Our hypothesis (H6) led us to expect *increased* attention and *more positive* evaluations given to the Reform and Progressive Conservative parties and *less* attention and *more negative* evaluations given to the New Democratic Party (NDP) following the sale of the various chain-owned newspapers to Hollinger. Finally, Table 3.7C shows the combined coverage given to all political parties, at both federal and provincial levels.

For the ex-Thomson newspapers, very few data in Table 3.7A(i) confirm hypothesis H6 dealing with increased attention to and support for parties on the right. The only federal political party to obtain any significant press attention was the governing Liberal party, but any increases in coverage under Hollinger ownership were modest and the coverage decreased marginally on the front page. In the ex-Thomson papers, evaluations of the Liberals became more positive in editorials and letters to the editor, while they became more negative in front-page stories and features.

The parties on both the right and left of the Canadian political spectrum garnered very little attention in any category of content. The high-water mark was 7.6% for features dealing with the Progressive Conservative party (PCs) under Thomson ownership; this fell to 5.2% following the sale to Hollinger. The Reform party also achieved its highest percentage of coverage in editorials under Thomson ownership (6.5%), falling off to 2% after the sale. Both the Reform and PC parties were evaluated positively in the few front-page stories and letters to the editor in the ex-Thomson papers after their sale to Hollinger; however, this trend did not extend to editorials and features. Coverage of the NDP was minimal under both owners, and evaluations of the party tended to be negative as well.

In terms of overall interest in federal political parties, there were no clear trends evident as a result of the ownership change: for front pages and editorials, interest was down slightly, while for features and letters to the editor, interest was up even more slightly. Perhaps the most significant finding was that the Thomson papers (both before and after their sale) ran far more political commentary on federal political parties in their editorials and features than appeared in their control paper.

Table 3.7A(ii) presents data on the coverage and evaluation of federal political parties in ex-Armadale papers and their control paper. In the Prairies, as in Atlantic Canada, the Liberal party received the greatest amount of media attention. Moreover, this held true for both ex-Armadale papers and their control paper, although this coverage dropped in editorial and feature material during the post-acquisition period. Press attention did not tend to be focused on parties of the right and, with the exception of feature material in the ex-Armadale papers and letters to the editor in their control paper, attention

TABLE 3.7A(ii) Coverage and evaluation of federal political parties, by ownership, pre- and post-acquisition (ex-Armadale papers and control paper)
(evaluation coded -1=negative evaluation; 0=neutral; +1=positive evaluation)

		% mentioned		eval (-1.0 to +1.0)		% mentioned		eval (-1.0 to +1.0)	
Federal Party	Pre/ post	Ex-Armadale	Control	Ex-Armadale	Control	Ex-Armadale	Control	Ex-Armadale	Control
		Front page				Editorials			
Liberals	Pre	5.2	3.1	-.71	0.0	22.7	23.1*	-.33	-.44
	Post	5.0	7.8	-.33	-.20	16.9	5.9*	-.60	0.0
Reform	Pre	1.5	1.6	+1.0	-1.0	4.5	7.7	-1.0	-.33
	Post	.8	0.0	+1.0	—	3.2	2.9	-1.0	-1.0
PC	Pre	1.5	1.6	-1.0	+1.0	9.1*	7.7	-.33	-.33
	Post	.8	0.0	-1.0	—	0.0*	0.0	—	-.33
Bloc Quebecois	Pre	1.5	1.6	0	-1.0	7.6†	2.6	-.20	-1.0
	Post	.8	0.0	-1.0	—	0.0†	2.9	—	-1.0
NDP	Pre	2.2	1.6	+1.0	-1.0	1.5	2.6	+1.0	+1.0
	Post	1.7	0.0	0.0	—	0.0	0.0	—	—
All fed. parties	**Pre**	**6.0**	**6.3**	**-.28**	**-.33**	**36.4†**	**33.3***	**-.35**	**-.26**
	Post	**5.9**	**7.8**	**-.29**	**-.20**	**20.3†**	**8.6***	**-.67**	**-.33**
		Features				Letters			
Liberals	Pre	20.2	7.7	+.50	-.75	8.1	10.4*	-.50	-.64
	Post	14.5	4.5	-.60	-1.0	10.9	3.0*	-.71	-.40
Reform	Pre	6.0	1.9	-.20	-1.0	.7	3.8	-1.0	-1.0
	Post	4.3	4.5	-.33	-1.0	2.3	1.5	-1.0	0.0
PC	Pre	10.7	3.8	-1.0	0.0	6.0*	5.7*	-.78	-.33
	Post	5.8	2.3	+.50	-1.0	.8*	.8*	-1.0	-1.0
Bloc Quebecois	Pre	6.0	3.8	+.20	-1.0	0.0	3.8*	—	-1.0
	Post	2.9	4.5	-1.0	-1.0	.8	0.0*	-1.0	—
NDP	Pre	4.8	0.0	-1.0	—	2.0	2.8	-1.0	-.33
	Post	1.4	0.0	-1.0	—	1.6	.8	0.0	-1.0
All fed. parties	**Pre**	**29.8**	**15.4**	**-.36**	**-.75**	**14.1**	**13.2†**	**-.67**	**-.48**
	Post	**18.8**	**15.9**	**-.35**	**-1.0**	**14.8**	**6.1†**	**-.68**	**-.50**

*Pre- and post-acquisition differences significant at the .05 level
†Pre- and post-acquisition differences significant at the .10 level (suggestive of trends)
Italics: fewer than 10 cases

to the Reform and PC parties declined in the second three-year period of the study. Attention to the federal NDP also declined for both categories of papers over the study period.

Evaluations of federal political parties in the ex-Armadale papers are at best ambiguous with respect to our hypotheses. In both periods, in front page coverage, Reform was evaluated at +1.0 while the PCs were evaluated at -1.0. In editorials and letters to the editor, however, Reform was evaluated at -1.0 in both pre- and post-acquisition periods, while for features the -0.20 recorded under Armadale fell to -0.33 under Hollinger ownership. Attention to all political parties remained constant for front pages and letters to the editor in the

TABLE 3.7A(iii) Coverage and evaluation of federal political parties, by ownership, pre- and post-acquisition (ex-Southam papers and control papers)
(evaluation coded -1=negative evaluation; 0=neutral; +1=positive evaluation)

		% mentioned		eval (-1.0 to +1.0)		% mentioned		eval (-1.0 to +1.0)	
Federal Party	Pre/ post	Ex-Southam	Control	Ex-Southam	Control	Ex-Southam	Control	Ex-Southam	Control
		Front page				Editorials			
Liberals	Pre	7.9*	6.1	+.17*	+.45	16.7	15.3	-.32	-.31†
	Post	17.0*	7.0	-.16*	+.33	12.1	20.7	-.23	+.35†
Reform	Pre	2.0*	4.6*	-.17	0	3.0	5.9	-.60	-.60†
	Post	15.5*	.6*	0	+1.0	6.6	1.2	-.33	-1.0†
PC	Pre	2.3*	2.2	-.57*	-.75*	4.2	4.7	-.71	-.25
	Post	12.9*	.6	0*	+1.0*	4.9	1.2	-.22	-1.0
Bloc Quebecois	Pre	3.3*	3.4	+.01	+.17	5.4	7.1	-.56	-.67
	Post	12.3*	1.2	0	-.5	2.2	1.2	-.25	-1.0
NDP	Pre	1.2*	2.2	0	+.50	0	0	—	—
	Post	12.3*	.6	0	+1.0	2.2	0	-.25	—
All fed. parties	**Pre**	**9.8***	**10.6**	**+.02**	**+.13**	**24.4†**	**23.5**	**-.49**	**-.37***
	Post	**18.2***	**7.6**	**-.12**	**+.40**	**16.5†**	**20.7**	**-.37**	**+.29***
		Features				Letters			
Liberals	Pre	11.5*	17.5	-.11	-.30	5.6	6.6	-.54	-.52
	Post	28.1*	18.8	-.24	-.48	4.4	6.6	-.76	-.57
Reform	Pre	5.4*	3.9	-.53*	-.67	3.9*	2.2†	-.53	0
	Post	20.1*	5.5	-.16*	-.56	.9*	.7†	-1.0	-.33
PC	Pre	4.8*	5.8	-.80*	-.56	2.6*	4.4*	-.09*	-.56
	Post	19.2*	6.7	-.14*	-.18	.5*	2.1*	-.33*	-.67
Bloc Quebecois	Pre	10.9*	3.9	-.79*	-.17†	3.7	1.7	-.50*	-.29†
	Post	17.8	4.8	-.22*	-.88†	2.3	.7	-1.0*	-1.0†
NDP	Pre	2.2*	1.3†	-.14	0	1.6*	2.2	+.14†	-.22
	Post	16.6*	4.8†	-.05	-.38	.4*	.2	-1.0†	-1.0
All fed. parties	**Pre**	**20.1***	**22.1**	**-.55***	**-.35**	**10.7***	**9.1**	**-.57†**	**-.45**
	Post	**31.7***	**23.6**	**-.32***	**-.47**	**7.0**	**9.5**	**-.86†**	**-.57**

* Pre- and post-acquisition differences significant at the .05 level
† Pre- and post-acquisition differences significant at the .10 level (suggestive of trends)
Italics: fewer than 10 cases

ex-Armadale papers, while it increased slightly for front-page news and remained the same for features in the *Winnipeg Free Press.* Sharp declines were posted for editorial commentary in both categories of papers: for feature material in the ex-Armadale papers, and for letters to the editor in the control paper.

It is clear that, with respect to federal political parties, at least for front-page stories and features, the ex-Southam papers showed a marked increase in attention to parties of all stripes, as every party recorded significant increases for both types of content. For editorials, there was a decline in attention paid to the Liberals and an increase in attention given Reform. For letters to the editor, however, decreases were recorded for every party. On this dimension, the control papers behaved uniquely: on their front pages and in letters to the editor, attention to parties declined except for the Liberal party, which received slightly increased coverage during the second three-year period. Editorial attention also increased only for the Liberals, while in features every party scored modest increases.

On the dimension of evaluation, in the ex-Southam papers we see evidence of the hypothesized (H6) positive shift with respect to Reform and, to a lesser extent, the PCs. On the front pages, a -0.17 evaluation for Reform under Southam ownership improved to 0 under Hollinger; for editorials, the evaluation improved from -0.60 to -0.33, while for features it improved from -0.53 to -0.16. Only for letters to the editor was there a negative trend, a decline from -0.53 to -1.0. While evaluations also improved for the PCs, at best the parties on the right tended to be evaluated neutrally under Hollinger ownership. As was the case for other parties, attention to the NDP increased in ex-Southam papers, but in this case evaluations tended to remain the same or to become more negative; for letters to the editor, a +0.4 evaluation under Southam fell to a -1.0 under Hollinger ownership. The two control papers actually evaluated the Reform and PC parties more positively than did the ex-Southam papers in their front-page coverage: we observed +1.0 for both in the second three years of the study. This did not, however, extend to other types of content, where all parties except the Liberals came under fire; instead, the Liberals came under fire in features and letters to the editor.

At the provincial level, the analysis shown in Table 3.7B(i) is complicated not only by the fact that the newspapers chosen for the comparison were located in three different provinces, but also by the fact that the Liberal and Progressive Conservative parties were closer competitors in Atlantic Canada than they were federally during the period of the study. As well, because the Reform Party had never sanctioned provincial counterparts, any pro-conservative spin at the provincial level would have had to be directed toward the PCs alone.

The one relationship that confirms the party hypothesis (H6) is found with respect to increased attention to, and positive evaluation of, the PCs in editorials in the ex-Thomson papers (an increase in attention, from 1.9% to 12.2%, combined with a shift in evaluation of that party from 0.0 to +1.0). However, these trends do not appear in other types of content. Interestingly, the NDP also showed a similar, though less robust, trend with respect to editorials (an increase in the level of attention from 1.9% to 4.9%, and a shift in evaluation from 0.0 to +1.0). For both the PCs and the NDP, it must be emphasized that the measurement of evaluations is based on fewer than ten cases.

TABLE 3.7B(i) Coverage and evaluation of provincial political parties, by ownership, pre- and post-acquisition (ex-Thomson papers and control paper)
(evaluation coded -1=negative evaluation; 0=neutral; +1=positive evaluation)

		% mentioned		eval (-1.0 <> +1.0)		% mentioned		eval (-1.0 <> +1.0)	
Provincial Party	Pre/ Post	Ex-Thomson	Control	Ex-Thomson	Control	Ex-Thomson	Control	Ex-Thomson	Control
		Front page				Editorials			
Liberals	Pre	5.9	6.8†	-.27	-.60	15.4	29.9†	0	-1.0
	Post	7.4	16.2†	-.27	-1.0	26.8	15.5†	-.45	-1.0
PC	Pre	0*	1.4	—	-1.0	1.9*	0	-1.0	—
	Post	4.1*	2.7	0	-1.0	12.2*	4.2	+1.0	-1.0
Bloc Quebecois	Pre	4.3	1.4	-.88	-1.0	0	0	—	—
	Post	0	0	—	—	0	0	—	—
NDP	Pre	.5	0*	-1.0	—	1.9	0	0	—
	Post	0	9.7*	—	+.71	4.9	4.2	+1.0	-.33
Any prov. party	**Pre**	**10.1**	**6.8***	**-.58**	-.60	**19.2†**	**29.9†**	**-1.0**	**-1.0**
	Post	**11.5**	**17.6***	**-1.0**	**-.51**	**34.1†**	**18.3†**	**0**	**-.92**
		Features				Letters			
Liberals	Pre	5.4	22.0	-1.0	-.82	14.0	25.3†	-.89	-1.0
	Post	7.8	14.3	-1.0	-1.0	7.9	16.4†	-.75	-1.0
PC	Pre	1.1	0	-1.0	—	2.3	.6	-.33	-.20
	Post	3.9	7.1	-.33	-1.0	2.0	3.0	-1.0	-1.0
Bloc Quebecois	Pre	5.4	0	-1.0	—	0	0	—	—
	Post	1.3	2.4	-1.0	-1.0	0	1.8	—	-1.0
NDP	Pre	5.4	0	-.2	—	0	.6	—	1.0
	Post	1.2	2.4	1.0	-1.0	0	1.2	—	-1.0
Any prov. party	**Pre**	**16.3**	**22.0***	**-.8**	**-.82**	**14.7**	**23.5**	**-.79**	**-.97**
	Post	**14.3**	**19.0***	**-.63**	**-1.0**	**9.9**	**19.4**	**-.80**	**-1.0**

*Pre- and post-acquisition differences significant at the .05 level
†Pre- and post-acquisition differences significant at the .10 level (suggestive of trends)
Italics: fewer than 10 cases

That Saskatchewan had an NDP government and Manitoba a PC government is no doubt the major explanatory factor underlying the distribution of data in Table 3.7B(ii), since governing parties naturally draw more attention in the press and coverage tends to be more critical as the press fulfills its watchdog function. In that both of these governments ran into difficulties in the years after 1996, it is not surprising that press attention to the NDP increased in every category of content in the ex-Armadale papers in Saskatchewan, while the same held true for the PCs in the *Winnipeg Free Press*. In both categories of papers, provincial parties as a whole received more attention in the post-acquisition period of the study.

Furthermore, when we examined evaluations of provincial political parties, we found that negativity was the general order of the day—there was scarcely a positive balance in the evaluation of any provincial party in any type of content, in either category of paper.

TABLE 3.7B(ii) Coverage and evaluation of provincial political parties, by ownership, pre- and post-acquisition (ex-Armadale papers and control paper)
(evaluation coded -1=negative evaluation; 0=neutral; +1=positive evaluation)

		% mentioned		eval (-1.0 <> +1.0)		% mentioned		eval (-1.0 <> +1.0)	
Provincial Party	Pre/ Post	Ex-Armadale	Control	Ex-Armadale	Control	Ex-Armadale	Control	Ex-Armadale	Control
		Front page				**Editorials**			
Liberals	Pre	.7	0.0	+1.0	—	4.5	5.1	.33	-1.0
	Post	1.7	0.0	0.0	—	3.4	5.9	-1.0	1.0
PC	Pre	5.2	1.6	-1.0	-1.0	1.5	7.7	-1.0	-1.0
	Post	2.5	6.3	-.31	-1.0	6.8	14.7	0.0	-.20
Bloc Quebecois	Pre	0.0	3.1	—	-1.0	3.0	2.6	-1.0	-1.0
	Post	0.0	0.0	—	—	0.0	2.6	—	-1.0
NDP	Pre	2.2*	0.0	+.33	—	9.1	0.0*	-.33	—
	Post	8.4*	1.6	-.60	+1.0	18.6	11.8*	-.27	-.50
Any prov. party	**Pre**	**7.5**	**4.7**	**-.50**	**-1.0**	**15.2**	**12.8**	**-.40**	**-1.0**
	Post	**10.1**	**6.3**	**-.58**	**-.75**	**23.7**	**26.5**	**-.38**	**-.11**
		Features				**Letters**			
Liberals	Pre	4.8	1.9	-.50	0.0	1.3	4.7*	1.0	-.60
	Post	8.7	2.3	-1.0	-1.0	1.6	0.0*	1.0	—
PC	Pre	2.4	3.8*	0.0	-.50	3.4	2.8	-.30	.33
	Post	2.9	5.9*	-1.0	-.43	1.6	7.6	0.0	-.60
Bloc Quebecois	Pre	3.8	3.8	-1.0	-1.0	0.0†	.9	—	-1.0
	Post	8.7	2.3	0.0	-1.0	2.3†	0.0	-1.0	—
NDP	Pre	15.5	3.8	-.55	0.0	7.4	2.8	-.45	-.33
	Post	17.4	4.5	-.50	0.0	10.9	3.0	-.57	0.0
Any prov. party	**Pre**	**19.0**	**9.6***	**-.83**	**-.60**	**9.4**	**9.4**	**-.43**	**-.30**
	Post	**26.1**	**22.7***	**-.56**	**-.50**	**14.1**	**8.3**	**-.55**	**-.55**

* Pre- and post-acquisition differences significant at the .05 level
† Pre- and post-acquisition differences significant at the .10 level (suggestive of trends)
Italics: fewer than 10 cases

An examination of provincial party coverage and evaluation in the ex-Southam and their control papers was without doubt the most complicated of the tasks we set ourselves. The papers in this comparison represented four provinces (stretching from Quebec to British Columbia), which were ruled at various times by a wide array of parties, from the NDP to the Parti Quebecois to the Progressive Conservative (in their more conservative incarnations, under Ralph Klein in Alberta and Mike Harris in Ontario).

As with federal parties, we found marked increased attention was paid to all provincial political parties in the ex-Southam papers after the Hollinger takeover, a trend especially evident on front pages and in features. For the control papers, there was a significant increase in interest shown to the PCs in front-page stories, editorials, and letters to the editor. This was most likely

TABLE 3.7B(iii) Coverage and evaluation of provincial political parties, by ownership, pre- and post-acquisition (ex-Southam papers and control papers)
(evaluation coded -1=negative evaluation; 0=neutral; +1=positive evaluation)

Provincial Party	Pre/ Post	% mentioned Ex-Southam	% mentioned Control	eval (-1.0 <> +1.0) Ex-Southam	eval (-1.0 <> +1.0) Control	% mentioned Ex-Southam	% mentioned Control	eval (-1.0 <> +1.0) Ex-Southam	eval (-1.0 <> +1.0) Control
		Front page				Editorials			
Liberals	Pre	4.9*	.6	-.33*	0.0	8.3	3.5	-.43*	+.33
	Post	14.1*	1.7	+.02*	+.67	3.8	1.2	+.29*	+1.0
PC	Pre	3.9*	1.1*	-.50*	+.50	6.0	4.7*	-1.0*	-1.0
	Post	13.8*	5.8*	-.06*	-.20	4.9	14.6*	-.33*	-.67
Bloc Quebecois	Pre	4.9*	2.8	-.40†	-.40	11.9	5.9	-.90	-1.0
	Post	13.5*	1.7	-.13†	-.33	8.2	3.7	-.80	-1.0
NDP	Pre	4.3*	2.2	0.0	-.25	4.8	7.1	0.0†	-.33
	Post	15.0*	1.2	-.12	-.50	5.5	1.2	-.70†	-1.0
Any prov. party	**Pre**	**12.8***	**5.0**	**-.41†**	**-.22**	**26.8***	**17.6**	**-.71**	**-.53**
	Post	**18.5***	**7.0**	**-.20†**	**-.17**	**16.5***	**18.3**	**-.67**	**-.73**
		Features				Letters			
Liberals	Pre	11.2*	3.9	-.14	-.83	2.8*	2.9*	0.0*	-.25
	Post	19.2*	4.2	-.04	-.71	.4*	.5*	-1.0*	-1.0
PC	Pre	7.0*	7.8	-.55*	-1.0	4.9	7.9*	-.71	-.53
	Post	21.3*	11.5	-.19*	-.84	4.9	12.3*	-.86	-.63
Bloc Quebecois	Pre	9.9*	4.5	-.84*	-.43	4.2	2.9*	-.67*	-.58
	Post	17.2*	1.8	-.26*	-1.0	3.9	.9*	-1.0*	-1.0
NDP	Pre	9.9*	6.5†	-.59*	-.60	3.7	5.2*	-.63†	-.29
	Post	23.1*	2.4†	-.22*	-.50	3.5	.9*	-.90†	-1.0
Any prov. party	**Pre**	**26.2**	**17.5**	**-.63***	**-.74**	**11.1**	**12.8**	**-.77***	**-.51**
	Post	**30.8**	**17.6**	**-.36***	**-.83**	**12.5**	**13.7**	**-.92***	**-.67**

* Pre- and post-acquisition differences significant at the .05 level
† Pre- and post-acquisition differences significant at the .10 level (suggestive of trends)
Italics: fewer than 10 cases

due to the location of both control papers in Ontario, a province that elected a controversial conservative government in the "Common Sense Revolution" in the Spring of 1995. While evaluations of the PCs remained negative in both types of papers over both periods of the study, evaluations tended to become less negative in both the ex-Southam and their control papers during the second three-year period of the study. This trend held true for every category of content except for letters to the editor, where evaluations became more negative. While we speculate on this point, perhaps this reflected the manifestation of opposition in letters to the editor as editorial content grew friendlier to governing parties.

Among the ex-Southam papers, front page, editorial, and feature coverage increased for the NDP, while letters to the editor remained at the same level.

TABLE 3.7C Coverage of all parties combined (federal and provincial), by ownership, pre- and post-acquisition

i)	Ex-Thomson Papers		Control (Halifax CH)	
	Pre-acquisition	Post-acquisition	Pre-acquisition	Post-acquisition
Front page	13.3%	14.9%	9.5%*	23.0%*
Editorials	34.6%	48.8%	38.8%*	21.1%*
Features	43.5%	42.9%	28.0%	21.4%
Letters	20.9%	15.8%	28.4%	25.5%
ii)	Ex-Armadale Papers		Control (Winnipeg FP)	
	Pre-acquisition	Post-acquisition	Pre-acquisition	Post-acquisition
Front page	12.7%	16.0%	9.4%	14.1%
Editorials	43.9%	39.0%	41.0%	32.4%
Features	45.2%	40.6%	21.2%†	36.4%†
Letters	20.1%	25.0%	18.9%	14.4%
iii)	Ex-Southam Papers		Controls	
	Pre-acquisition	Post-acquisition	Pre-acquisition	Post-acquisition
Front page	19.7%	24.0%	14.5%	12.8%
Editorials	42.2%*	30.2%*	37.6%	36.6%
Features	39.3%	44.4%	35.7%	37.6%
Letters	19.0%	17.4%	19.9%	22.2%

* Pre- and post-acquisition differences significant at the .05 level
† Pre- and post-acquisition differences significant at the .10 level (suggestive of trends)

Evaluations of the NDP became more negative in all categories of content except for features, where evaluations became somewhat more positive; evaluations of the party, however, remained on the negative side of the ledger even in features. In the two control papers, coverage of the provincial New Democratic parties declined in all categories of content, while evaluations of the parties tended to be negative, and became increasingly negative throughout the period of the study.

Table 3.7C combines data for all political parties at both the federal and provincial levels. We present these data to establish benchmarks of attention paid to political parties in general; differences in coverage from one party to another reflect shifts in partisanship rather than attention to partisan politics in general. Indeed what these data show is considerable stability in patterns of attention paid to political parties: attention to parties was particularly pronounced for editorials and features, with less coverage appearing in front-page stories and letters to the editor. As well, there is remarkable consistency among all newspapers studied—the Hollinger-acquired as well as their control papers—before and after the Hollinger acquisitions. The only statistically significant pre/post changes are seen for front-page and editorial interest in political parties in *The Chronicle Herald*, and for editorial interest among the ex-Southam papers.

TABLE 3.8 Left/right orientations of content, by ownership, and pre- and post-acquisition (far left=1; centre=3; far right=5)

i)	Ex-Thomson Papers		Control (Halifax CH)	
Location	Pre-acquisition	Post-acquisition	Pre-acquisition	Post-acquisition
Front page	2.54	2.93	2.80	3.10
Editorials	3.12	2.90	3.00	3.10
Features	2.92	2.76	2.82	2.75
Letters	2.76	2.67	2.97	2.89
ii)	**Ex-Armadale Papers**		**Control (Winnipeg FP)**	
Location	Pre-acquisition	Post-acquisition	Pre-acquisition	Post-acquisition
Front page	3.03	2.93	3.22	3.00
Editorials	3.15	3.00	3.25	2.95
Features	3.10	3.02	2.76	2.83
Letters	2.78	3.09	3.25	2.74
iii)	**Ex-Southam Papers**		**Controls**	
Location	Pre-acquisition	Post-acquisition	Pre-acquisition	Post-acquisition
Front page	3.24	3.09	3.10*	2.91*
Editorials	2.89*	3.23*	3.13	2.92
Features	2.72*	3.25*	2.99	2.90
Letters	2.83	2.84	2.57*	2.79*

* Pre- and post-acquisition differences significant at the .05 level
† Pre- and post-acquisition differences significant at the .10 level (suggestive of trends)

Our final table, Table 3.8, introduces data showing the overall ideological orientation of all four categories of content appearing in the newspapers, as measured on a 5-point scale on which "far left" was coded "1," centre was coded "3," and "far right" was coded "5."[7]

With the ex-Thomson papers, data point to a moderate shift to the right (from 2.54 to 2.93) with respect to front-page stories, matched by a shift to the right on the part of the control paper (from 2.8 to 3.1). This movement to the right was not, however, evident in editorials and features, where the orientation moved slightly toward the left. Ideological shifts in the control paper were less noticeable. In fact, in the post-acquisition period there is very little ideological distance between the ex-Thomson papers and their control paper. Both types of papers were positioned close to the midpoint of the scale.

With the ex-Armadale papers, contrary to hypothesized trends, data show them tending to move slightly toward the left after their acquisition by Hollinger: from 3.03 to 2.93 for front pages, from 3.15 to 3.0 for editorials, and from 3.10 to 3.02 for features. Only in the category of letters to the editor do we see the hypothesized shift to the right, from 2.78 to 3.09. Interestingly, a similar small shift to the left is evident in the control paper, as only in the category of features did the *Winnipeg Free Press* move slightly to the right, from 2.76 to 2.83.

The ex-Southam papers add evidence pointing to inconsistency with respect to ideological trends among Hollinger-acquired papers. The ex-Southam papers moved significantly to the right, as predicted, in editorial and feature content (from 2.89 to 3.23 and from 2.72 to 3.25 respectively), remained unchanged in letters to the editor, and moved from right of centre toward the left of centre in front-page material. In this comparison, the two Toronto control papers moved to the left in ideological orientation in three categories of content: front-page stories, editorials, and features (with the change in front-page material, from 3.10 to 2.91, statistically significant). Letters to the editor, on the other hand, saw a statistically significant shift to the right, from 2.57 to 2.79.

Let us attempt to put these data on ideological change into perspective. For the final three years of the study, for all content studied in the twelve papers in the sample, the mean ideological orientation was 3.01. This represents a minuscule shift to the right from the 3.00 calculated for the first three years. However, when we aggregate data from all Hollinger-acquired papers on the one hand and from all control papers on the other, we do see some evidence pointing to differences. On all four types of newspaper content studied, the Hollinger-acquired papers as a group showed a shift in ideological orientation to the right, moving from 2.86 to 3.01, while data from all the control papers moved in the other direction, shifting to the left from 3.04 to 2.9. These figures reflect not only that there were four ex-Southam papers, as opposed to two each from Thomson and Armadale, but that the Southam papers were a good deal larger and ran far more material than did the smaller Thomson and Armadale papers. These figures also reflect that there were eight Hollinger-acquired papers as opposed to only four control papers. Two of these control papers were *The Globe and Mail* and the *Toronto Star*, the latter of which has a declared liberal orientation.

Two items, one related specifically to Hollinger ownership and one more generally concerning trends in newspaper performance, merit some elaboration. The first has to do with perceptions generated by Mr. Black's critics at the time of his rapid and unexpected rise to domination of the Canadian newspaper industry. These critics predicted that his ownership would entail an ideological shift to the right *regardless* of where the newspapers he purchased were already positioned.

In a line of research separate from this project, scholars at the University of Windsor have, since 1988, administered three mail questionnaires to Canadian daily newspaper editors, the latest of which was administered in

2000. In 1995, editors were first asked to identify the editorial position of their newspaper on a left/right ideological continuum. In that year, 7% of editors placed their newspaper's position on the left, 67% placed it in the centre, and 25% placed it on the right. Significantly, in the 2000 survey, while about the same percentage (9% in 2000; 7% in 1995) placed their newspaper's position on the left, only 45% placed it in the centre, and 45% placed it on the right. These data indicate a self-reported ideological shift to the right of 20% over a five-year period (Soderlund, Lee, and Gecelovsky, 2002; also see Martin, 2003 and Taras, 2001 for a confirming view regarding the ideological direction of Canadian newspapers).

Of importance to the issue at hand is that, contrary to what one might have expected, it was not the editors of newspapers acquired by Hollinger between 1995 and 2000 who led the charge to the right. Hollinger newspaper editors were actually more centrist than editors of newspapers owned by rival chains, especially those at newspapers in the Sun chain. This observation is consistent with what we found in newspapers studied in the research presented in this chapter. Evidence pointed to movements to the left among ex-Thomson and ex-Armadale papers that were almost equal in strength as the movements to the right among ex-Southam papers after their acquisition by Hollinger.

The second consideration deals with the overall negative evaluation given to political parties. Negative evaluations predominated for all political parties, federal as well as provincial, whether they were on the left, right, or centre of the political spectrum.

There were 240 opportunities for political evaluations: evaluations of 5 federal parties, in 4 categories of content (front-page, editorials, letters, and columns), for 2 types of newspapers (chain v. control), for 3 chain comparisons (ex-Thompson, ex-Armadale, and ex-Southam), over 2 periods of study (pre- and post- sale). Of the 240 opportunities, 154 evaluations of federal political parties, accounting for 64% of the total, were on the negative side of the ledger; only 13% were positive, while 23% were either neutral or could not be evaluated. For provincial political parties, the situation is even more negative: of 192 opportunities for political evaluations of the 4 parties active at the provincial level, 154 possible evaluation points were negative, accounting for 66% of the total; only 10% were positive, and 24% were either neutral or contained no evaluation. Clearly, political parties of all ideological orientations and at both levels of government were portrayed in a pervasively negative manner in the nation's press.

These findings are not reassuring to those who believe that public confidence in those who govern is a crucial ingredient to the successful workings of democratic system (Soderlund, Romanow, Briggs, and Wagenberg 1984). Negativity is a phenomenon long associated with media treatment of politics and has been linked to voter cynicism and apathy (Ansolabehere and Iyengar, 1995; Romanow et al., 1999). Its prominence with respect to political parties in this study of newspaper content across Canada over a six-year period is disquieting, to say the least.

Four

An Assessment Of Conrad Black's Ownership

Walter C. Soderlund and Kai Hildebrandt

How can we assess the impact of Conrad Black's ownership on the content and ideological spin, based on four categories of newspaper material from a sample of eight newspapers that were purchased by Hollinger in 1996 from three different chain owners: Thomson, Armadale, and Southam? Our conclusion, which is derived from our analysis of newspaper content over a six-year period, contradicts the expectations advanced by critical theorists. We found that, while there were changes in the content and evaluations contained in these newspapers during that period, on balance the thrust of the critical school premise cannot be confirmed. At least it cannot be confirmed for *this* sample of papers, acquired by Hollinger from three different chains.

Our findings, which are complex and contradictory, can best be described as *inconsistent* with respect to support for our hypotheses (see Chapter 3). In some instances, data confirmed critical expectations; in other instances, they disconfirmed predicted trends. In most instances, though, data were simply inconclusive. Furthermore, in many instances trends similar to those in the sample papers were also evident in the various control papers studied. This was true of both confirming and nonconfirming data, and it calls into question whether ownership change was in fact the primary driving force behind the discovered changes in newspaper content. The data thus suggest that other factors, either industry-wide or region-specific, were at work. (See Shoemaker and Reese, 1996 for a discussion of the full range of influences on media content.)

Lydia Miljan and Barry Cooper argue that *journalists'* opinions are an important component of the news content emerging from media organizations, and that these opinions may offset strong ownership views in the determination of content. Based on a study of 626 English-speaking and 178 French-speaking journalists employed by a variety of media outlets ranging from the CBC to *The Globe and Mail,* Miljan and Cooper conclude that "coverage of public policy issues in the Canadian media reflects journalists' opinions to a far greater extent than the views that cultural critics presume to be held by managers and owners" (2003, pp. 167). In addition, Barry Cooper has pointed out that:

> Whatever the purpose of media ownership—chiefly, if not exclusively, profits—the media "system," owners *plus* journalists, may be internally balanced as a result of the attitudes of journalists.... Thus, whatever the owners may think or try to do in the area of profit maximization, they have their intentions modified by the opinion of their employees. What would be very odd would be congruence between owners and journalists. (Personal communication, Cooper, June 16, 2004; emphasis in the original).

As well, what we might call "the local news imperative"—the reality that only with respect to local news do newspapers hold a competitive advantage over competing media—may account for the continuation of locally oriented material appearing on the front page. Despite a particular owner's wish to trim expenses by cutting local staff, this material can be written only by local staff.

As one might predict, though, based on the advantages accruing from economies of scale, feature columns—which do not need to be written by local staff—tended to move in the anticipated direction, toward the homogenous content engendered by chain-wide production and distribution of the Hollinger-acquired papers.

In summary, we found in this study of Hollinger-acquired and control papers, first, that while there were changes in content, few of these changes were statistically significant. Second, for those changes that were statistically significant, not all moved in the same direction and they could not reasonably be seen to follow discernible and consistent patterns. Finally, statistically significant changes tended to be found almost as often in papers that did not change owners as in those that did. While it is possible to selectively choose particular pieces of evidence that tend either to confirm or to disconfirm the hypothesized impact of Hollinger ownership (for example, changes in treatment of labour or business issues in editorials), we do not see this as a particularly useful exercise.

If looked at systematically and in its totality, the evidence presented in Chapter 3 clearly shows that some changes in newspaper content did occur during the course of the study. Furthermore, it is reasonable to suggest that some of these changes (for example, a decrease in attention paid to political issues and an increase in attention paid to economic issues, seen in a majority of the Hollinger-acquired papers, and an ideological shift to the right, seen in the ex-Southam papers) are at least partly related to Conrad Black's ownership. However, given all the instances of non-change together with some contradictory findings, it is hard to reach the conclusion that Lord Black's ownership had the predicted impact on content in the full range of newspapers that were examined for this study.

Indeed, reflecting on the reality of a constantly changing news environment (at local, provincial, national, and international levels), and adding to this the dynamic nature of the media industry itself, findings that indicate change but point to no overall clear pattern in that change are really not all that surprising. Change is to be expected—what is uncertain is the magnitude, consistency, direction, and origin of that change.

Interestingly, our findings appear consistent with those of Yorgo Pasadeos and Paula Renfro, who attempted to document a "Murdoch style" among newspapers acquired in the United States by Rupert Murdoch's News Corporation. While their findings did indicate statistically significant short-term and long-term increases in sensationalism and local content among Murdoch acquisitions, the researchers concluded that "fears articulated in the 1970s about Murdoch's impending corruption of American journalism have not been realized" (1997, p. 43). At least with respect to his impact on the Thomson, Armadale, and Southam newspapers included in this study, we can reasonably make the same statement for Conrad Black and Canadian journalism.

Views of Journalists

Writing midway in Mr. Black's four-year tenure as the dominant newspaper owner in Canada, John Miller and Vince Carlin assessed his contribution to Canadian newspapers quite differently—Miller being overtly critical, and Carlin being on the whole supportive.

Miller characterizes Black's rise to the status as the largest newspaper owner in Canada as "a nightmare long feared by critics of newspaper concentration" (1998, p. 61) and goes on to make the case that the nightmare did indeed become reality:

> For decades, the ultimate defence used by chain owners to justify their wide holdings of newspapers was that they never used this power to influence what their papers printed.... Black makes no such pretense. In fact, he wasted no time in showing that he is prepared to use his dominant position as newspaper owner to trumpet his own political, social and personal views. Many of his papers have adopted more conservative editorial policies and their opinion pages are dominated by columnists with markedly conservative views. Even more worrisome, journalists who run afoul of Black often find themselves silenced and without any other place to work. (1998, p. 68)

According to Miller, Black's control was most often exercised through personnel decisions. He lists Joan Fraser, Blair Fraser, Christopher Young,

James Travers, and Peter Calamai as either having resigned or having been removed in order to effect ideological change. Miller goes on to cite Barbara Amiel, Andrew Coyne, and Giles Gherson as additions to personnel on Black's newspapers to effect the same purpose (1998, pp. 68–77). Miller's overall evaluation of Mr. Black's performance is disparaging: "For now, Black has the newspapers to carry out his mission: a voracious appetite for more; and the bully's ability to intimidate, second-guess and silence journalists who get in his way" (p. 80).

Carlin, though, points out that "quality in newspapers does not arise spontaneously from below; it has to be encouraged and rewarded from above." Moreover, he argues that it is necessary to examine how dominant chains actually work "before we can automatically conclude that concentration is necessarily bad." In his evaluation, he concludes that "throughout the Hollinger/Southam chain, the look and feel of the larger papers changed, most often for the better," although he acknowledges that "some of the improvements have come at the expense of the smaller newspapers in the group" (1998, p. 106). As for layoffs, Carlin agrees with Miller that smaller papers were affected by large-scale layoffs, but he maintains that the only application of the "Radler formula"[1] to large papers occurred in Regina and Saskatoon. In those cases, he says, the "papers haven't declined in quality and that their former employees have started up new papers in both cities" (p. 107). Over all, Carlin's evaluation of Mr. Black's record tends to be far more balanced than Miller's:

> In fact, many of the negative effects predicted for Black-controlled enterprises have not materialized. There is no doubt that Black is an aggressive, opinionated owner. There is also no doubt that many of the properties he has acquired have not declined, and many have improved. We did have to endure a lengthy treatise on international affairs authored by owner Black in the magazine *Saturday Night*, and highly respected editor Joan Fraser resigned from the *Montreal Gazette* when Black took over, but there has not been the wholesale ideological bloodletting that many predicted. (Carlin, 1998, p. 107)

Interviewed during the financial scandal that forced Black's resignation as CEO of Hollinger International in 2003, Kenneth Whyte, Black's choice as founding editor of the *National Post,* claimed that:

> He left [Southam] in much better shape when he sold out than when he came in....
>
> I think [Conrad] demonstrated how narrow and lethargic the political conversation was in Canada until he came around.... He enlivened it immeasurably. He made journalists, editors, writers, columnists matter more than

> they had in generations. And he improved the quality of not only his own papers but all competing proprietors [by prompting them] to recognize that they'd perhaps been paying too little attention [to] their editorial operations. (Whyte, as quoted in Zerbisias, 2003, p. A9)

For his part, Mr. Black attributes much of the controversy surrounding his management style to what he sees as his critics' failure to understand the link between the business and editorial functions of a newspaper. These he explains as follows:

> [In no other industry] would chief executives have consented to be praised for having absolutely nothing to do with the quality, nature or content of the product. Nor should the publishers and corresponding executives in other media be lightly excused for allowing the Left in the working press successfully to represent proprietary vigilance for professional standards as abusive interference with editorial integrity. This insane segregation of commercial and editorial management was elevated into a cardinal virtue as editors and journalists praised noninterventionist newspaper executives while they highjacked their products and became either bland or antagonistic to the communities being served. This was like the head of Coca Cola saying he didn't care how his beverages tasted, or the head of General Motors saying he didn't care what his cars looked like or whether they actually worked. (Black, 1998, p. 96)

Views of Newspaper Executives

Over a three-month period in the summer and fall of 2002, we interviewed, in person, just under a dozen senior executives of the newspapers that were included in this study, as well as some senior executives representing the companies that owned those papers.[2] Copies of the content analysis study, more or less as it appears in Chapter 3, were sent to each executive prior to the interview. First, we asked the respondents for their impressions of the study in terms of how accurately the findings reflected the reality of content change in their newspaper over the study period. For the Hollinger-acquired papers, we then asked how news of Mr. Black's impending ownership had been viewed by personnel in their respective papers and finally we asked to what extent and how Mr. Black actually exercised editorial influence.

With respect to the inconclusive findings of the study, most respondents were not surprised that Mr. Black's ownership stamp appeared as lightly as it had. As noted by one respondent, "the influence of an owner is less than most people think." Two main reasons were offered to support this view. The first was that a newspaper's ownership is only one factor among many that may influence content change. It was pointed out that "newspapers change all the time for a number of reasons." New patterns of competition, changes in publishers and editors, broad societal trends, and dramatic events of the day all have an impact on content at least as great, if not greater, than changes in ownership. Also, owners "understand from a business point of view that a newspaper has to have credibility" and therefore resist what might be perceived as heavy-handed imposition of control.

Another factor involves the reality that implementing a desired change is far more difficult than it may seem. On this point, one respondent told us that when he was hired as editor it had been his goal to make changes to his newspaper rather quickly. He found effecting the changes far more difficult and time-consuming than he had imagined—it took three to five years, and even then he was not successful in accomplishing all of the desired changes. Thus, even if an owner *wants* to change a paper's content, the path to accomplishment is neither easy nor automatic. As one editor phrased it, "ownership influence works through a 'trickle-down' process—messages may be sent, [but] how they are carried out is another matter." It was pointed out that in the real world "compliance with ownership directives is often based on agreement over the issue at hand, combined with the personal relationships between the editor, publisher, and owner."

The question regarding how Mr. Black's announced ownership was greeted in affected newspapers across the country elicited some interesting, and on the whole consistent, responses. While some interviewees pointed out that it was the "idea of being sold," with all its unknowns, rather than the idea of "being sold to Mr. Black specifically" that caused apprehension, most acknowledged that Mr. Black's reputation added to the level of concern.[3]

Clearly, Mr. Black's critics had made an impact. One editor offered that Black had "the persona of an ogre," another that "if he's as bad as they say, this could be terrible," while a third used the metaphor "the Huns are at the gate" to describe the reaction to Black's impending ownership at his newspaper. In general, it is safe to say that acquisition by Mr. Black was "viewed with some concern," as it was perceived that "he would exercise more influence than ordinary owners." Such fears tended to be tempered by the fact he was "a newspaper man" or that "at least, he knew newspapers." Importantly, respondents claimed that apprehension ran highest in the upper management of the newspapers. As one editor put it, with a change of owners, "management in particular gets nervous, as previous allegiances and understandings disappear."

The field of respondents was divided as to whether Mr. Black's ownership resulted in a "chill" in the newsroom. Most reported that fears of a "chill phenomenon" among working reporters were overblown. It was pointed out that journalists are a "particular breed of human being," in that "most are not interested in corporate advancement"; also that "questioning of owners is seen as a part of the job."[4] Some, however, did acknowledge that there was at least a "subliminal message as to what will get them ahead, and what is career-limiting." One editor explained that journalistic behaviour ranges between "sycophancy and insubordination" and that, in making decisions regarding what to write and how to write about it, reporters are likely to avoid the latter, reasoning that "we're not going to get into that kind of trouble."

Our final line of questioning dealt with the respondents' actual experience with Mr. Black's ownership style. On this point it quickly became obvious that Mr. Black operated very differently with respect to the so-called "Big Five" papers—papers in Vancouver, Edmonton, Calgary, Ottawa, and Montreal—than he did with newspapers in smaller communities. In the smaller communities, his editorial style was definitely "hands off." One editor in a small community reported that frankly he had "expected to see more direction" than he received and that Mr. Black "did not pay close attention to editorial policy." Another agreed that "editorial management was left in the hands of local people." One confessed that "he had never seen the man," and had "never received as much as a phone call or an e-mail from him." Moreover, in two cases it was reported that under Black's ownership considerable improvements were made to the newspapers' physical facilities. It became apparent to us that with smaller papers, Mr. Black's control, exercised through David Radler, was largely financial. Budgets were established and financial targets set, which were expected to be met, but there was no pressure to make editorial changes.

With the big city papers, Mr. Black's ownership style was definitely more involved—but here too there was a good deal of editorial autonomy.[5] One executive of a rival newspaper chain acknowledged that "for Conrad, serving the community is big," and that Black had "never believed in central office monitoring." These observations were confirmed by editors working for Mr. Black on big city papers. For these papers there was editorial guidance, but not of the sort feared by Mr. Black's critics.

Owner influence over large dailies, whether exercised by Mr. Black or by other owners, was described to us as working through a "parameter of ideas"—a statement of "the things this newspaper is going to stand for." For Mr. Black, first and foremost, this involved having "a clear sense of the core values of the community" in which his newspapers were located. For Black, one ideological template did not fit all, and he insisted that his newspapers be "a relevant voice in their communities." As one respondent commented, "Conrad wanted you to be the newspaper your community wanted you to be." Beyond this,

Mr. Black "wanted editorial diversity in his newspapers." One editor reported that there has been "too much made of [Mr. Black's] ideology—his biggest 'ism' is journalism." While Black expected his conservative views to be reflected in the papers he owned, he cautioned his editors: "Don't ignore the left." What he really wanted was "sharper and better stuff—'soft right-wing pap' was seen as no better than 'soft left-wing pap.'" In fact, one editor reported that Mr. Black had cautioned him about the "law of anticipated reaction" and had warned him to guard against it; that is, Black had felt journalists might "spin" their writing to conform to his reported views, which he understood might be "over-interpreted."

Occasionally, Mr. Black did make his views known in the newspapers that he owned. When he did so, his method was simple and direct: editors reported receiving signed opinion pieces with Mr. Black's byline, accompanied with instructions "to publish it on the op-ed page of Saturday's newspaper."

It was reported that Mr. Black was primarily interested in an increase in the level in the "quality of writing and thinking" that went into his newspapers. As one editor put it, "there was definite pressure to perform at a higher level—to be imaginative and adventurous." His advice to one editor was to "hire great writers." Black was not reluctant to invest money in his newspapers, and he did not "squeeze" journalistic resources for profit. Without exception, executives reported they were satisfied working for him, although a number spoke of Mr. Black's "fondness for provoking a response." As one editor put it, "he knew what strings to pull." Another editor described him as "a very good proprietor for a journalist to work for—he liked newspapers," while another volunteered that "he was one of the best owners we ever had."

In summary, with respect to Mr. Black's influence on the content appearing in his newspapers, the interview data collected from those who worked for him tended to confirm the results of the content analysis reported in Chapter 3. While Mr. Black had a reputation as a fierce ideologue, in the area of editorial control he was not a "hands on" manager.

Postscript

On November 18, 2003, front page headlines in newspapers across Canada reported that Lord Black had been forced to resign his position as CEO of Chicago-based Hollinger International. Although he was the company's major shareholder, its stock was publicly traded on the New York Stock Exchange, and the company's second largest shareholder (New York-based investor Tweedy, Browne) had in the spring of 2003 objected to "more than $200-million in fees and other compensation paid to management" (Shecter, 2003, Oct. 18, p. FP3), including Lord Black. Tweedy, Browne had also questioned the relationships among Black's private holding company Ravelston, Toronto-based Hollinger Inc., and Hollinger International. In June 2003, a special Hollinger board committee was tasked with the investigation of Hollinger's finances (Pitts, 2003; Shecter, 2003, Oct. 18, p. FP3; Wells, 2003).

On November 17, this committee reported that $32.2 million in "non-compete" payments made in the United States—which had purportedly been paid to Hollinger by the purchasers of Hollinger International-owned community newspapers—had in fact been paid "to Lord Black, three of his executives and a Toronto-based company he controls." It was also reported that "after a prolonged meeting...of Hollinger's board of directors, Lord Black tendered his resignation effective Friday [November 21] and agreed along with two of the other ousted executives to repay the unauthorized personal payments" (McNish and Waldie, 2003, p. A1). Still remaining to be reported on were similar non-compete payments (in the reported amount of $58.1 million U.S.) made to Hollinger by CanWest Global in 2000 and the Osprey Media Group in 2001 in connection with their purchases of Canadian newspapers (DeCloet, 2003). On November 22, reports confirmed earlier speculation that the U.S. Securities and Exchange Commission (SEC) would launch its own investigation into the unauthorized payments (Blackwell, 2003, Nov. 18), and on December 9 it was reported that shareholder Cardinal Capital Management had "asked a Delaware judge to approve a lawsuit that would allege wrong-doing by directors and executives of Hollinger International Inc. and some affiliated companies" (Shecter and Tedesco, 2003, p. FP5). Christopher Browne, a managing director at Tweedy, Browne, made it clear that his firm's problems with Hollinger International went beyond Lord Black and declared that the board of directors must be held accountable as well (Browne, 2003, Dec. 13; for an account of Tweedy, Browne's role in the unravelling of Hollinger Inc., see McDonald, 2004).

Lord Black, although self-described as "chastened but purposeful," claimed that "there was no suggestion these payments were illegal—they were not sufficiently documented or finalized." Under the terms of the resignation agreement, he was to remain as Hollinger International's "non-executive chairman" (Shecter, 2003, Nov. 18, p. A1). A week after Lord Black's resignation from Hollinger International, four independent members of the board of directors of Toronto-based Hollinger Inc. resigned over his refusal to step down as CEO of that company. Those resignations left "the Toronto company's board without an audit committee" (Canadian Press, 2003, Nov. 25, p. D6), further complicating "the regulatory situation now facing Black's media empire" (Maich, 2003, Nov. 25, p. A21).

In the wake of his resignation, speculation centred on the future of Lord Black's remaining newspapers, including such properties as *The Daily Telegraph* (Great Britain), *The Jerusalem Post*, and the *Chicago Sun-Times.* It was reported that the Hollinger International board of directors favoured a course of action that would see the media properties auctioned off individually, while Lord Black's preference was to find one corporate buyer for them all. A Delaware court subsequently ruled that the properties were to be sold individually. Toward the end of June 2004, it was announced that the Barclay brothers were the successful bidders for *The Daily Telegraph* at $1.33 billion U.S. (Shecter, 2004, June 23). Whatever the outcome of the sale of these properties, Lord Black continued to be involved with Hollinger in a number of capacities (Kirchgaessner and Burt, 2003); as well, he remained an investor with David Radler in Horizon Publications Inc. (Wells, 2003, p. A7). As 2003 came to an end, Conrad Black's company Hollinger Inc. also faced a $25 million lawsuit by CanWest Global related to Hollinger's failure to cover future operating losses at the *National Post* (Shecter, 2003, Dec. 18).

In spite of his having been named the 2003 Canadian Press business newsmaker of the year (Canadian Press, 2003, Dec. 29), Lord Black's days as a major player in the Canadian newspaper industry now appear to be over. Given the SEC investigation—which, in light of a possible violation on an earlier "consent decree" signed with the SEC, might result in criminal charges (Gumbel, 2003), given shareholder and CanWest lawsuits, and given the resignation of the Hollinger Inc. audit committee, "Black's troubles may just be beginning." This indeed was the observation of Linda McQuaig upon hearing the news of Black's forced resignation as CEO of Hollinger International (2003, Nov. 23, p. A12).

Indeed, it does appear that Lord Black's legal problems are growing increasingly serious over time. On December 23, 2003 it was reported in the *Financial Post* that Lord Black, in his first appearance before the SEC, "exercised his Fifth Amendment right against self-incrimination by refusing to testify before U.S. regulators." This was explained by his lawyer as follows:

> In light of the very early stage of the investigation, the lack of time to adequately prepare, and the uncertainty regarding the nature and scope of the investigation, we advised Lord Black that he should exercise his constitutional right not to testify. (As quoted in Shecter, 2003, Dec. 23, p. FP 1)

The Globe and Mail put the story on its front page, quoting a former SEC lawyer who said that invoking the fifth amendment "is not the norm, but it's not uncommon." The lawyer went on to say, however, "that taking the fifth can make

SEC officials want to pursue a case more aggressively" (as quoted in McKenna and Stewart, 2003, pp. A1, A8).

Of further significance, in early May 2004, Hollinger International Inc. amended a previous lawsuit

> seeking US $125-billion from Conrad Black and others connected to the publishing company, alleging racketeering and "fraudulent diversion of company funds" for allegedly selling newspapers to related companies for less than market value.... The new complaint alleges violations of the U.S. RICO Act (Racketeer Influence and Corrupt Organizations Act), and seeks "treble" damages under its provisions. (Shecter, 2004, May 8, p. FP1)

In a May 15, 2004 column, Anne Kingston revealed details of the $125 billion lawsuit, which

> alleges Conrad Black, his wife, Barbara Amiel Black, and a number of close associates "freely plundered the coffers of the company to subsidize their own lifestyles".... Devastating allegations abound...among them that Black and others took $204-million in "excessive" management fees; that more than $88-million was transferred to individuals in "non-compete" fees; that $90,000 of company money was spent in refurbishing Black's 1958 Rolls Royce Silver Wraith. (Kingston, 2004, p. SP1)

As well, the company was charged for the Blacks' household staff: "chefs, senior butlers, chauffeurs, housemen, footmen and security personnel." The final indiscretion claimed was "that Lady Black gave a tip to the doorman of a swank New York department store and charged it to Hollinger" (Kingston, 2004, p. SP1).

Toward the end of May 2004, in press interviews in Toronto, Lord Black indicated that he would "formally respond to racketeering charges levied by Hollinger International Inc. 'in a few weeks' [indicating that] it is 'not a completely unreasonable inference' that further litigation is likely." Lord Black also suggested that "the multi-million-dollar claims against him from shareholders and Hollinger International will be resolved 'satisfactorily' " (Schecter, 2004, May 28, p. A1). In October 2004, a U.S. judge dismissed the RICO allegations against Lord Black (Corcoran, 2004, Oct. 9).

On September 1, 2004, the special Hollinger Board of Directors Committee released a report to the U.S. Securities Commission bearing the title *A Corporate Kleptocracy.* The report claimed "that over seven years, Lord Black and his closest associates used their position at Hollinger International...to line their pockets with more than $400-million of company money," which constituted a major portion of the company's profits over the period 1997 to 2003. Revelston Corp., which was controlled by Black, responded to the charges by characterizing the report as " 'recycling the same exaggerated claims laced with outright lies that have been peddled to the media and over-reaching lawsuits for months" (Shecter and Dabrowski, 2004, p. A1). On October 2, Lord Black's lawyers "served notice under the Libel and Slander Act of Ontario" to the authors of the report of a $1.1 billion lawsuit over allegations contained in the report (Shecter, 2004, Oct. 2, p. FP5).

In mid-November 2004, based on the Hollinger International Report, the U.S. SEC filed a civil lawsuit against Lord Black, David Radler, and Hollinger Inc., charging that they had "engaged in a fraudulent and deceptive scheme to divert cash and assets" from Hollinger International and "concealed their self-dealing" from the company's shareholders. At issue was an attempt to recover $85 million in what were described as "ill-gotten gains" as well as steps to wrest control of Hollinger International from Lord Black by banning both Black and Radler from serving as an officer or director of a public company in the United States. As well, the SEC asked "the Court to appoint a trustee to vote the 18% stake (which accounts for 68% of the voters) through which Lord Black controls Hollinger International, publisher of the *Chicago Sun Times* and *The Jerusalem Post*" (Tedesco and Shecter, 2004, p. FP1). A day later, it was reported that *The Jerusalem Post* had been sold to a fifty/fifty partnership between an Israeli publisher and CanWest Global Communications (Brent, 2004, Nov. 17, p. FP1). Speaking through Ravelston Corp., Lord Black called the SEC action "regrettable" and indicated that he expected to be vindicated on the latest charges. For its part, "the SEC served notice that it could file further charges" (Tedesco and Shecter, 2004, FP2).

In summary, the lawsuits and counter suits that dominate the legal relationship between Hollinger International, the Securities and Exchange Commission, and Lord Black could take years to resolve. As well, Lord Black has begun a process of privatizing Hollinger Inc. through a $73-million buyout of shareholders. This was explained as a plan "to take his Canadian holding company... away from the scrutiny of increasingly angry regulators" (Hodgson, 2004, p. FP5). In fairness to Lord Black, it must be pointed out that, throughout the period of intense controversy that began in November of 2003, he has consistently maintained that he has done nothing wrong, and as of the end of November 2004 no charge levelled against Lord Black has resulted in a court conviction.

PART TWO

Convergence: The Aspers and CanWest Global

Five

Media Convergence and CanWest Global

Kai Hildebrandt, Walter C. Soderlund, and Walter I. Romanow

In a remarkably prescient article published in 1990, Anthony Smith outlined the rationale behind what has since become known as *convergence*:

> Publishers want to be in a position to exploit a work of talent across the whole media landscape; they have come to fear the consequences of being excluded from an audience if they do not have a finger in every kind of media pie. Furthermore, it is becoming easier in technological terms to become involved in a wider range of media. Transnational media empires are thus coming into being to exploit new opportunities and as protection against possible loss of opportunity. Newspapers, film businesses, radio, television and publishing are passing into the same institutional hands. (Smith, 1990, pp. 8–9)

CanWest Global, the television broadcasting company controlled by Winnipeg's Asper family, literally operationalized Smith's formula in the summer of 2000 with its purchase of the major portion of Conrad Black's Hollinger-owned Canadian newspapers. In hindsight, it seems obvious that government regulators and the Canadian public alike should have paid more attention to what lay ahead. By adding the country's largest group of newspapers to its already substantial holdings in television broadcasting, CanWest Global became the largest media conglomerate in the country (Nesbitt-Larking, 2001, pp. 110–111). As observed by Gordon Pitts:

> Before the Aspers, there had never been owners who enjoyed such broad access to Canadian mainstream media—through the ownership of most major newspapers (commanding nearly 35% of the country's daily newspaper circulation), its second-largest private television network, and Canada.com, a significant Internet news source. (Pitts, 2002, p. 3)

In the heady context of globalization, concerns over the overlaps in market penetration created by what had previously been referred to as "cross-media ownership" (which, in Canada, in the early 1980s had been restricted by CTRC regulations) tended to be ignored. It was argued that, in a world increasingly dominated by giant multimedia conglomerates, the advantages of size and the benefits of the synergies of convergence were essential to successful competition (see Gerbner, Mowlana, and Schiller, 1996; Jack, 2003; McChesney, 2000; Tuck, 2003). Moreover, in the deliberations of the Standing Senate Committee on Transport and Communications a committee member noted that

> "I do not think anything has consumed our time more in our discussions with our various witnesses than cross-ownership." Certainly, [the report continued] for many of the witnesses, cross-media ownership was the central issue. (Canada, 2004, p. 91)

As CanWest Global announced on its web site: "If You Can Watch It, Read It, Hear It or Download It—We Want to be the Source" (CanWest Global, 2002).

Convergence as a Concept

Gordon Pitts has described convergence as a vague concept (2002, p. 4), and his description is not without justification. In reality, the term is used to refer to a number of related but different phenomena. In his analysis, Canadian academic media analyst David Taras identifies "four realms of convergence: the convergence of technologies, the convergence of corporations, the convergence of information with entertainment, and convergence of cultures" (2001, p. 61).[1] It is the second of these four realms, the convergence of corporations, that is of primary interest to us.

The term *convergence* appears to have had its origins in the technological domain. Specifically, following the development of fibre optics, microwave, and satellite technologies, the distinction between broadcasting and telecommunications had become blurred. In that broadcasting and telecommunications were at the time subject to different sets of governmental regulation, convergence as a product of technological change had to be addressed (Romanow and Soderlund, 1996, pp. 145–147; see also Baldwin, McVoy, and Steinfield, 1996; Carlin, 2003; Winseck, 2002).

While governments struggled to come up with fair regulations to deal with what in the 1990s was referred to as the "carriage vs. content" dilemma, corporations attempted to deal with the problem themselves, and the concept of corporate convergence was born. Convergence differs from the earlier type of horizontal integration characteristic of pure newspaper chains described in earlier chapters of the book and, as Anthony Smith had predicted, it brought together different types of media under the umbrella of a single corporate owner.

Pitts maintains that the January 2000 merger between AOL and Time Warner marked the beginning of the push for corporate convergence in Canada:

> The world woke up on January 10, 2000 to the largest corporate merger ever, but even more significantly, the first giant convergence deal, one that blended print, music and broadcast content, and the potential of cable networks, with the magic of the Internet. [Pitts claims that the true impact of the merger lay in the revolutionary concept of integrating] "content" assets—a term for everything from entertainment to news and sports—with companies that controlled "the pipes" of cable, satellite, wireless and telecommunication links. The two sides needed each other:...That's what the AOL Time Warner deal was all about, and that dream would soon come to obsess Canada's media owners as well. (2002, pp.4–5)[2]

It is in this sense of aggregating a variety of content-producing and content-distributing media assets *under a single corporate owner*, that we use the term convergence in this book. We must bear in mind, however, that the convergence of newspaper and television properties under one owner will exert a strong push for the increasing convergence *of news and entertainment*—that is, Taras' third realm of convergence.

Arguments For and Against Convergence

In his discussion of the implications of convergence for content, former CanWest Global executive Kenneth Goldstein points to the explosion in the number of media choices available to Canadians. For example, he reports that in May 2002, 717,921 Canadians were registered with NYTimes.com (*The New York Times* on-line). This figure, he points out, is "larger than the average daily circulation of any daily newspaper in Canada.... and is surely a powerful indication that Canadians are not in any way limited in their media choices" (2002, June 14, p. 3). He further clarifies the size of the audience potentially realizable by CanWest, which he points out has been consistently exaggerated by the corporation's critics:

> We own 27 daily newspapers [as of November 2004, 13 daily newspapers] out of a total of 102 dailies in Canada [about 26%].... The Canadian Community Newspaper Association considers 41 of our papers to fall within their definition of a community newspaper, out of a total of 1,061 community newspapers in Canada [about 4%].... And our television services account for about 15 per cent of the television tuning by English-speaking Canadians. (2002, June 14, p. 12)

With regard to the television audience, Goldstein argues that critics of CanWest have confounded the corporation's reach (reported as being up to

97.6% of Canadians), which is "a measure of *potential* audience, *not* a measure of *actual* audience" (2002, June 14, pp. 14–15; emphasis in the original) with its actual audience. CanWest's actual television audience is 15%, second to CTV (which has 18%), but ahead of CBC (which has 7%). As for newspapers, Goldstein holds that:

> the circulation of all of the CanWest dailies combined is equivalent to 15% of Canadian households. The circulation of all of the CanWest dailies that run the national editorials [to be discussed in detail in Chapters 6 and 7] is equivalent to just over 10% of Canadian households. (2002, June 14, pp. 14–15)

Marni Soupcoff likewise does not see ownership consolidation and concentration among conventional mass media as problematic, in part because of the growth of new sources of information:

> *Fact: When one looks at the media as a whole (cable and satellite television, radio, daily newspapers, weekly newspapers, Internet sites, web-based newsletters), there are more alternative voices available to Canadian consumers than ever before.* Today, Canadians have access to news and entertainment from a wide array of sources, including the Internet and innumerable digital cable channels that cater to everyone from the Anglophile mystery freak to the francophone music lover. (2003; p. 8, italics in the original)

Numerous witnesses quoted in the *Interim Report* of the Standing Senate Committee on Transport and Communications made the same point. For example, Charles Dalfen, Chair of the CRTC, referred to research done by the regulating body on media concentration in four major markets from 1991 to 2001:

> In every case, in practically every medium, you will find that there are a larger number of owners and a larger number of broadcasting and newspaper outlets over that 10-year period. Even though it may sound counterintuitive, that, in fact, is the case when you focus them in. (As quoted in Canada, 2004, p. 66)

However, not all assessments of the new media landscape are positive. Writing about the situation in the United States, Robert McChesney makes the case that ownership convergence works to nullify the myriad of voices purported to accompany new media outlets. He argues that the proliferation of new media (satellite and cable TV, plus the ubiquitous Internet) relays the false impression that a corresponding proliferation of voices and ideas is reaching audiences. For McChesney, this is not happening; he describes a process whereby the old media are dominating the new:

> It is ironic that the media giants use the rise of the Internet and the prospect of new competition to justify their mega-mergers because, if anything, the Internet is spurring more concentration in media ownership, as well as other corporate sectors. I argue...that the Internet will not launch a wave of commercially viable challengers to the existing media giants. Merely being able to launch a website is not sufficient to contend with the enormous market advantages of the media giants as they colonize the Internet. (2000, p. xxii)

David Taras points to essentially the same problem occurring in Canada as McChesney has identified in the United States:

> Despite the surface impression that Canadians now have the world at our fingertips because we enjoy more media choices than ever before—that we are media wealthy—the reality is that Canadians are becoming media poor. Simply having a larger assortment of the same thing is not the same as having many different choices. The situation is made worse by the failure of media moguls to put the needs of the country and its citizens on at least a par with their own interests and governments and a regulatory system that have failed to curtail their power—that have allowed a few powerful individuals and corporations to call the tune. (2001, p. 2)

There is no doubt that more channels of information are now available to Canadians than was the case in the past. Nor is the question of the quality of the content produced under convergent ownership the issue. On this point, Soupcoff quotes a U.S. study showing "[TV] stations with cross-ownership in which the parent company also owns a newspaper in the same market tended to produce higher quality newscasts" (as quoted in Soupcoff, 2003, p. 9). The problem centres on the limited range of opinions available in the media to Canadians, and on this point Vince Carlin observes that "you can fit everyone who controls significant Canadian media in my office.... This is not a healthy situation" (as quoted in *The Washington Post* and cited in Winter, 2002).

The question that confronts us, then, is not whether the content transmitted through the various channels controlled by this small ownership elite is better or worse than before convergence, but whether it presents a variety of views or is largely homogeneous. As argued by Carlin, "despite the plethora of services, we may actually be hearing a narrower range of views from fewer people" (2003, p. 52). While we do not maintain that this is in fact happening, it seems clear that convergence for the purpose of creating economies of scale (for instance, by combining news-gathering and news-editing functions across different types of media) creates the possibility that the resulting *content* (which is then distributed through various media types and outlets, all controlled by a single owner) may be much less diverse than the media platforms on which it appears.

Fragmentation as a Concept

David Taras has rightly pointed out that convergence is being challenged by "a countervailing phenomenon, an opposing rhythm called fragmentation" (2001, p. 61). In this context, Romanow and Soderlund have pointed to a change in terminology, from "mass communication" to "segmented mass communication," arguing that "in today's society, with a multiplicity of competitive media, audiences seek out the media and media content that display life spaces with which they are familiar" (1996, p. 64). Stephen Chaffee and Miriam Metzger have analyzed the fragmentation problem further:

> [The] characteristics of the new media are cracking the foundations of mass communication. Today, media institutions are changing such that mass production is less mass. The explosion of available channels afforded by the new technologies contributes to the demassification of the media diffusing the audience for any particular media product. This has resulted in channel specialization, and the old model of broadcasting to the masses has given way to market segmentation and targeting to niche audiences. (2001, p. 369)

In the context of these developments, Kenneth Goldstein made the point that to understand convergence one has to appreciate what really motivates it: convergence, he said, is "a response to fragmentation in order to compete and maintain economies of scale" (2002, June 14, p, 8). In earlier research, he had concluded that

> while there are a number of reasons that go into corporate decisions relating to consolidation, one theme clearly emerges.... In total, *the media market is more fragmented than it has ever been in the past, and media are consolidating in an attempt to re-aggregate the fragments.* (2002, Jan., p. 2; emphasis in the original)

According to Goldstein, market fragmentation has put a "downward pressure on unit costs" (2004, p. 9). With the aid of Harold Innis (1972, p. 6), Goldstein outlines the relationship between the "costs of transportation" (or, in this case, the costs of channels of communication) and the costs of material being transported (in this case, media content). Goldstein rewrites Innis' analysis as follows:

> As the costs of *channels* declined, *less costly programs* emerged as staples—*long-form drama...variety programs*...and finally *reality-based shows*.... [Thus] content sharing across a number of outlets is a response to fragmentation and the resulting pressure on costs. (Goldstein, 2004, Mar. 5, p. 10; italics indicate Goldstein's modifications to the Innis text)

Data taken from a Gallup Poll published in February 2002 show that, in the extensive contemporary mix of media available to Canadians, conventional media are losing ground to the Internet—see Table 5.1. In fact, specialty TV news channels (up 6%) and the Internet (up 16%) were the only media registering gains in use over the four-year period (1998–2002) covered in the poll, while daily newspapers were down (8%) and TV network news was down (8%) as cited sources of information (Hartley and Mazzuca, 2002).Thus, to reach an audience of comparable size to that of a decade ago, a media owner now needs access to a wider range of media platforms.

TABLE 5.1 Sources consulted by Canadians for news, 1998 and 2002 (percentage indicating source used)

SOURCE	1998	2002
Nightly local news	81%	74%
Nightly network news	81	73
Specialty television news channels	67	73
Daily newspapers	73	65
Radio news programs	63	58
Television news magazines	65	52
Through the Internet	15	31
Weekly news magazines	27	18

Source: Hartley and Mazzuca, 2002

This analysis is reinforced by Soupcoff, who, based on data from Statistics Canada analyst Heather Dryburgh, argues that newspapers in particular are losing readers to the Internet:

> Statistics Canada has found that in 2000, an estimated 13 million Canadians (53 percent of Canadians over age 15) had used the Internet in the past year, while 90 percent of 15- to 19-year-olds had used the Internet.... Fifteen percent of the Internet users surveyed reported that they spent less time reading

> books, magazines, and newspapers due to their Internet use, and 55 percent of the Internet users surveyed said they used the Internet to view online news sites such as those offered by newspapers. (2003, Oct., p. 9)

The Senate Committee agrees: "Audiences have fragmented; today no single news source, be it print or electronic, can have the mass impact that the news giants had thirty years ago" (Canada, 2004, p. 3). On the basis of such evidence, one can understand the legitimate concerns of media owners about being left behind as the audience shifts in ways that make past business practices economically non-viable.

Convergence: The Canadian Experience

Gordon Pitts (2002) identifies five "Kings of Convergence" in Canada: Jean Monty, Pierre-Karl Peladeau, Israel (Izzy) Asper, Ted Rogers, and the Shaw family. Only the first three, however, presided over the type of newspaper/television convergence that is the focus of this book. In 2000, Jean Monty, head of Bell Canada Enterprises (BCE), combined the assets of CTV and *The Globe and Mail* to create Bell Globemedia. In his comments on Bell Globemedia, David Taras points out that BCE also "owns Bell Canada, Telesat, ExpressVu satellite TV, the Sympatico-Lycos Internet portal and sites such as YellowPages.ca and VMP.com" (2001, p. 231).

Quebecor's Pierre-Karl Peladeau added Le Groupe Vidéotron (a major cable provider) to the corporation's previously held Sun newspaper chain and TVA network.[3] Of this conglomerate, Taras observes that, in addition, "Quebecor is the largest commercial printing company in the world and has a strong presence on the Internet through its Canoe and Netgraphe portals" (2001, p. 234).

CanWest Global's Israel (Izzy) Asper purchased a substantial portion of Conrad Black's Canadian newspaper holdings, the Internet portal Canada.com, and half of the *National Post* to add to his Global TV holdings; Global TV had just achieved the reach of a national network through the acquisition of Western International Communications' TV stations in British Columbia and Alberta (Pitts, 2002, p. 135). With respect to these acquisitions, Taras notes that CanWest Global "now owns TV stations as well as newspapers in almost every major city in Canada" (2001, p, 231; see also Cohen-Almagor, 2002; Winseck, 2002).

The impact of convergence on newspapers, as Chris Dornan notes, was that "by 2002, with only a handful of exceptions, every major daily Canadian newspaper was the property of a parent owner with interests that extend far beyond newspaper publishing" (2003b, p. 100).

TABLE 5.2 Cross-media ownership, in Canada by corporation

	Astral	BCE	Brunswick	CanWest	CHUM	Cogeco	Corus	Craig	Power Corp.	Quebecor	Rogers	Shaw	Torstar	Transcontinental
Print Media														
Dailies		+	+	+					+	+			+	+
Weeklies			+	+						+			+	+
Magazines		+								+	+		+	+
Broadcast Media														
TV: Conventional		+		+	+	+	+	+		+	+	+		
TV: Pay and Specialty	+	+		+	+	+	+	+		+	+	+	+	
Production*		+		+	+	+	+			+	+		+	
Radio	+		+	+	+	+	+	+		+	+			
Distribution														
Cable						+				+	+	+		
Satellite		+										+		
Other (Incl. ISP)		+				+	+	+		+	+	+		
Other Media														
Internet (Webportals and sites)	+	+	+	+	+	+	+	+	+	+	+		+	+

* Production refers to facilities for making TV programs
Note: Table is from Canada, 2004 p. 36

Table 5.2, prepared for the Senate Standing Committee on Transport and Communications, shows the degree of media cross-ownership in Canada by corporate owner. It shows that Quebecor and BCE are most advanced toward the integration of all types of media (print, broadcast, distribution, and Internet), while CanWest Global, Rogers, and Torstar have a significant presence in print and electronic media as well as on the Internet.

Table 5.3, originally prepared for the House of Commons Standing Committee on Canadian Heritage and reproduced in the *Interim Report on the Canadian News Media* (Canada, 2004, p. 37), shows the market share of daily newspaper circulation and viewership of supper-hour television newscasts controlled by the three convergence conglomerates CanWest Global, Bell Globemedia, and Quebecor. These data show that the impact of

TABLE 5.3 Market share and cross-ownership in nine local markets, 2002

Market	Ownership Group	Market Share (%)	
		Newscasts	Dailies
Quebec City	Quebecor	47.1	56.2
Toronto	Bell Globemedia	43.8	18.3
	CanWest Global	33.0	11.5
Anglophone Montreal	CanWest Global	5.0	100.0
Francophone Montreal	Quebecor	37.1	60.4
Regina	CanWest Global	28.3	100.0
Saskatoon	CanWest Global	15.3	100.0
Calgary	CanWest Global	32.2	57.8
Edmonton	CanWest Global	39.7	60.0
Vancouver	CanWest Global	70.6	100.0

Note: Table is from "Media Ownership in Canada," Report prepared for the House of Commons Standing Committee on Canadian Heritage (Feb. 5, 2003), by the Centre d'études sur les médias. (As cited in Canada, 2004 p. 37)

convergence varies widely across the country. The Standing Senate Committee on Transport and Communications analyzed the data as follows:

> If one excludes anglophone Montreal, Regina and Saskatoon, which are markets with just one local daily, it can be seen that Vancouver, francophone Montreal and Quebec City were the markets where certain owners enjoyed the highest cross-media share. CanWest's market share dominance in Vancouver reflects the fact that it owns the most viewed local broadcaster as well as the two local dailies. Quebecor's francophone Montreal and Quebec City dominance is because the company owns the most popular daily newspaper and the most viewed local television station in both cities. (Canada, 2004, p. 36)

Within a year, convergence had arrived full-blown on the Canadian media scene. From an economic perspective, the experience with convergence has been less than reassuring. For example, Jean Monty was forced to resign as CEO of BCE in April of 2002 (Pitts, 2002, 323)[4]; as of November 2003, "Bell Expressvu has not made a dime of profit" (Lamey, 2003, p. A21); and, perhaps most significant of all, BCE's new CEO Michael Sabia appeared dubious of the premises underlying convergence (Damsell, 2002).[5] In addition, one cannot fail to mention the mega-meltdown of the trend-setting AOL Time Warner merger in 2003 (Associated Press, 2003; see also Carlin, 2003).[6]

Yet, in spite of these setbacks, the Aspers appear undeterred. For example, at an April 2002 Canadian Newspaper Association Conference in Calgary, Donald Babick, then CEO of CanWest's Southam Publications, stated that

> there are significant opportunities in the convergence world and probably we see the biggest opportunities in operational convergence.... We're having lots of success sharing back and forth between our television operations and our newspaper operations.... In the longer term, we see tremendous advantages as these initiatives evolve...we will be able to better serve the emerging multimedia consumer. (As quoted in Scotton, 2002, p. A9)

In early 2003, CanWest Global announced major changes to its management structure, intended to facilitate convergence, and it appeared that Mr. Babick became a casualty of the very convergence strategy that, less than a year earlier, he had praised. Babick (then president of CanWest Publications) and Gerry Nobel (Global Television's CEO) were reported to be leaving their positions by the end of August 2003. Rick Camilleri was slated to

> take over direct responsibility for executive management of CanWest's television, newspaper and other media operations. [With respect to this move,] CanWest CEO Leonard Asper said...the executive changes are intended to further CanWest's convergence strategy by having a single executive oversee newspapers and television. (McFarland and Damsell, 2003, p. B3)

The strategy appears to be working, as a *Maclean's* article on the financial problems of the *National Post* mentioned that

> in recent months...more *Post* reporters have been showing up on TV screens, and the content of the chain's daily papers across the country has become increasingly standardized—a trend that seems sure to intensify as the company struggles to get out from under a $3.6-billion debt load. (Gigliotti, 2003, p. 16)

Kenneth Goldstein has identified five areas where operational convergence may operate at the corporate level: "Integration of 'back office' functions; Convergence of consumer-relations activities; Cross-promotion; Cross-media advertising sales; and Sharing and re-positioning of content" (Goldstein, 2002, June 14, p. 10). While it is not possible to chronicle here all CanWest policies designed to further the success of convergence, we believe that the CanWest national editorial policy and the CanWest News Service, which will be discussed in later chapters, can in fact be categorized as such.

Another initiative clearly related to convergence involves changes to CanWest newspapers' on-line editions. At the end of October 2003, the corporation's on-line division CanWest Interactive announced a restructuring of the on-line editions of its newspapers, beginning with *The Ottawa Citizen* in November, followed in December by the corporation's flagship paper, the *National Post*. The described restructuring consists of a system whereby on-line information is provided in proportion to fees paid—*free access* providing "breaking news…, a selection of key stories…, headlines and the lead paragraphs from most news stories and use links to weather reports and other sites"; *seven-day subscriptions* providing "all news stories, columns and features in the newspaper for which the Citizen has online rights…[as well as] archived information from the previous seven days"; *the electronic newspaper* providing "an online replica of all news, features and advertising in the daily newspaper…available at 5,am ET" (CanWest News Service, 2003, p. C2). The electronic newspaper was to cost the same as a monthly subscription to the hard copy version of *The Ottawa Citizen* ($18.99) and be available to the newspaper's regular subscribers for an additional $4.99 per month.

Two motivations can be cited as prompting this move. The first surely involves the protection of classified advertising revenues from outside Internet competition. Chris Dornan has argued that classified ads are

> the bread and butter of the newspaper industry…an ad market that amounts to some $900 million per year. [He further points out that classified ads] are superbly suited to the Internet…. So what happens to the newspaper industry when classified can be unhitched from the paper-and-ink product of the daily paper? What happens when it's splitsville for the seamless marriage between editorial content and the largest single source of revenue for the newspaper as we know it? (2003a, Feb. 13–15)

The electronic newspaper may be seen as CanWest's response to the questions posed by Professor Dornan.

The second motivation for the change stems from the reality that, for Canadians with Internet access—an estimated 50% of Canadians at the beginning of 2002 (Goldstein, 2002, Jan., p. 14)—publishing a free electronic newspaper creates a disincentive for customers who would otherwise purchase the hard copy. This problem was identified by a number of newspaper executives whom we interviewed in 2002. Respondents who commented on their on-line editions claimed that they were money-losing ventures, designed to provide a service for emigrants from the community or for regular subscribers on vacation. These respondents recognized that the more information they provided for free in the on-line edition, the more they were undermining their regular subscription base; as one respondent put it, "it's hard to sell something that you can get for free." In this context, another related the story of a lapsed subscriber who had called him to complain about a reduction of material appearing in the free on-line edition of the paper.

Thus far, profits associated with the Internet have been largely illusory; the announced restructuring strategy, in addition to preserving CanWest's classified ad revenue, also appears to be the company's attempt to make the Internet pay its own way. In a June 2004 speech to the Canadian Newspaper Association Super Conference in Vancouver, CanWest CEO Leonard Asper emphasized the need "to embrace change" in order to extend the reach of newspapers and to "hang onto readers in a digital age." In so doing, Asper made it clear that CanWest was not in business to provide free content:

> We insist at CanWest that we must not give away our content for free. If we blow this, if we just throw all our stuff on the web and give it for free, we will blow one of the greatest opportunities we have. Others may be doing it, but I think they will either fall by the wayside, or they will start charging. (CanWest News Service, 2004, p. B7)

Interviews with Newspaper Executives

In our interviews with newspaper executives conducted over the summer and fall of 2002, we asked respondents, in an open-ended question, for their views regarding convergence. While their responses touched on each of the final three operational areas of convergence identified earlier by Goldstein (cross-promotion, advertising synergies, content sharing, and content repositioning), most of the comments were directed at the last of these: content sharing and content repositioning.

Responses were generally tentative, although on balance more skepticism than confidence was expressed with respect to the ultimate success of convergence. Most felt that while convergence "has potential," it was "too early to judge the final outcome." Typical responses were that "too much was expected of it" and that "it's not as big a deal as people thought it was." At least one interviewee commented that the concept had gone from being "overhyped" to being "discredited" and that reality lay somewhere in between. Executives tended to focus on the purported synergies to be created by melding print and electronic journalistic functions, and their views on this topic are revealing. A number of respondents pointed out that it had long been common for the various media to carefully monitor one another, with one respondent claiming that even before convergence "the morning newspaper was the source material for TV news."

Most felt that television stood to gain the most from the content-sharing dimension of convergence, especially where a company owned both a newspaper and a local-news-generating TV station in the same city. Since newspapers tend to have larger news-gathering staffs than TV stations (see Canada, 2004, Tables 28, 29, and 30, pp. 42–43), it was claimed that TV news "can add credibility and depth to its coverage" by incorporating material gathered by print journalists. On the other hand, respondents felt that newspapers stood to gain more from the potential for cross-promotion inherent in convergence: television audiences could be directed to the newspaper for in-depth examination of issues featured in two-minute television news stories.

Executives also pointed out that differences in the functions and cultures of print news and electronic news could lead to problems in understanding how each could use the other constructively. Television was seen essentially as an entertainment medium, but also as a medium that could bring breaking news to people very quickly. On the other hand, the print medium was characterized as a medium to which "people go for understanding and verification of what happened," especially for larger and more important stories.

Respondents were divided on whether journalist resources could be effectively shared; in other words, "can the same guy do the same story for TV and newspapers?" Judgments on this question varied widely. It was pointed out that TV and newspapers have "different cultures of presentation," and that working in each required "different skill sets" (information-gathering and writing skills as opposed to presentation skills). Here it was generally felt that "most newspaper reporters can't do TV"; one interviewee went so far as to claim that "TV ruins print journalists." On the other hand, it was pointed out that universities were producing a new set of journalists with a wider range of skills, which would make them comfortable working in a multimedia environment; the argument was that "only when the young of today become reporters, can you get convergence."

One respondent shifted the discussion from personnel to content, arguing that for convergence to work it was necessary to figure out "how to make more money out of the same content." He was not optimistic that this was possible, maintaining that "it is hard to find ideas that work in both media—there are print pieces and there are TV pieces."

Advertising was held as another area in which both chain ownership and convergence offered considerable advantages. Indeed, one respondent claimed that "convergence is all about advertising." The older form of horizontal integration, characteristic of chain ownership, had created the ability to attract national advertising accounts. Convergence was seen as leading to the creation of so-called "synergy packages," whereby newspaper and TV advertising could be combined in a single ad campaign. As with much about convergence, reality has not lived up to theoretical expectations; one respondent claimed that "nobody has made it work." Another executive explained that the problem with advertising was the need "to find new pools of advertising revenue." When offered to clients, synergy packages tended to elicit the "where's the discount?" response, and consequently there has been "no substantial rush to spend more on ads." The increased spending that would enable convergence to produce increased profits did not come about.

In spite of the less than enthusiastic endorsement of convergence overall on the part of our interviewees, the idea of the need to be a "multi-platform media company" to succeed in the current environment is far from dead. As a response to the problem of the fragmentation of media audiences, one interviewee held that, at minimum, it was reasonable to "take old media to see if we can extract reasonable economic profit and make use of their interconnections." While maintaining that convergence was "an idea still in the proving stage," an executive of a newspaper not yet involved in a convergence merger offered the judgment that "in the future, for a media company to survive, it has to have access to multimedia."

Assessments

In his introduction to *How Canadians Communicate,* David Taras offers the following critical assessment of convergence:

> Convergence has created a new set of problems for Canadian media corporations. First, in order to make these acquisitions, corporations have saddled themselves with debt. The irony is that, as they have grown larger, they have also become weaker and more vulnerable. Arguably, their ability to take chances, to invest heavily, and to promote Canadian magazines, music, TV shows, or newspapers has been weakened. But convergence has also raised questions about the nature of journalism and its role in ensuring that the country benefits from a lively and open debate about the issues that are critical to the future. Critics contend that, when ownership falls into too few hands, abuses of power are more likely to occur. (2003, p. 16)

Although the bloom is off the convergence rose and the leaves are somewhat droopy, the plant still shows distinct signs of life.[7] In the conclusion to *Kings of Convergence,* Gordon Pitts notes that:

> Convergence is a story that has run through a few introductory chapters, and has lost and gained a few characters, but the plot has yet to unfold entirely. As it does, it will be shaped by the factors of technology, strategy and ego.... That potent mix was present in all my conversations with the titans of Canadian communications—and never more so than with Izzy Asper. (2002, p. 331)

In spite of obvious disappointments and problems with the concept, the faith of the Aspers and CanWest Global in convergence continues to appear unshaken. For example, at CanWest's annual meeting near the end of January 2004, CEO Leonard Asper indicated that the company was on the hunt for possible new media acquisitions, describing CanWest as being

> "conceptually interested in anything that moves" in the sector.... We have to be part of the mix, and we have to find a way to be a part of any asset changes. I don't think we want to sit idly by and see our competitors grow. (As quoted in Silcoff, 2004, p. FP6)[8]

In March 2004, CanWest's convergence strategy was further clarified by Leonard Asper as

> operating in five media areas—television, print, outdoor advertising, radio and online.... This provided consumers with CanWest content anytime, anywhere.... Owning assets and building powerful brands in these categories allows us to leverage the sales, cross promotion and content creation opportunities in order to gain market share. [Asper went on to comment on how content can be shared:] Content at CanWest is never thrown out. There is no longer material on the cutting room floor that can get swept away. (Wilson, 2004, Mar. 12, p. FP5)

Mr. Asper gave the example of a two-hour interview with a celebrity that might become an 800-word story in a newspaper, and also run as a full transcript on that newspaper's on-line premium tier. "And you'll probably get the video of that interview as well" (Wilson, 2004, p. FP5).

Speaking at an e-content conference later in the same month, Rick Camilleri, then Chief Operating Officer for CanWest, outlined how CanWest's convergence strategy, which he described as horizontal, differed from the vertical type of convergence characteristic of the failed AOL Time-Warner merger. Following Leonard Asper's definition, horizontal convergence was defined as "branded content exploited over different media platforms." Camilleri summarizes his own argument regarding convergence as follows:

> Horizontal convergence involves merging different types of media, such as television and print, as is the case with CanWest. Vertical convergence occurs when the company owns both the media as well as the pipeline, or infrastructure, to deliver it.... Companies must come to grips with the fact that the balance of power has shifted from media companies to consumers.... Consumers have limitless access to content, anytime, anywhere, on demand. (Camilleri, as quoted in DaCruz, 2004, p. FP7)

In light of Leonard Asper's conception of how content could be shared among CanWest's many types of media, it appears to us that a simple horizontal/vertical dichotomy understates the complexity of CanWest's convergence model. In that content creation is clearly a factor in the mix, perhaps "vertical convergence of content over horizontally distinct multimedia platforms" more accurately catches the essence of what is involved in CanWest's convergence strategy.

On October 4, 2004, CanWest Global announced the birth of a new corporate entity, CanWest MediaWorks, designed "to integrate our media operations and leverage our media across platforms" (Brent, 2004, Oct. 5, p. FP1). Hired as part of this restructuring, in which Mr. Camilleri was retained as president, were five high-profile media executives from the United States including Kathleen Dore as president of television and radio operations, Michael Williams as president of publications (including newspapers), and Joseph Mangione as president of sales and marketing. A *Globe and Mail* story placed the following spin on the restructuring:

> Analysts see the changes as a move by CanWest chief executive Leonard Asper to boost Mr. Camilleri's role and add experienced managers to realize Mr. Asper's vision of a firm where broadcasting and print content are profitably resold in a variety of forms. (Blackwell, 2004, p. B1)

A further development related to CanWest's convergence strategy was reported on November 17, 2004, this being CanWest's acquisition from Hollinger International of 50% ownership of *The Jerusalem Post* in partnership with the Israeli company Mirkaei Tikshoret Group (MTL). Although sentiment was not the whole reason for the purchase, in part this acquisition could be explained as fulfilling a long-held dream of Izzy Asper's (Fisher, 2004, p. FP2). Leonard Asper indicated that CanWest was

> delighted to work with MTL to unleash the considerable untapped potential of the Jerusalem Post Group and to extend the reach of the Group's flagship

> newspaper and other properties around the world, but particularly in North America where CanWest's strong printing, sales and marketing expertise can be utilized. (Brent, 2004, Nov. 17, p. FP1)

More specifically, it was reported that

> Can West was looking at printing the North American edition of the prestigious daily in Montreal, Ottawa or Windsor, Ont., to achieve cost savings and an effective way to penetrate the big U.S. market that exists along the eastern seaboard from Boston to Washington. (Fisher, 2004, Nov. 18, p. FP2)

Whatever may be the economic rewards and the ultimate outcome of convergence, for newspapers the strategy has some clear implications: convergence tends to absorb or negate what have normally been regarded as the newspaper's unique strengths—its traditional, distinctively separate, and specialized presentation of news and views to readers. This uniqueness has been under attack for some time and is constantly being eroded as newspapers compete for audience with emerging media, especially television (Hildebrandt and Soderlund, 2002; Romanow and Love, 1989). As convergence proceeds, undoubtedly there will be increased pressure to unite newsrooms and news staffs from the different media involved in the process.

Such pressure may be viewed in the context of April 2001 CRTC licence renewal hearings. Both CanWest Global and CTV were queried regarding the extent to which broadcast properties would be merged with newly acquired newspaper holdings, and the CRTC considered whether the separation of broadcast and newspaper properties would be a condition of licence renewal—a condition rejected by both national television networks. Ivan Fecan, CEO of CTV, while acknowledging that it would be possible to merge broadcast and newspaper newsroom functions, stated that "we would not accept it on any level." Kirk Lapointe, CTV's president for news (since October 2003, managing editor of the CanWest-owned *Vancouver Sun),* was less definitive, claiming:

> that there are opportunities to collaborate...and to share resources will provide a very real improvement in news quality—and in diversity. We have not seen a single piece of concrete evidence that there is an existing threat to diversity of voices. (Southam News, 2001, Apr. 26, p. A9)

In spite of assurances to the contrary, we believe that convergent television and newspaper ownerships will, to the extent possible, merge the news gathering and news editing functions of their print, Internet, and broadcasting properties to lower the unit costs of information (see Wendland, 2001). The unfortunate consequences of this will be a decline in the number of independent voices and the loss of the distinctive qualities of newspapers as providers of information. We must also appreciate that the "convergence plot" is in the process of unfolding within a particular context—that of globalization. And in this global context it is clear that people, especially the young, are turning increasingly to the Internet as a source of daily information.[9]

Six

CanWest Global's National Editorial Policy
Round One

Walter C. Soderlund, Ronald H. Wagenberg, and Walter I. Romanow

In the summer of 2000, when Conrad Black's Hollinger announced the sale of substantial Canadian newspaper holdings to CanWest Global Communications, headquartered in Winnipeg, the overwhelming reaction of Canadians concerned with the impact of ownership on media content was one of relief. For the preceding four years, Conrad Black had controlled just over half of the country's daily newspapers, accounting for over 40% of daily circulation (Saunders, Mahood, and Waldie, 1996, p. B1). Now it seemed that the era of Mr. Black's ownership of Canadian newspapers had come to an end with no serious infringements on freedom of editorial expression (see Chapters 3 and 4, this volume). Moreover, in CanWest Global a Canadian owner had emerged to buy Mr. Black's newspapers, erasing fears that no potential Canadian purchaser would have enough capital ($3.2 billion) to buy the majority of the Hollinger Canadian newspaper empire—a circumstance that would have placed pressure on the government to relax foreign ownership restrictions. In May 2000, among rumours of a pending sell-off of Hollinger newspapers, Heritage Minister Sheila Copps had announced that the government was thinking of setting up "a blue-ribbon committee" to study the possibility of relaxing foreign ownership restrictions, claiming that "the issue of diversity of voices is a very important one.... If you have one owner who owns the majority of newspapers in the country, is that true competition?" (as quoted in Craig, 2000, p. A9).[1]

While there were some early indications of attempts by the Aspers to assert editorial influence on their newly acquired newspapers, these efforts did not appear to go beyond the level of editorial influence traditional for owners of Canadian newspapers. With any change in ownership, some changes in strategic direction and a consequent reshuffling of personnel could be expected (Marotte and Peritz, 2001). The Aspers now owned the newspapers—they paid the salaries, were responsible for damages resulting from lawsuits, expected profits, and were entitled to be comfortable with their newspapers' management.

However, on December 6, 2001, CanWest Global initiated a national editorial policy for its major Southam newspapers, fundamentally redefining the relationship between individual chain-owned newspapers and the chain's head office with respect to control of editorial content.[2] In a marked departure from journalistic tradition and past North American practice (and from assurances given the federal government regarding editorial autonomy[3]), CanWest Global announced that "national editorials" on questions of national and international importance would be written by Southam news personnel and would run in the chain's major newspapers. While the policy was justified in terms of stimulating debate—"on some issues, having a view point appear across the country can be of great value to the national discourse" (Gazette, 2001, pp. A1–A2)—editors of individual newspapers were also instructed that they could not run editorials that expressed views contrary to the "core positions" taken in the national editorials. Even though contrary op-ed pieces and letters to the editor were permitted, to many observers of the nation's media the "no contradictory editorial opinions" edict seemed more likely to shut off debate on important issues than to stimulate it. Moreover, the policy was seen as the precursor to a "chill" in Southam newsrooms across the country, as it was feared that journalists would self-censor to remain in the good graces of those who issued their paycheques.

The national editorial policy occasioned a furor among journalists (at home and abroad), as well as with media critics, academics, politicians (federal and provincial), and concerned citizens (see Allmand, Atwood, Berton, Branscombe, Broadbent, et al., 2002; Baxter, 2001; Canadian Press, 2001, Dec. 20; Ha, 2001). Journalists at *The Gazette* withheld their bylines in protest and three former editors of *The Gazette* in a letter to the editor of the paper claimed that

> our alarm is compounded by the fact that the newspapers' own editorials will not be permitted to disagree with the corporate line. Over time, as the corporate editorials cover more and more public issues, the range of topics on which local papers may express their views will diminish dramatically. (Fraser, Webster, and Harrison, 2001, p. B6)

The national editorial policy caught the attention of *The Washington Post*, which reported the conclusion of the National Conference of Editorial Writers: that the policy was "likely to backfire with readers who are accustomed to editorials on national and international subjects that take account of the diversity of views in their communities" (Brown, 2002, p. A25).

In spite of the controversy sparked by the policy, it was vigorously defended by the Aspers (Asper, 2001; Shecter, 2002). The policy was strongly supported and its detractors castigated in one of the national editorials, which read:

> We seek to bring Canadians together through national discussions of ideas. We believe that exploring issues from a Canada-wide perspective, rather than only regionally is good for the country. But in the worst manifestation of closed

> minds, critics have condemned it before even seeing the initiative develop. (Southam News, 2002, Jan. 29)

The research reported in this chapter accepts the challenge of "seeing the initiative develop." We present here our assessment of the thirty-one editorials the national editorial policy produced.

CanWest Global continued to publish national editorials through the winter and spring of 2002, although far fewer such editorials appeared than originally announced (on average one per week, rather than the three per week promised). When *Ottawa Citizen* publisher Russell Mills was fired in mid-June 2002, a firestorm of criticism erupted although the firing technically did not stem from a violation of the national editorial policy.[4] CanWest Global seemed to have had second thoughts about its policy and no national editorials appeared between June 17 and the end of September 2002.

The national editorial policy and the firing of Mr. Mills provoked torrents of journalistic commentary dealing with the impact of ownership concentration on freedom of expression in Canadian newspapers and the adverse effect this impact had on the health of Canadian democracy (see Canadian Press, 2002, June 19; Lunman and McCarthy, 2002). However, remarkably little analysis has been published of the actual content of the CanWest-written national editorials. While in no way seeking to dismiss the importance of the broader issues of ownership concentration and freedom of expression (which will be discussed in the concluding chapter), the focus of the research reported here is an analysis of what was actually contained in those Southam national editorials. Specifically:

1. What was the distribution between national and international topics in the series of national editorials?

2. What major issues were addressed in the editorials?

3. What were the "core positions" taken in the editorials (that is, those positions that were not to be challenged by counter-editorials in individual newspapers of the chain)?

4. What political parties and politicians were mentioned, and how often were they mentioned?

5. Was a clear partisan political direction evident in the editorials?

Background

The Southam newspaper empire dates from 1887, when founder William Southam acquired control of *The Hamilton Spectator.* A newspaper chain began to take shape with the 1897 addition of *The Ottawa Citizen*, followed prior to 1930 by the *Calgary Herald,* the *Edmonton Journal,* the *Winnipeg Tribune*, and the Vancouver *Province* (Kesterton, 1967, p. 78). The corporation continued to augment its newspaper holdings, bringing its holdings to seventeen newspapers by 1991 and twenty by 1996. As well, it expanded into other areas of "the communication-information industry," mainly in broadcasting and printing (Canada, 1981, p. 92).

In 1980, Southam, along with rival Thomson Newspapers, was the subject of an inquiry under the Combines Investigation Act for closing its *Winnipeg Tribune* at the same time that Thomson closed its *Ottawa Journal* (as mentioned in Chapter 1), leaving the surviving papers (the *Winnipeg Free Press* and *The Ottawa Citizen*) in monopoly positions in their respective cities. Other than triggering the Royal Commission on Newspapers (the Kent Commission), these newspaper closings led to no governmental action. However, as Chris Dornan argues, the Kent Commission "established a climate in which media companies could not behave with impunity in closing titles, purchasing competitors, or venturing into cross-media ownership" (1996, p. 79).

In terms of the quality of journalistic content, Southam newspapers fared well in comparison with competing chains. In 1986, during hearings regarding a stock transfer agreement between Southam and Torstar designed to ward off a potential hostile takeover, Royal Commission on Newspapers Chairman Tom Kent praised Southam for its journalistic integrity, claiming that it "always had a policy of sacrificing profit in order to publish higher quality newspapers" (as quoted in Greenspon, 1986, p. B4). In fact, there was little doubt that the Southam papers (particularly the "Big Five" located in Vancouver, Edmonton, Calgary, Ottawa, and Montreal) represented the best that there was with respect to Canadian newspaper chains.[5]

Speculation as to whether Paul Desmarais' Power Corporation or Conrad Black's Hollinger (both minority shareholders in Southam) might attempt a takeover of Southam ended in 1996, when Mr. Black bought out Mr. Demarais' Southam shares. The Southam acquisition (in addition to newspapers purchased from the Thomson and Armadale chains), added to his Hollinger holdings, made Mr. Black Canada's dominant newspaper owner. It was these newspaper assets (excluding 50% of the *National Post,* which he had launched in October 1998) that were purchased by CanWest Global in the summer of 2000.[6]

Methods

The research for this study is based on a combination of qualitative and quantitative text analyses. First, a list of national editorials was compiled and verified for completeness. All editorials were then read and analyzed by a minimum of two of this chapter's authors to determine the level of focus (national or international), the issues addressed, and the core positions taken. In addition, mentions of political parties or politicians were recorded for each editorial, and a judgement was made as to whether the editorial took a clear partisan position with respect to any of the major political parties. A high level of agreement (over 90%) was achieved on the coding of all of the above dimensions, consistent with standards established by Ole Holsti (1969, p. 140); the few differences of opinion that did arise were resolved to the satisfaction of all authors.

Findings

The thirty-one CanWest national editorials that form the data base for this study were published between December 6, 2001 and June 17, 2002. Nearly three-quarters (74%) of the editorials (twenty-three) dealt with national issues, another four (13%) were judged to have combined an international issue with an issue of Canadian foreign policy, while the remaining four (13%) focused exclusively on international issues.

The editorials can be grouped into five issue areas, in which two or more editorials appeared, plus a miscellaneous group of editorials dealing with a variety of policy themes. Issues of government spending, debt, and taxation, and the effects of those issues on the economy generated by far the greatest number—seven—editorials (22.5%). Following in numerical importance were editorials dealing with the complex of issues surrounding international terrorism, Muslim-Western conflict, and the Israeli–Palestinian conflict—these were the subject of four editorials (13%). Questions of journalistic practices in Canada, especially as they related to the Liberal party's leadership succession, were the subject of two editorials, as were the topics of parliamentary reform and violent street protests against globalization. The remainder of the editorials dealt with issues such as health care, property rights, support for the military, the *Indian Act*, securities regulation, water exports, procedural matters related to party leader selection, prosecutorial misconduct, and the need to unite the parties of the right. As previously mentioned, one editorial defended the national editorial policy.

National editorials appear to have been used by CanWest Global to imprint the owners' views across the chain's newspapers with the exception of the *National Post.* This use was augmented by the directive that individual newspapers in the chain could not present editorial views that contradicted the core positions expressed in the Winnipeg-written national editorials. In all the national editorials that were run, this edict had the most significance for the question of journalistic practice and the politics of Liberal leadership succession. While the challenge of Paul Martin to Prime Minister Chrétien's continued leadership, along with the question of if or when Mr. Chrétien ought to relinquish office, emerged as far and away the leading domestic political story of the summer of 2002, the Southam editorials admonished newspapers (their own prominently included) not to engage in idle speculation based on theories of what might happen. "The issue of Liberal party leadership is a matter between party members and their leader, Jean Chrétien.... For now the rhetoric and inflammatory language should be cooled" (Southam News, 2002, June 3). Editorials, claimed Southam, were supposed to consist of informed opinion based on competent research: "The public is entitled to expect the prime minister to provide leadership to the government, the government to tackle the real issues of our time, the media to report and opine based on facts, not theories" (Southam News, 2002, June 4). The impact of this policy, if its directives were followed, would be that Southam papers, including major dailies in thirteen Canadian cities, were restrained from commenting editorially on what was undoubtedly the most important domestic political issue of the day, if not of the year—whether Mr. Chrétien should stay or go.

The major foci of the national editorials were the closely related themes that governments were too involved in areas not specifically related to governance, that consequently government spending was too high, and that it was this excessive level of spending that necessitated an excessive level of taxation. These conditions, the editorials argued, interfered with the free market economy, and the free market was the system that could best provide solutions for Canadian society's problems and promote Canada's competitive position in the international economy. Some examples of such arguments follow:

> Over the last four decades the footprint of government on the economy has grown to that of a thousand pound gorilla, and a clumsy one at that. (Southam News, 2001, Dec. 6)

> In debates on public policy, especially within governments, there is a reflex that says if something isn't working well, spend more. (Southam News, 2002, Jan. 24)

> In stumbling over each other to get more loonies from taxpayers, all governments forget there's only one pocket to pick from. (Southam News, 2002, March 21)

> The journey to better productivity will only begin when the government acknowledges the link between performance, investment and people keeping more of what they earn. Until then, the outlook for Canada is more of the same: lower living standards, a sinking dollar and the emigration of citizens the country should keep. (Southam News, 2002, April 18)

> To truly prepare Canada to compete internationally in the new economy, governments need to constrain spending and make real tax cuts. (Southam News, 2002, March 21)

In addition to providing the primary focus of seven editorials, these points of view found their way into numerous other editorials that dealt with a wide range of specific policy concerns, including enshrining the right to private property in the constitution, instilling the norm of charitable giving into the national value system, reforming the *Indian Act*, reforming health care, and exporting water.

Taxes, in addition to being too high, were portrayed as unfair. At least two editorials urged the adoption of the flat tax. For example:

> Tax reform should be simple, equitable and efficient. One rate for all meets the criterion of simplicity. A flat tax is equitable since it taxes all income similarly. People with larger incomes pay a larger amount of tax. That's fair. And one rate eliminates the disincentives that arise as people move from one tax bracket to the next. (Southam News, 2002, April 25)

Support for the flat tax was one area where the Southam editorial position was overtly supportive of Stephen Harper and the Canadian Alliance Party.

The question of alleged unfair treatment of private charitable foundations for tax purposes was raised in the very first national editorial, and was dealt with peripherally in another:

> The chief distinction between private foundations and public ones is that the latter tend to draw donations from multiple sources...while private foundations tend to have fewer donors. There are legal definitions of differences on their board, but those are largely obsolete. Neither difference justifies this tax discrimination. (Southam News, 2001, Dec. 6)

The very first editorial claimed that donations made to public foundations were eligible for a tax deduction approximately 30% higher than the deduction for donations made to private charities. It is surprising that discrimination against private charities was deemed to be a national concern worthy of the inaugural editorial. The fact that the Aspers had established a private charitable foundation (The Asper Foundation) prompted some critics to question the degree to which the editorial was tailored to promote the particular tax interests of the Asper family (Weston, 2001). Such criticisms brought forth a strong response from the Aspers (Asper, 2001; Robb, 2001).

National editorials were mildly supportive of, and rarely overtly critical of, the Liberal party. It was the profligate spending and deficits of the Mulroney years that were singled out for criticism: "Debt service costs were as high as 40 per cent of spending [under Mulroney]" (Southam News, 2002, May 23). However, the general intrusiveness of governments and their propensity toward high spending were themes that constantly surfaced. In that the Liberals had been in power since 1993, for most Canadian readers, criticism of "government" in general, the "federal government" specifically, and references to "Ottawa" likely brought to mind the Liberal government. Consequently, this type of editorial could hardly be seen as promoting support for that party. The critical position taken toward "government" seems almost at odds with the directive that the chain was to leave Prime Minister Chrétien alone, and let him decide to leave office as he saw fit.

On the international dimension, the editorials dealing with terrorism and Middle East politics left no doubt of CanWest's hard-line attitude toward both terrorists and Yasser Arafat. Arguments that economic and social root causes of terrorism needed to be addressed were dismissed in favour of calls for a harsh military response:

> One hundred days after the horrors of Sept. 11, the worst banalities mouthed in response still have astonishing currency. Chief among these are that "violence doesn't solve anything," and that the leaders of the free world should instead negotiate a resolution to the crisis we face. These are absurdities.... The civilized world cannot negotiate with hate-filled terrorists. (Southam News, 2001, Dec. 20)

Support for Israel was as unequivocal in the national editorials as was the condemnation of Yasser Arafat:

> The 168 countries that pay only about 14 per cent of the costs regularly use the UN to attack western democracies, especially Israel. There are more

> than a dozen one-sided UN resolutions criticizing Israel, most relatively silent about misdeeds by the Palestinian Authority or Arab states. (Southam News, 2002, Jan. 31)

> Like his terrorist underlings, Arafat sees the lives of children—Palestinian and Israeli both—as fodder for the Arab mission to ignite a regional war that will destroy Israel. He and his supporters must be isolated internationally, beaten down militarily and made to understand that Palestinians can never hope to have a country so long as they embrace the apocalyptic creed under which suicide bombers—and Palestinians who cheer them on—explode themselves. (Southam News, 2002, April 2)

As well, Mr. Arafat was described as "corrupt," "incompetent," and "a dictator" (Southam News, 2002, May 30). On these issues the personal views of the Aspers appear most evident, whoever may have actually committed them to words. Presumably, any alternative editorial view on this most complicated of international situations, perhaps one that saw the need for negotiations between the parties, was proscribed for CanWest newspapers.

On the issues of parliamentary reform and violent protests against globalization, the national editorials adopted mainstream positions (saying that parliamentary reform was needed and protests against globalization were harmful). These were not likely to have occasioned opposing editorial views, even if individual CanWest papers had been free to write as they pleased:

> If MPs become somebodies again, and electing them made more difference to how the country was run, perhaps the 40 per cent of electors who have given up on casting ballots might even return to the voting booth. That would be especially good for the health of our democracy. (Southam News, 2001, Dec. 27)

> Attacking policemen with shards of concrete and glass is not a form of free expression. Neither is tearing down a fence erected to protect politicians and their staff from the same weapons. And it does not become free expression merely because the perpetrators say they are motivated by "rage" and "frustration" over how governments govern. (Southam News, 2002, May 2)

These editorial positions, and with some exceptions[7] those put forward in numerous other policy editorials categorized as miscellaneous, tended to be unremarkable. As well, the range of topics on which editorials was written was rather narrow, with an inordinately heavy concentration on two issues:

government spending and taxes and the Middle East conflict. Conversely, the list of significant topics that were *not* dealt with was a long one. Notably absent were editorials dealing with Canada's relations with the United States.

In terms of ideological orientation, the national editorials reflect a set of right-of-centre views that had emerged in Southam papers long before the "law according to Winnipeg" was laid down. Indeed they were characteristic of the editorial positions held by Canadian newspapers more generally at the time.[8] In fact, other than giving expression to a western (some would say an Albertan) regionally oriented point of view that might otherwise not have been present in eastern CanWest newspapers (for example, favouring the Triple-E Senate and the flat tax), the national editorials' contribution to democratic debate is questionable.

Interestingly, the editorials were not especially strong in partisan attack or support. As mentioned, the Progressive Conservatives (under the leadership of both Brian Mulroney and Joe Clark) tended to be the objects of much criticism and little praise. The PC party was referred to as "cadaverous," while Mr. Clark was described as "a former, not a future prime minister. His career delusions cannot obstruct Canadian democracy" (Southam News, 2002, Apr. 4). While the Liberals came off somewhat better, they must have borne the brunt of frequent, non-party-specific anti-government, anti-federal-government, and anti-Ottawa sentiments—for example, "the federal government's tax and spend culture" (Southam News, 2002, Apr. 18).

The effect here is hard to calculate. For example, while Minister of Foreign Affairs Bill Graham was characterized as a "naive do-gooder" for meeting with Yasser Arafat, the fact that Mr. Graham was a Liberal cabinet minister was not mentioned. Did this editorial then reflect negatively on the Liberal party? Our guess is that most readers were able to make the connection.

The Alliance/Reform party was both praised and criticized. For its financial policies, it was singled out for praise:

> The strength of the Alliance, and the Reform party before it, has always been its willingness to advocate new policies. Under Preston Manning's leadership, Reform was the first national party to champion fiscal common sense through balanced budgets. He recommended tax cuts as a means to improve Canada's economic prospects. (Southam News, 2002, Apr. 25)

For its social attitudes it was chastised:

> [Alliance/Reform] has a checkered history of such nonsense [racial intolerance] and of flailing about rather that dealing with it. (Southam News, 2002, Jan. 18)

The New Democratic Party and the Bloc Québecois received almost no editorial attention. It is therefore difficult to make any assessment of the evaluation of those parties by CanWest other than by pointing out their perceived irrelevance.

In terms of actual mentions by name, we were struck by the relatively few editorials that mentioned political parties. The governing Liberal party was cited in only seven editorials (22.5%), the Alliance/Reform party in five (16%), and the PCs in four (13%). The NDP and the Bloc Québecois were each mentioned only in a single editorial.

The list of specific politicians mentioned by name is interesting as well, both because few politicians were explicitly mentioned and because no one politician can be said to have dominated. As might be expected, the list is headed by sitting Prime Minister Jean Chrétien, mentioned in seven of the editorials (22.5%); followed by his leadership challenger, Paul Martin, mentioned in four (13%); by opposition leaders Stephen Harper and Joe Clark, each mentioned in three (10%); and by John Manley, Alan Rock, and Yasser Arafat, each mentioned in two (6%). The list of single-editorial mentions includes a host of contemporary lights and lesser lights (primarily Liberal cabinet members), a brace of social activists such as Jaggi Singh, Naomi Klein, and Maude Barlow (all referred to in a negative context in an editorial dealing with violent protest), as well as such historical luminaries as James Madison, Vladimir Lenin, and Wilfrid Laurier.

Discussion

The Aspers' national editorial policy brought to a boil the issue raised in 1996 by Conrad Black's rise to a dominant position as a newspaper owner: What would happen if owners actually used the considerable power available to them through chain/conglomerate ownership, to attempt to dictate the content of the media outlets under their control? It was always clear, hypothetically at least, that owners held this power. However, as Robert Dahl has cautioned, it is important to distinguish between "potential influence" and "actual influence" (1991, pp. 20–25).

With the national editorial policy, this distinction disappeared. For the first time, we were faced with actual owner influence, and this on a large scale—planned, open, clearly spelled out, and justified—rather than with potential influence. In short, "the Aspers [took] media concentration to places it had never been before" (Smith, 2002, p. 48).

What were the Aspers trying to achieve by instituting the national editorial policy? There is no reason not to take them at their word and accept that their primary purpose was to present a national viewpoint across the country and thus to stimulate debate. However, given the universally recognized economic diversity of Canada coupled with the political fragmentation evident since the 1993 election, one must ask whether there is, or even can be, a national viewpoint on critical issues affecting the country.[9] Our answer to this question lies somewhere on the continuum between "no" and "not very likely."

Traditionally, newspapers have viewed themselves as champions of the locality in which they are published. The huge geographic expanse of Canada and consequent economic and political differences between provinces and the communities within them have meant that editors tend to highlight different problems; if they address the same issue, they do so from different perspectives. For example, among CanWest newspapers, one would expect to see discussions of possible government subsidies to attract automobile plants in *The Windsor Star*, of the impact of the Kyoto Protocol in the *Calgary Herald*, and of the operation of the Canadian Wheat Board in the Saskatoon *StarPhoenix*.

But are there pan-Canadian issues on which a national editorialist could express a viewpoint that speaks to a national community? Fiscal policy, defence policy, foreign affairs, and health care all seem to be issue areas that transcend parochialism. However, the historical and contemporary reality in Canada is such that even these national concerns tend to be viewed from different perspectives in different parts of the country. For instance, many CanWest Global editorials have as a focus (and a number of other editorials have as subtext) the argument that the scope of government is too broad; if one accepts that argument as valid, it follows that one also accepts that there should be fewer civil servants. That point of view, published in an editorial in *The Ottawa Citizen,* can hardly be thought of as championing the views of the paper's subscribers. If national editorial writers had decided to weigh in on the Kyoto Protocol, whose perspective would have been presented as the national one?

CanWest owners can commission national editorialists to write on any subject they choose to, but to claim that these so-called national editorials express a truly national perspective (and then to preclude any of their local papers from taking a contrary editorial view) stretches credibility. This would be the case even had the national editorials showed a much higher level of insight and sophistication than was evident in the editorials that were published.

Beyond the "national point of view" argument, one may speculate whether the national editorial policy represents a conscious importation to newspapers of a concept that had developed in television over the previous decade: that of "corporate branding" (Hannigan, 2002). In television, branding (as seen in the network logo in the lower right-hand corner of the TV screen) represents a conscious attempt by networks to build viewer loyalty, and to legitimize and add credibility to what is being broadcast through its identification with the network (Kim, 1999). CanWest executive Donald Babick lends support to the case for the branding motive in his remarks to the 2002 Canadian Newspaper Association conference: "At the end of the day we're really helping build significant brand presence for each of our properties.... Brand identity is a key factor in attracting younger readers, viewers and consumers" (as quoted in Scotton, 2002, p. A9). In this context, the inclusion of the Southam torch logo, which accompanied all national editorials, appears to be a case of direct borrowing from television of the concept of network branding (Shields and Soderlund, 2001).

The question becomes: how appropriate is the transfer of this branding concept from one medium to another? We suggest that the concept did not travel well at all. As Chris Dornan has observed, "in the end, all news is local" (2003b, p. 120), and newspapers, as opposed to television networks, are essentially local institutions. While readers realize that their local newspaper is owned by somebody, and, as established by the data reviewed in Chapter 1, Canadians are well accustomed to chain ownership, no one wants to be reminded on an ongoing basis that the local newspaper is both owned—and its content to some extent dictated—by people who live outside the community. Whether that owner is in Winnipeg, Vancouver, Halifax, or Toronto appears to us to be beside the point. We would argue that corporate branding of newspapers, which after all live or die by how well they serve their communities and reflect local interests, offers no advantage and is inherently alienating to local editorial staffs and newspaper readers alike.

Another question that must be addressed is: how likely was it that the goals of the CanWest owners would be met by the positions articulated in the national editorials? Judging by its relative absence, overt support for or criticism of particular political parties (with the exception of the deprecation of the PC party and its leaders) was apparently not a major goal of the national editorial policy. In terms of the policy's impact on public opinion, the issue that most immediately comes to mind is the attempt to spare Prime Minister Chrétien from the ravages of journalistic speculation regarding the date of his retirement. The impression gained from reflecting on the intent of this set of editorials (but not necessarily from their specific text) is that, while *not insisting that Mr. Chrétien should stay*, they were instructing their newspapers *not to say that he should go.* If the intent of these editorials was to bolster Mr. Chrétien's position with the public—and editorials are after all meant to, and do, make some impact on public opinion (Fridkin Khan and Kenny, 2002)—the effort failed miserably. The firing of *Ottawa Citizen* publisher

Russell Mills in mid-June focused extraordinary attention on Mr. Chrétien's future (as well as on the legitimate extent of a newspaper owner's power to control content), and most of this commentary was not supportive of the prime minister's continued indefinite reign. As the summer months went by, both the Canadian public and the Liberal party seemed to reach the conclusion that the prime minister ought to retire. Indeed, on August 20, 2002, in advance of a scheduled fall leadership review that many predicted he was unlikely to survive, Mr. Chrétien appeared forced into announcing that he would retire in February 2004 (although he actually retired on December 12, 2003).

The broader question, whether the CanWest national editorial policy in its first round of application constituted a threat to freedom of expression, is not as easily answered. In the controversy over the policy, the issue of freedom of expression far outstripped any discussion of the impact the editorials may have had on specific policies (Lorinc, 2002). Thus, one of the factors prompting this research was our interest in discovering the substance of the editorial views transmitted to the Canadian public through this controversial policy. We have pointed out that, with a few exceptions, the topics of the first set of editorials were not especially remarkable and the positions taken in them were neither ground-breaking nor memorable. The editorials did not offer much in the way of opinion that CanWest newspapers had not already adopted or would not have been likely to adopt as editorial policy had the national editorial policy not been established.

Furthermore, one might have expected national editorials to be characterized by a keen sense of which issues were truly worthy of being designated as national. In the case of the CanWest national editorials, however, far too many were written on topics that appeared marginal or esoteric, and this worked to depreciate the impact of the set of editorials as a whole. With a somewhat predictable, if not weak, selection of topics (within the thirty-one editorials there was considerable redundancy), even the one editorial per week that appeared on average was, in our opinion, more than could maintain credibility with readers over an extended period of time. As well, one would have expected that national editorials would show deep insight into the nature of complex problems and would be characterized by excellent writing. Our admittedly subjective conclusion is that these characteristics tended to be decidedly absent from CanWest national editorials, which often resembled "shots from the hip" rather than well-thought-out pieces.

Thus we are faced with a paradox: if editorial autonomy was to be openly challenged by a corporate owner, as the Aspers did with the national editorial policy, it is indeed fortunate that the challenge was carried out so poorly as to discredit the entire initiative. We would hope that other chain owners, who certainly do not lack intelligence, have learned what not to do. On this point, we are reminded of George Bain's cogent assessment of the motives behind Conrad Black's drive for newspaper control in 1996: "Something I am prepared to assume is that he has not made himself the owner of more newspapers in Canada than anyone else for the purpose of running them into the ground" (Bain, 1996, p. 48). Owners do have important choices to make, between treating their newspapers as profit-making businesses or treating them as vehicles to further a particular ideological point of view. In light of the Aspers' negative national editorial policy experience, it is our feeling that most newspaper owners will have little difficulty in deciding to opt for the former over the latter.

Indeed, critics have questioned the level of business understanding brought to their newly acquired newspaper properties by the CanWest Global owners. Although no obvious benefits accrued to the conglomerate from the national editorial policy, there has been a significant public relations cost. Regardless of how the Aspers feel about the national editorial policy, the bottom line is that it was rejected by the rest of the Canadian newspaper community and was the object of serious concern among politicians and academics. The Aspers are, in effect, isolated. Even Conrad Black is reported to have described the Aspers' policy as

> ham-handed, perhaps out of inexperience with the politics of newspapers or possibly from bad advice. They should have stated their intentions from the beginning and engaged in open discussion with the people from their own newspapers. Instead they issued editorials and edicts from on high, and when they were met by a negative reaction hunkered down and traded wild accusations with their critics. This botched strategy allowed their media rivals to seize the high ground on the censorship issue. (As quoted in Pitts, 2002, p. 268)

In their review of developments in journalism across the Commonwealth during 2002, for Canada, Murray Burt and Derek Ingram describe the "coast-to-coast across the country, editorial interference by chain owners and resultant ethics issues [as continuing] to set journalism on its ear in what is usually a media-placid nation" (2002, p. 468). Burt and Ingram appeared less concerned with the financial and control implications of the Aspers' acquisition of the Hollinger properties than they were with the "single CanWest head-office fiat about editorials that ignited enormous journalistic harrumphing and a campaign of full-page advertisements by former Southam News luminaries, scorning the new owners' interference and seeking government action" (2002, p. 473). Even so staunch a defender of media convergence as Marni Soupcoff used the word "lamentable" to describe the Aspers' national editorial policy (2003, p. 10).

It is hard to reach any conclusion with respect to the Aspers' national editorials other than that they were a mistake, and that CanWest should cease and desist. The Aspers should restore editorial autonomy to their newspapers, and they should do so sooner rather than later. The policy was a bad idea—from the perspectives of democratic theory and of media practice. Fortunately, it was implemented so ineptly that, other than having raised the issue of free expression to a critical level of attention, it was of little consequence. Certainly it will be seen as hardly having been worth the negative publicity it created for CanWest Global, and thus it stands as a powerful example of what to avoid rather than what to emulate. Ironically, in this sense, the CanWest national editorials ultimately may have made an unexpected positive contribution to the cause of freedom of expression in this country.

Seven

The Firing of Russell Mills, Round Two of National Editorials, and the CanWest News Services Initiative

Walter C. Soderlund and Walter I. Romanow

The Firing of Russell Mills

During the winter and spring of 2002, the CanWest national editorial policy continued to draw criticism. It was, however, when *The Ottawa Citizen* carried a feature article critical of Jean Chrétien's financial dealings, along with an editorial calling for the prime minister's resignation, that the issue of ownership control over editorial content reached a crisis point. Two weeks after the appearance of the article and editorial, CanWest Global fired the newspaper's publisher, Russell Mills.

The feature article and accompanying editorial published in the June 1 (Saturday) edition of *The Citizen* were truly exceptional pieces of hard-hitting journalism. The feature, headlined "Double Standard" and written by Graham N. Green, the *Citizen*'s Deputy Editorial Page Editor, was an extraordinary op-ed piece that ran four full newspaper pages in length. It focused on Chrétien's financial dealings with respect to his ownership of shares in a golf course adjoining the Auberge Grand-Mére in Shawinigan, located in the prime minister's riding. Green traced in detail the complicated, murky financial transactions, describing how Mr. Chrétien's shares in the golf course had supposedly been sold in 1993 but were not paid for until 1999. In the meantime, the prime minister had personally intervened to secure federal loans for the troubled adjoining hotel—loans that would sustain the value of the golf course—and that would likely not have been granted without his personal intervention. The conclusion reached by the article's author was clearly presented and devastating to the prime minister:

> A detailed review of the prime minister's own words—and those of his ministers and closest advisors in his defence—over the past three years shows that he has been the one ignoring the facts. It is hard to reach any other conclusion but that Mr. Chrétien knew what he was saying was untrue and chose to deliberately offer explanations he knew to be false.
>
> Only one word—lying—describes this behaviour and that's what Mr. Chrétien has done in these situations. (Green, 2002, p. B2)

As if it was not enough to accuse the prime minister of lying, an editorial headlined "Time to Go" appeared in the same issue of *The Citizen*. The editorial used extraordinarily harsh and blunt language, charging that "Chrétien's own behaviour inspired government rot." Referring specifically to the Green article, the editorial concluded that Mr. Chrétien's less-than-satisfactory reactions to allegations of Cabinet misbehaviour

> constitute a persuasive case for his swift and unceremonious departure. But there is a more powerful reason this prime minister must step aside: his own disgraceful behaviour.... [The editorial concluded with the exhortation] Mr. Chrétien, we ask you to step down—for the good of the country. If you will not, we urge the Liberal party to throw you out. (*Ottawa Citizen*, 2002, June 1, p. B6)

In spite of his having received an honorary degree from Carleton University for excellence in journalism the day before, on Sunday, June 16, in an evening meeting with David Asper, Russell Mills was fired (CBC News, 2002, June 17).[1]

In many ways, Russell Mills seemed an unlikely candidate for the role of chief trouble-maker at CanWest Global. He was a long-time Southam employee, having joined *The Ottawa Citizen* in 1971 as a copy editor and moved up the corporate ladder, to be named editor in 1977 and publisher in 1986 (Southam Newspapers, 2002, June 18, p. A5). He also appears to have developed "more than his share...[of] advanced survival skills." As John Miller recounted, when Conrad Black took control of the *Citizen* in 1996, "everyone knew that the man whose head was probably first on the block was Mills" (Miller, 1988, pp. 74–75); yet at that time it was not Mills but Jim Travers, the newspaper's editor, who was fired.

CanWest's and Mr. Mills' accounts of the reasons for Mills' firing differed significantly. Mr. Mills stated that the reason for his dismissal was his failure to pre-clear the "Time to Go" editorial with the Aspers: "They wanted to see it in advance and they felt I should have submitted it to them for approval. I had no way of knowing that was their expectation" (as quoted in Southam Newspapers, 2002, June 18, p. A5). The Aspers cited long-standing differences over

> news and editorial coverage of federal politics. [Leonard] Asper said the *Citizen's* publisher was not fired because he published a single editorial or news story critical of the prime minister, but because he was in charge of consistently one-sided coverage. Mills was fired for "repeated non-compliance" with requests to make the paper more diverse. (*Ottawa Citizen* Staff, 2002, June, 21, p. D11)

This explanation notwithstanding, given the two-week interval between the editorial and the termination, and given the odd hour and circumstance of the actual firing, Mills' account has the louder ring of truth:

> I was given the option of retiring, but it would have required signing a confidentiality agreement and just putting out a short statement that I had retired. In my view, I couldn't do that after so many years in journalism, to put out a statement that was inaccurate. (Southam Newspapers, 2002, June 18, p. A5; see also Mills, 2002, July 1)

As mentioned in the previous chapter, it was the firing of Russell Mills that crystallized opposition to the national editorial policy. *Citizen* reporters withheld their bylines for a week and politicians spoke out. NDP leader Alexa McDonough asked: "How many more (voices) will be silenced before this government moves to protect journalistic independence from media concentration and convergence?" Liberal MP John Bryden personally attacked the Aspers: "This whole sorry story shows alarming immaturity on the part of the Aspers, owners of CanWest, who appear not to have the foggiest notion of the concept of press freedom in a democracy" (Canadian Press, 2002, June 19, p. 18). The issue even attracted the attention of the International Press Institute (IPI) in Vienna, a global network organization involving 110 countries. IPI Director Johann Fritz described Mills' firing as

> an attack on press freedom by an unholy coalition between politics and big business.... Many believe that it is only in autocratic countries of the Third World or in countries in transition that democracy and a free press is in danger. But the Mills affair will have a chilling effect on critical reporting in Canada and will bring an increase in self-censorship. (As quoted in Lunman and McCarthy, 2002, p. A1)

Earlier, on June 6, the broader Canadian journalism community had joined the public policy debate. Forty former Southam newspaper executives took out full-page ads in a number of non-CanWest newspapers, including *The Globe and Mail,* criticizing CanWest's national editorial policy on a number of grounds:

> First, the gag order is ominous and the list of forbidden perspectives grows longer as time passes. Second, this change has already skewed editorials, commentary and coverage about domestic and foreign issues. Third, we are

> deeply opposed to any trend that diminishes Canada's diversity of voices.... We can picture a time when one or two multi-channel media giants, each with a single national voice, will be telling us all what to think. (As quoted in *The National Newspaper Guild*, 2002, June 14)

For its part, Canadian Journalists for Free Expression called upon CanWest to rehire Mr. Mills, in part at least to restore its own credibility:

> CanWest, like any newspaper proprietor, has the right to impose an editorial line on its newspapers. But it has abused this right by dismissing or disciplining not just a publisher but reporters and columnists who dare to challenge its corporate views in public. CanWest readers are also within their rights to ask why Canada's largest newspaper chain chooses to suppress divergent perspectives developed by its own employees, who are highly respected journalists with a long tradition of serving their communities. (Canadian Journalists for Free Expression, 2002, June 17)

The firing of Mills was also linked to the prime minister himself, through his friendship with Israel (Izzy) Asper. Citing reports that Mr. Chrétien had met with the senior Asper on the day the editorial had appeared, Progressive Conservative party leader Joe Clark saw the firing in the context of an "alarming pattern which I think needs to be investigated." He added, "These are questions that go to the root of freedom of the press and the root of democracy." The Aspers denied any prime ministerial influence, and Leonard Asper claimed that CanWest Global "has no 'special relationship' with the prime minister" (*Ottawa Citizen* Staff, 2002, June 21, p. D11).

As a consequence of Mills' firing, the Canadian Association of Journalists reported that:

> many CanWest reporters have already told us about the editorial chill they feel [and told us they believe that] the removal of Mills will only add to the self-censorship by journalists that is removing important stories and ideas from the pages of some of the country's biggest and most important newspapers. (Canada News Wire, 2002, June 17)

It was also reported that *The Citizen* lost "more than 6,000 copies daily in the three months after the controversial dismissal. Average Saturday sales were down about 9,000 copies over the same period" (Galloway, 2002, p. A16). The Canadian Senate began preparations for a "public inquiry into the concentration of media ownership" (Winsor, 2002, June 19, p. A4); an interim report stemming from that inquiry was released in April 2004 (Canada, 2004). Whatever the motivation behind the suspension of national editorials, the one published on June 17 (dealing with the negative impact of anti-establishment demonstrations) ushered in a twelve-week hiatus. National editorials would not reappear until the end of September 2002.

National Editorials: Round Two

The attention initially focused on the national editorial policy was due largely to the resistance of Southam journalists, and to efforts of competing newspaper chains to turn the policy into an issue of freedom of expression. For CanWest Global, the difficulty was compounded by the fact that it lacked an adequate disaster control plan to deal with the predictable fallout from Mills' firing. The question then became: could we be comfortable that the owners of CanWest Global would not make other attempts to control newspaper content?

Unfortunately, the answer to this question was no. As we have mentioned, the Aspers stopped publishing national editorials for twelve weeks, over the summer of 2002, most likely in response to the extensive negative public reaction to the firing of Russell Mills and the negative reactions from their own papers. Although its critics may have hoped that the policy would remain shelved and that CanWest Global would return to accepted journalistic practice in the operation of its newspapers, national editorials reappeared in the fall of 2002 although with the announcement that there would be fewer than initially planned.

David Estok, Adjunct Professor of Journalism at the University of Western Ontario, reported that, as before, "reaction to the Aspers' national editorials from journalists and media observers was swift and negative." It was Estok's interpretation that, in resuming the editorials on a reduced scale, CanWest "is quietly backing away from a controversial policy…[that] sparked a public relations nightmare last year" (2002, p. B11).[2] However, Estok was not optimistic regarding the Aspers' attempts to exercise control in the future:

> That the Aspers wanted to use their newspapers to express their opinions about current events on the editorial pages is normal and perfectly natural. That the Aspers used such a blunt instrument, bullying tactics and firing people to get their way is less so. Don't expect the Aspers' views to disappear from their editorials and, maybe even subtly, their news coverage. Expect only that we may hear and see less of it so openly. (Estok, 2002, p. B11)

The first of this second round of editorials again took up the politics of Liberal party leader succession. "An editorial from Southam News," headlined

"Liberal party needs real leadership race," appeared in *The Windsor Star* on September 30, 2002, calling on Jean Chrétien to free his cabinet ministers from the "no campaigning for leader" edict issued in June. Mr. Chrétien lifted the ban in October 2002, freeing other potential candidates to vie with Paul Martin for the leadership of the party and the prime minister's job. Of interest in the editorial is this statement: "The candidates and their party owe Canadians a level of transparency far beyond the usual manipulation of the news media. We will act on behalf of our readers to scrupulously seek out candidates' clear positions on issues" (Southam News, 2002, Sept. 30, p. A6).

A second editorial, "Rate hikes risky," appeared with the Southam torch logo on October 26 in the *Edmonton Journal*; it argued that the Bank of Canada should take a cautious approach with respect to raising interest rates (Southam News, 2002, Oct. 26).[3] The final editorial of 2002 appeared shortly after it was reported that Chrétien's communications director, François Ducros, had referred to U.S. President George W. Bush as a "moron" in the context of Bush's policy toward war with Iraq. A front-page editorial from CanWest Publications[4] (a new source of editorials) appeared in *The Windsor Star*, stressing the importance for Canada of good relations with the United States (CanWest Publications, 2002, Nov. 28). The editorial argued that "responsibility for the intellectual climate that encouraged a senior Canadian official to casually utter a crude and inappropriate insult about the president of the United States is widely shared." It further pointed out that the

> country's public culture and political history are steeped in cheap and wrong-headed anti-American sentiment...[and expressed the hope] that this incident will have a salutary effect—it has at least brought Canada–U.S. relations to the forefront of public discourse and perhaps it can lead to positive change. (CanWest Publications, 2002, Nov. 28, pp. A1, A8)[5]

For whatever reason, as mentioned in Chapter 6, the theme of Canadian–American relations had been conspicuously absent in the first round of national editorials.

The first editorial of the new year appeared in the *Edmonton Journal* on March 11, 2003, headlined "Clear choice on Iraq." The editorial argued that, while Saddam Hussein "gives a bit here and there," fundamentally he had never intended to comply with promises made at various times to disarm. As a consequence, he should no longer enjoy the benefit of the doubt:

> No further hand-wringing is necessary.... The indictment against the Iraqi regime has been proven over and over. When war comes, and ends, it is

> essential that Canada will have stood unequivocally with the coalition of the willing, and been counted as a reliable friend to Britain and the U.S. (CanWest Publications, 2003, Mar. 11, p. A12)

Jean Chrétien chose to ignore this advice, and Canada did not join the coalition forces seeking to disarm and depose the Iraqi leader.

On the domestic side, an editorial headlined "Quebec albatross off the PM's back" appeared in *The Windsor Star* on April 22, following the defeat of the Parti Québecois at the hands of the Liberals under Jean Charest. The editorial praised the "healthy dose of 'tough love' " delivered to Quebec by the Chrétien government in the form of the *Clarity Act*. It went on to enumerate the reasons Mr. Chrétien should be pleased with his accomplishments, but criticized the prime minister's penchant for defending the United Nations, the "cavalier" manner in which Canada's relations with the United States had been handled after September 11, and the waste of money incurred by the gun registry program. However, the editorial concluded that "no government, and no leader, gets everything right [and] Canadians have reason to be in a good mood, and to celebrate their good fortune with the prime minister" (CanWest Publications, 2003, Apr. 22, p. A6).[6]

The CanWest News Service Initiative

In addition to resuming national editorials, albeit in reduced numbers, on January 20, 2003, CanWest Global announced the formation of a "Canada News Desk" (ultimately named CanWest News Service). To be located in Winnipeg (home of CanWest Global), the news desk was designed to replace existing Southam News operations in Ottawa. It was described as serving "as a news hub for the Southam newspaper chain, co-ordinating stories and coverage of CanWest's 12 big-city newspapers.... The chief goal is to improve efficiency by ending duplication of editorial coverage throughout the 126-year-old Southam [chain]" (Damsell, 2003, Jan. 20, p. B2).

Fears were immediately raised that editorial autonomy, already challenged by the national editorial policy and the firing of Russell Mills, would be further compromised, as "assignment editors across the country will work for both their local supervisors and the Winnipeg desk" (Damsell, 2003, Jan. 20, p. B2). Roger Bird, a professor of journalism at Carleton University described the news desk initiative as

> an appalling idea.... The only possible reason to do this would be to have closer control of the news by head office. I'm sorry, Winnipeg is a wonderful city, but

> it's not one of the news capitals of the country, very much and very often. (As quoted in Damsell, 2003, Jan. 20, B2)

Stephen Kimber also described the news desk as a further attempt by CanWest Global to tighten "the editorial noose":

> [CanWest] recently opened a centralized news desk in Winnipeg with an Internet-based date book system to allow editors in Winnipeg to track every reporter on every assignment in every CanWest paper, while "bat" phones provide Winnipeg with direct entry into every newsroom in the country. At some point, the news desk is expected to begin providing its homogenized hodge-podge of news, features and opinions to the chain's TV and Internet outlets, too. (Kimber, 2003)

In March 2003, Keith Damsell reported the creation of a five-person "arts team… comfortable working in both print and TV" in Winnipeg, with responsibilities to cover television, film, and pop culture. Although Gordon Fisher, CanWest's president of news, reported that "there are no plans to reduce CanWest's arts coverage or shift editorial control to the company's Winnipeg head office," critics were skeptical. For example, Peter Murdoch, vice-president for media for the Communications, Energy and Paperworkers Union of Canada charged that "CanWest continues to treat its newspaper customers as though they were buying dog food—bigger box, less food. What do the dogs know?" (as quoted in Damsell, 2003, Mar. 20, p. R5).

In June 2003, CanWest announced that the *National Post*'s Ottawa and foreign bureaus had been integrated into the CanWest News Service, and that only those reporters attached to the *Financial Post* section of the *National Post* would remain "directed from Toronto." CanWest spokesperson Gordon Fisher indicated that "the rest of the journalists at the Post's Ottawa bureau are now working for the CanWest News Service, a Winnipeg-based operation that distributes stories to all the newspaper in the organization, including the Post" (Paddon, 2003).

Beyond its impact on CanWest media properties, the creation and growth of the news desk, combined with an announcement by CanWest in July 2003 that its flagship newspaper the *National Post* might withdraw from the Canadian Press news co-operative "next summer" gave rise to "speculation that the media company might pull out of CP [the Canadian Press news co-operative] and rely instead on reports from its 11 dailies, shunted through a Winnipeg news desk established earlier this year."[7] While the loss of the *National Post* would involve a reduction in CP 2005 revenues of only 2%, the loss of the entire

CanWest chain would result in a crippling 24% reduction of the co-operative's membership based on circulation figures (Smith, 2003, p. A14). CanWest explained the possible move purely in terms of cost-cutting (the *National Post* had lost over $200 million since it began publishing in 1998); however, given its commitment to convergence and in light of the newly created CanWest News Service, we would be prudent to keep in mind CanWest's desire to be pre-eminent in all aspects of information dissemination.

In his comments on the news desk initiative as it was initially presented, Russell Mills pointed to "two significant fears." The first fear was that "this is the first step in a broader strategy to reduce editorial staff and budgets of individual newspapers," while the second was that Southam's "Ottawa bureau, which covers the federal government and politics, will report to the news desk in Winnipeg," thereby allowing the politically active Asper family an opportunity to influence news coverage (Mills, 2003, Jan. 21, B11).

Mills also pointed to the need for newspapers to have "strong and unmistakably local voices. The Montreal Gazette should not read like the Vancouver Sun or vice versa" (Mills, 2003, Jan. 21, p. B11). As evidence of sound newspaper business practice, he cited the case of *The Boston Globe*, which for the past ten years had been owned by *The New York Times:*

> Although it would be much cheaper for the Globe to rely on the excellent reporting staff of the Times for national and world coverage, this does not happen. The New York Times allows the Globe to maintain its own foreign correspondents and Washington bureau and the paper retains a distinctive voice that appeals to Boston. (Mills, 2003, Jan. 21, B11)

With some Southam newspapers "producing profit margins of more than 30 per cent," the implicit question posed by Mills is why tamper with a formula that appears to be working? In assessing the reasons underlying this policy change, a convergence strategy comes to mind, as it is evident that the news desk is intended to service far more than CanWest's newspaper properties.[8] Mills also commented on another change in CanWest's organizational structure that can be interpreted as facilitating convergence, namely the retirement of "the title of 'publisher.' Newspapers in future will be run by 'general managers,' who will likely have less autonomy than their predecessors and less control over what the subscribers in their communities get to read" (2003, Feb. 13–15).

Gordon Fisher, as president for news for CanWest, replied to Mills' criticisms, claiming they were "the journalistic equivalent of a child insisting there might be a boogeyman under the bed.... Only a Central Canadian snob could say that something is lesser by virtue of being in Winnipeg than in

Toronto or Ottawa." Contrary to the fears expressed by Mills, Fisher argues that "the desk will have greater numerical strength than has previously been devoted to encouraging that the very best journalism produced by the company gets the biggest audience, which is its main mission." On the question of ownership interference, Fisher also reassures:

> There is no reason to worry that anyone will "interfere" now any more than when Mr. Mills ran the newspaper company from its head office in Toronto, or when he was publisher of The Ottawa Citizen just down the hall from the newsroom—or that it could happen with the Honderichs of the Toronto Star or the Grahams of The Washington Post or any proprietors. (Fisher, 2003, Jan. 29)

Views of Newspaper Executives

As part of the interviews we conducted with newspaper executives in 2002, we explored their views on the Aspers' national editorial policy and the firing of Russell Mills. In that many of the respondents worked for CanWest newspapers, this was obviously an extremely sensitive part of the interview, and we appreciate the honesty of their responses to our inquiries.

Although one respondent saw the policy as "a threat to journalistic independence," in general, the concept of "national editorials" per se, while not enthusiastically endorsed, was not seen as a big problem. The edict not to disagree with the positions expressed in the editorials was, however, viewed critically. Most respondents were not fundamentally opposed to CanWest expressing points of view in national editorials; indeed, one offered the opinion that "*The Globe* writes national editorials every day." Nor was the national editorial policy seen by most as part of a "grand Machiavellian scheme" or as "a major conspiracy." Rather, the policy was attributed to the fact that "the Aspers were new to newspapers." This was seen as a case of "cultures colliding"; as a consequence, "[the Aspers] failed to understand how journalists and readers relate to newspapers." One respondent working for a non-CanWest paper reported that the editorials were "viewed more with surprise" than anything else.

While the national editorial policy did not perhaps fall into the category of a serious problem, most of the interviewees did not think national editorials were an "especially good idea." One respondent characterized the Aspers' policy as "a throw-back to the era of partisanship," while another noted "there was nothing to gain" in a business sense from publication of the national editorials. As to whether the editorials constituted a threat to free expression, most held the view that they posed only a minor risk. One described them as "slap-dash" and another indicated that they "were immediately discounted by readers."

Respondents were, however, almost unanimously both puzzled by and opposed to the "no contradiction policy" that accompanied the editorials; they felt newspapers "should be able to disagree." One saw the national editorial policy, and especially the firing of Russell Mills (those who would talk about the firing felt it was handled badly[9]), as a "threat to journalistic independence." For that respondent, the role of the press was to provide opposition to government and as such "it needs to raise questions and to make politicians accountable for what they do." This sentiment was echoed by another interviewee who maintained that "the press has to be rude to government, come what may."

It was also pointed out that the national editorial policy would likely damage CanWest's bottom line, as "people do not like naked displays of power." As well, the no-contradiction policy could be seen as "stifling community opinion"; this in turn would diminish the newspaper's credibility. "Smart owners understand a newspaper has to have credibility [and to achieve this] they have to leave newspapers free to disagree." It was also felt that the national editorial policy was likely to stifle local creativity: "You can't micro-manage newspapers. Journalists are not like other people—to get the best work out of them, at best you can set broad guidelines and manage trends."

In that the interviewees were senior newspaper executives, it is not surprising that all of them acknowledged the right of the Aspers to implement the national editorial policy. The statement "Owners have rights—this is hard to disagree with as long as there is diversity of opinion" was typical of the point of view expressed. At least one respondent, however, while agreeing that the Aspers "have the right to do it," pointed out that "it is simply foolish." Another sentiment typically expressed was that "while exposure to other editorial views is a good thing, individual newspapers have to have their own views." To these observations, we add the views of Russell Mills:

> The news media are often described as a public trust in private hands. CanWest now owns a large share of Canada's news media and the Canadian people have a right to some answers about how the company plans to handle this great public responsibility it has assumed. (2003, Jan. 21, p. B11)

As Hugh Winsor observed, "David Asper may well wish that he had never made that Sunday night visit to Ottawa to can the most successful publisher in his empire" (2002, June 19, p. A4).

Conclusion

Ownership Rights Vs. Social Responsibility

Defining an Appropriate Role for Newspaper Owners

Walter C. Soderlund, Ronald H. Wagenberg, Kai Hildebrandt,
and Walter I. Romanow

Writing in the context of the United States toward the end of the 1990s, Robert McChesney argued that "the issue of who controls the media system and for what purposes is not a part of contemporary political debate" (2000, p. 7). Nothing could be further from the case in Canada. Perhaps because the extent of media ownership concentration here far exceeds that south of the border, debate on the issue is far more vibrant, as evidenced by the McGill Institute for the Study of Canada's February 2003 conference, *Who Controls Canada's Media?* and the ongoing investigation of the Senate Standing Committee on Transport and Communications. We would like to end this book with our contribution to this debate—a discussion of what we see as an appropriate role for chain/conglomerate owners in influencing editorial and news content of their media properties in the era of convergence.

While we must reserve judgement regarding Lord Black's business practices (see the Postscript to Chapter 4), in terms of his impact on the content of the newspapers he acquired in 1996—acquisitions that for four years made him the dominant force in Canadian newspaper publishing—we can say, based on the data presented in Chapter 3, that no fundamental damage to the editorial autonomy of the individual newspapers under his ownership was evident. This conclusion acknowledges that, as John Miller has pointed out, the editorial direction of at least two Hollinger newspapers was changed through resignations and the removal of key personnel. We also take into consideration the arguments of media analysts that at least some papers became *stronger* under Black's ownership. Thus, in spite of Mr. Black's occasional penchant for overstatement and confrontational language, he did not monitor their content or, if he did monitor it, at least their content was not directed by corporate ownership. This is the case even with issues such as labour and free trade, where such policy direction might have been most expected.

The case of CanWest Global, however, is another matter, and it is indeed worrisome. CanWest national editorials appeared on the scene at a time when the concept of globalization had gained ascendancy. In the process of globalization, mass communication industries generally came under increasingly concentrated ownership, both within and across national boundaries. This was facilitated by a worldwide trend toward media deregulation, privatization, and convergence. In this context, widespread and growing concern was expressed over freedom of expression in media, including concern voiced by those working for the nation's newspapers. For Canada, in the 1990s, these anxieties increasingly centred on the issue of convergence, specifically on how convergence might limit the diversity of media content.[1]

Views on Ownership Influence: Journalists and the General Public

Some of the problems inherent in convergence are reflected in data from a study done by Stuart Soroka and Patrick Fournier (2003) for the previously mentioned McGill conference, *Who Controls Canada's Media?* Their study, based on a survey of over a thousand journalists working for nine leading Canadian daily newspapers, revealed that overall 91.6% of journalist respondents believed that owners of newspapers do "have views and interests they would like to see expressed" in their papers. Among the four CanWest Global newspapers included in the survey (the Montreal *Gazette, The Ottawa Citizen,* the *National Post,* and the *Vancouver Sun*), the average expressing this view was 98.8%, as opposed to 84.8% for the five non-CanWest papers in the study (*Le Devoir, The Globe and Mail,* the *Toronto Star, Le Journal de Montreal,* and *La Presse*). (Breakdowns presented here, by CanWest and other owners, were calculated from the published results; they were not part of the original data.)

Moreover, journalists working for CanWest papers reported much higher agreement than other journalists on certain questions. When asked "Are the owner's views and interests regularly reflected in newspaper content?" 96.4% of CanWest respondents, as opposed to 71.3% of non-CanWest respondents, said yes; when asked "Are the owner's views and interests regularly reflected in editorials?", 91.3%, as opposed to 62%, said yes; and when asked "Are owner's views and interests regularly reflected in news coverage?", 70.3%, as opposed to 42.8%, said yes.

As well, CanWest journalists appeared to be more accepting of ownership influence over content. Nearly half (47.0%) of the CanWest respondents agreed "in principle" that such owner influence was acceptable, while just over one-third (34.6%) of journalists from non-CanWest papers were comfortable with the proposition. Moreover, 45.9% of CanWest journalists agreed that the "owner's views should regularly be reflected in editorials," while only 36.9% of other journalists felt this was appropriate. Only with respect to news coverage, as separate from editorial content, did the views of the two groups of journalists converge in near unanimous condemnation of owner influence, with just 5.2% (CanWest) and 5.3% (non-CanWest) considering such influence legitimate.

With respect to the reality of owner influence on their own work practices, differences in responses given by the two sets of journalists were relatively small: 53.2% of CanWest journalists, as opposed to 49.7% of others, reported that "owner's views and interests have an impact" on what they write or edit, either "most" or "almost all the time." On the impact of owners' views on the issues and points of view journalists were able to "raise and pursue," 55.9% of CanWest journalists, as opposed to 42.1% of others, felt such ownership pressure either "most" or "almost all the time;" 10% of CanWest journalists felt this pressure "almost all the time," compared to only 2.2% of other journalists.

Finally, on questions dealing with the impact of "ownership concentration" and "convergence" on the "quality of newspaper content" and on the "public credibility of newspapers," the findings of the study are most interesting: 88.7% of CanWest journalists, as opposed to 64.9% of others, reported that *ownership concentration* decreased the quality of newspapers, while almost all (97.5% and 93.1% respectively) saw concentration as having a negative impact on newspaper credibility. On the effects of *convergence* (defined in the study as ownership of both TV and newspaper properties), again there was virtual unanimity: 92.6% of CanWest journalists, as opposed to 86.3% of others, felt that it had a negative impact on newspaper quality, while 97.3% and 89.7% respectively reported that convergence had a negative effect on a newspaper's credibility with the public. In short, while there was agreement on the negative impact of ownership concentration and convergence, it appears that the journalists most affected by both ownership concentration and convergence (that is, those working for CanWest newspapers) judged its effects more negatively (Soroka and Fournier, 2003).[2]

An Environics poll (Jedwab, 2003), conducted with just over two thousand Canadians (who were not journalists) at the end of 2002 and the beginning of 2003 and reported at the McGill conference, also addressed the issue of ownership concentration. On the question of editorial independence from media owners ("Generally speaking, do you believe that journalists and editors have a great deal, some, not much, or no independence at all from their media owners when it comes to control of news and editorials?"), 58% of responses fell into the "some" (50%) and "a great deal" (8%) of independence categories. The "not much" category accounted for 28% of respondents, while only 9% felt that journalists and editors had no independence at all; 5% fell into the "don't know/no answer" category.

When contrasted with the assessments of journalists themselves (see our analysis of the Soroka and Fournier data above), it is clear that the public somewhat overestimated journalistic independence and especially underestimated the indirect influence of ownership views and interests. About half of the journalists in both CanWest and other papers acknowledged that owners "have an impact on what they write or edit," whereas over half (58%) of the non-journalist respondents in the Environics study indicated they felt journalists had some degree of control over content independent of their newspapers' owners.

The Environics study also reported responses to the following question, which dealt more generally with views toward convergence:

> In recent years, an increasing proportion of Canadian media outlets have been purchased by a number of large media conglomerates, such as the purchase of the Globe and Mail and CTV network by Bell Canada Enterprises, or the purchase of the Sun chain of newspapers by Quebecor. Some people say that this is a good development because this allows for the creation of diversified, world-scale Canadian-based media corporations. Others say this is a bad development because this may concentrate the ownership of many media outlets among a few corporations. Which is closer to your own [view]?

Overall, 57% (61% in Ontario) saw it as a "bad development," 36% as a "good development, with 3% reporting that it was "neither good nor bad" and another 4% in the "don't know/no answer" category (Jedwab, 2003).

While the general public appeared somewhat less concerned with the effects of ownership concentration than were journalists, to argue in light of findings such as these that there are no problems associated with ownership concentration and convergence would appear to be ludicrous. However, as we have noted repeatedly, to take the opposite position and insist that newspaper owners should have no role in setting the editorial direction of their newspapers is likewise naive in the extreme. As long as newspapers are private businesses, their owners have a legitimate right to participate in decisions bearing on what might make those businesses more or less profitable. Moreover, as argued by Frances Russell, "owner influence is as old as the printing press" (2002, p. A14), and, indeed, the history of newspapers in Canada is one of owner-politicians and owners tied to political parties (Kesterton, 1967; Waite, 1962).[3]

An Appropriate Role for Media Owners

What then, we may ask, is an appropriate role for owners in influencing the content appearing in their newspapers? The basic issues that we need to address in arriving at an answer to this question appear to be: How great should ownership influence be? How should it be exercised? Will owners voluntarily adopt the concepts of the media as a public trust and of social responsibility? And, is there a role for government in the regulation of newspaper ownership?[4]

Let us begin the discussion by considering the final question. As was documented in Chapter 1, all the attempts to regulate newspaper ownership that emerged from the Davey Committee Report (Canada, 1970) and the Kent Commission (Canada, 1981) met with a long list of objections focused mainly on the negative impact of government interference on freedom of journalistic expression. Arguments against government involvement pointed out that regulation inevitably would result in an unfortunate outcome for a free press and for Canadian democracy alike. For better or worse, proposals forwarded to governments by Davey and Kent calling for various controls over chain ownership have not been enacted in legislation.

A report of the U.S. Twentieth Century Fund Task Force on the Government and the Media (1972) helps put this problem into perspective:

> In our discussions...the task force did not feel it necessary to dwell over-long on the critical linkages between democracy, which depends on an informed citizenry, and the press, which is the purveyor of information to the public. But we all were aware that the public has the biggest stake of all in seeing that the nation's press is protected against government intrusion or pressure. It is a truism that the public gets the newspapers it deserves, but we feel that the public has a right to fuller and fairer information than it has been getting. If government officials have sometimes been irresponsible toward the press, it is our view that the press has not always been responsible toward the public it serves. (Twentieth Century Fund, 1972, p. 7)

It is important to bear in mind that arguments against government regulation of chain ownership have always emphasized that editorial independence of local publishers and editors is the best guarantee that a multiplicity of voices will be heard in the nation's press, even if ownership itself devolves into fewer and fewer mega-chains. Such arguments were presented by media owners to both the Davey and Kent inquiries. As expressed by John Miller, "for decades, the ultimate defence used by chain owners to justify their wide holdings was that they never used this power to influence what their papers printed" (1998, p. 68).

McChesney contends that "professional journalism is arguably at its best... when elites disagree on an issue" (2000, p. 51) and concentrated ownership control over the content of individual newspapers cannot but reduce such disagreement. On this point, let us be clear—the cat is now out of the bag. The CanWest policy of national editorials, combined with its no-contradiction dictum, fundamentally undermines the validity of arguments, put forward in defence of chain and conglomerate ownership, that claim editorial autonomy for the constituent media properties.

Ownership has always had, and continues to bring with it, very powerful instruments of control: putting in place publishers and editors with compatible political and economic views; establishing budgets; setting expectations for journalists to follow; and the all important "power to hire, promote and fire" (Chomsky, 1999, p. 592). Imposing national editorial points of view and mandating a no-contradiction policy clearly exceeds the bounds of what Canadians should expect and accept from newspaper chain owners. If we accept that media ownership gives the owners the right to express their opinions in unsigned editorials that must be run across the country and cannot be contradicted, we are stepping back into the mid-nineteenth century, when newspaper owners were unapologetic polemicists for political parties (whose leading figures often owned the newspapers). This is a chapter in Canadian history that we feel should remain closed.

If we accept as legitimate that owners determine chain-wide editorial positions, what is to stop those owners from choosing the kinds of events and the parts of the world to be reported on, and the spin to be put on them in news coverage?[5] This is precisely the focus of the concern that stems from the CanWest News Service initiative. The selection of news items—the information-providing function of mass media—is the result of numerous gatekeeping decisions, a number of which are controlled directly by owners (see Romanow and Soderlund, 1996, pp. 70–71). Should the predilections of owners, as to whether particular news items get prominent coverage or none at all, be the final gate in this process? We sincerely hope not but, as the data compiled by Soroka and Fournier (discussed above) indicate, owner influence has already gone far beyond what most would consider a reasonable level of comfort.[6]

The issue of control over news content was evidently a sensitive one in the upper echelons of CanWest management as, in response to the widespread negative reaction to Russell Mills' firing in 2002, the editor and new publisher of *The Ottawa Citizen* reassured readers in a signed column on the second page that, while national editorials would "from time to time" continue to be published, owner influence would not extend into news coverage:

> Our proprietors have stated publicly that every decision about *news coverage* will be made right here by local journalists.... The owners have also reaffirmed their unqualified assurance that they will never direct or intervene in the *news coverage* of this newspaper. (Anderson and Fisher, 2002, p. A2; italics added)

The creation of the Winnipeg-based CanWest News Service can be explained as a business move, taken to use the advantages brought by convergence to achieve economies of scale and thereby reduce the unit costs of information—which no doubt it is, at least in part (see Goldstein, 2004). However, in light of CanWest's national editorial policy, the concerns voiced by the News Service's critics, who claim that its creation was motivated by CanWest's desire to exert control over news content, or at least that such control may be facilitated by the News Service, are understandable.

From the time of the Davey Committee, there have been proposals for governments to solve the problem of ownership concentration through the regulation of newspapers. However, (as with efforts to enact constitutional reform in Canada) given the failures of earlier attempts to do so, we must ask how realistic an option this is. For better or worse, answers to the question of whether government regulation is necessary range from "unacceptable" to "unnecessary" to "perhaps."

In his remarks at the *Who Controls Canada's Media?* conference, *Financial Post* Editor-in-Chief Terence Corcoran spoke unequivocally against any form of government regulation of the newspaper industry:

> We didn't do it in 1981—and we shouldn't do it now.... We should be moving in the other direction. We should be removing government control over the other media, not expanding it to newspapers.... It is time to begin scaling back government involvement and return the media to where freedom of the press dictates that it belongs. Freedom of the press is a property right. (2003, Feb. 13–15)

Speaking at the same conference, Gordon Fisher also made the case for non-regulation, based first on the right of owners "to direct their operations in terms of both content and ideology," and adding that he does not see how owners could abandon the direction of their operations. "Their commercial interests are, frankly about only one thing. Content. We are selling content. It is a commercial activity." He also expects media audiences to seek out the information they need:

> Readers and viewers are not victims: They pick and they choose. The owners—the Aspers, the Thomsons, the Honderichs, the Siftons, the Blacks (David, not Conrad), the Peladeaus—will all, ultimately face their judgment. And to expect those people to operate their businesses as if they were a blind trust is to suspend judgment..... [The Aspers are] not trying to direct the daily news operation of CanWest Publications or of Global Television News.
>
> But even if they had, so what. You have all heard about fragmentation and the multiplicity of sources. It's all true. There is just too much free information OUT THERE and our citizens are smart enough to get it. (Fisher, 2003; capitals in the original)

In his presentation to the conference, Russell Mills (2003) made the chilling point that technological advances have given owners the ability to control content, although he did not suggest that it was anyone's intention to do so:

> Technology is making it easier all the time. With the high-speed electronic connections that we have today, it would be easy for a determined owner of even a large number of media outlets to monitor and control virtually all content before it is published or broadcast... None do this, but it's certainly possible. (2003)

Mills went on to distinguish between three types of newspaper content: news, editorial board opinions, and "other opinions presented in columns, op-ed pieces and letters to the editor." He maintained that

> as far as news is concerned, owners should never interfere. This is factual material and its selection and its presentation should be delegated to professional journalists.... The facts should not be selected based on an owner's opinions....
>
> [Mills' prescription for the opinion categories was only somewhat less restrictive:] When dealing with opinion, a distinction should be drawn based on how many media outlets a proprietor owns. No one could object to the owner of a single newspaper expressing his or her views in editorials on the editorial page. That's how press freedom began. The more outlets a proprietor controls, however, the less defensible this becomes and the more restraint a proprietor should show....
>
> [He went on to criticize CanWest Global specifically:] The strong public views of some owners, such as CanWest, may be limiting the range of opinion that is presented. Editors selecting opinion pieces and letters should not have to worry about the owner's opinions. Their only concern should be keeping the public informed. All owners, whether they own a single medium or many, have an obligation to present the widest possible range of opinions in columns, op-ed pieces and letters to the editor. Priority should be given letters criticizing the newspaper or challenging its editorial opinions. This supports the marketplace of ideas and is simply a matter of good journalistic practice. (Mills, 2003)

In light of the potential for abuse inherent in the concept of convergence, combined with the example of one owner that has aggressively used its power to control editorial content, one might wish to consider Lord Black's proposal for placing some overall cap on media ownership. Given his conservative views[7], his position favouring a form of government intervention in the newspaper industry is an interesting one:

> Instead of agitating and litigating over percentages of Canadian newspapers or newspaper circulation, I suggest we take up the formula that has been recently discussed, though not yet adopted, in Britain and Australia. We should devise a system of estimating media units of circulation for all types of media, establishing a basis of equivalence for listening, viewing and reading statistics and imposing a limit of ownership, say 20 or 25 percent of all media. (Black, 1998, p. 94)

How Should Ownership Influence be Exercised?

If current ownership practices persist, some form of government regulation remains a possibility. However, we propose a solution that follows a different path—one that we believe is both reasonable and achievable. Our suggestions regarding the extent of legitimate owner influence are grounded pragmatically in two concepts: those of *elite social responsibility* and of *editorial autonomy* for newspapers. As noted in the introduction to this book, the foreword to the Report of the Commission on Freedom of the Press highlighted "the responsibilities of the owners and managers of the press to their *consciences* and the *common good* for the formation of public opinion" (1947, p. vi; italics added), and specifically pointed out that "the tremendous influence of the modern press makes it imperative that the great agencies of mass communication *show hospitality to ideas which their owners do not share*" (1947, p. viii; italics added). The commission also believed that "the press is not free if those who operate it behave as though their position conferred on them the privilege of being deaf to ideas which the processes of free speech have brought to public attention" (1947, p. 9). It concluded with a scenario that current Canadian media owners might ponder if they wish to avoid the imposition of government regulation: "freedom of the press can remain *a right of those who publish* only if it incorporates into itself *the right of the citizen and the public interest*" (1947, 18; italics added).

In this context, a reaction against measures to relax current restrictions on cross-media ownership is already evident in the United States.[8] Additionally, we believe it is highly unlikely that Canadian governments will continue to tolerate current levels of concentration of media power in the hands of those who show their commitment to use that power to control content. The potential downside is simply too great. In this context, in its *Interim Report,* the Senate Standing Committee on Transport and Communications acknowledged that "Canadians have been and are well served by their news media,… [and that] it is no part of our mandate to imperil that good fortune" (2004, p. 1). However, ten and a half pages of that report are devoted to discussion of various forms of government and private sector regulation; while much of this discussion is focused on broadcasting, newspapers are not exempted (2004, pp. 74–84).[9]

Is there still time for multimedia owners to understand the importance of the principle of freedom of the press, and correct what are obvious faults in their current behaviour? For the good of Canadian democracy, we hope so. One of the most perceptive students of the American political system, V.O. Key, Jr., analyzed the relationship between public opinion and democratic practice and concluded his study by pointing out the power of elites and stressing the concept of elite responsibility: "If an elite is not to monopolize power and thereby bring an end to democratic practices, its rules of the game must include restraints in the exploitation of public opinion" (1967, 538). He argues that these rules of the game "gain strength, not from their statement in the statutes and codes, but from their incorporation into the norms that guide the behaviour of the political activists" (1967, p. 539).

It is, then, on the basis of owner self-interest, combined with a sense of social responsibility, that we argue for a voluntary return to the practice of strict editorial autonomy for individual newspapers of a chain, albeit this autonomy would exist within a set of editorial guidelines laid down by the owners. Such guidelines should be framed in broad terms—not proclaimed on an issue-by-issue, party-by-party, or leader-by-leader basis.

It is important to recognize that newspaper owners do have a right to make their voices heard in the pages of the newspapers they own. Regarding this right, we suggest that, on those relatively rare occasions that owners wish to make their personal views on a subject known, they adopt the practice followed by Lord Black. As related by Russell Mills:

> In the four years I ran the Citizen under his ownership, I did not receive a single call from him or any of his colleagues about news or editorial comment. When Conrad was upset about a public issue he would send us a piece under his own byline and suggest we consider running it on our op-ed page. Of course we did. (2003)

In this context, it must be pointed out that Lord Black rarely exercised this right of ownership—he appears to have understood the perils of overexposure.

Not all commentators believe that the adoption of a posture of social responsibility by media owners is either achievable or necessarily beneficial. For example, while praising social responsibility for its "high ideals" and "laudable goals," Paul Nesbitt-Larking concluded that

> the social responsibility model of objectivity is insufficient to facilitate good political journalism. It permits journalists to hide behind a series of strategic rituals designed to give the appearance of comprehensiveness and balance, but that do little more than reproduce dominant assumptions. (2001, p. 374)

While this may be true when applied to individual journalists, our focus here is not on journalistic practice but on the issue of media ownership. Applied to ownership, social responsibility theory should lead to the hiring of many journalists from a diversity of backgrounds. When combined with the principle of editorial autonomy, this approach should result in the expression of a fairly wide range of opinion in the newspapers of a particular chain. Granted, Nesbitt-Larking is probably correct in the sense that the opinions expressed would largely lie within a range of social acceptability.

David Taras, on the other hand, while not employing the precise language of social responsibility, arrives at a conclusion with regard to the behaviour of media owners that is not far from our own:

> In *Power & Betrayal*, I argued that those who own, control, and regulate the Canadian media system have a grave responsibility to serve their country and the needs of its citizens. I also charged the system was out of balance—out of kilter—in some important ways and that reforms needed to be made.... The Canadian media system that has been built in the last few years has the potential to deliver great benefits. It also has the capacity to do considerable harm to our public life. The new super conglomerates are amongst the most powerful institutions in our society. *They have an obligation to ensure open debate, a competition of ideas, and the service of the common good.* (2001, p. 240; italics added)

Going back to the question of whether, with their national editorial/no contradiction policy, the Aspers overstepped the boundaries of reasonable owner influence, the answer is an unequivocal "yes." Unfortunately, what to do about the situation is not clear. As is evident in the divergent positions expressed at the *Who Controls Canada's Media?* conference, we are faced with a problem for which there are no easy or completely satisfactory solutions.

Government regulation has been advanced by some as a solution, but it is one that is complicated by a history of failure, by a *Charter of Rights and Freedoms* that guarantees "freedom of the press and other media of communication," by a climate in which regulations are softened or dismantled rather than enhanced, and by the possibility that the proposed cure might be more troublesome to democratic practice than the problem it seeks to rectify.

In this regard, Kenneth Goldstein in particular notes "the slippery slope" on the road to government intervention, arguing that

> despite the ringing calls for freedom of the press by all of the groups [opposing the national editorial policy] that have issued ads or petitions, their arguments betray a serious lack of understanding about what freedom of the press really means, and about the meaning of Canada's Charter of Rights and Freedoms. (2002, June 14, p. 20)

In an effort to deal with a problem that is mainly associated with the behaviour of one particular conglomerate ownership group, we must not forget that, in its original formulation, freedom of the press meant freedom *from government control* and that around the world, even in the twenty-first century, the worst abuses of press freedom are still carried out by governments. Vince Carlin has pointed to the need for a "reality test" regarding possible remedies for excessive ownership concentration:

> We might all agree that it would be preferable if newspapers were locally owned and run as public trusts, but we might also all agree that it would be preferable if all Canadians were bilingual. Both are laudable ideals; both are unachievable in the real world. (1998, p. 102)

In no sense do we see as acceptable a situation in which owners treat their media holdings simply as private property to do with what they please. The Aspers need to be reminded that having the right to do something does not necessarily mean it is the right thing to do. As mentioned, we see a return to owner behaviour based on principles of social responsibility as a reasonable and achievable option. However, if self-regulation (as it has been operationalized in the past by the newspaper industry) is accepted by media owners as an appropriate method of protecting editorial autonomy, we must point out that self-regulation implies self-restraint—*social responsibility has to be a part of the equation.* On this point it is again instructive to quote the words of V.O. Key, Jr.:

> The argument amounts essentially to the position that the masses do not corrupt themselves; if they are corrupt, they have been corrupted. If this hypothesis has a substantial strain of validity, the critical element for the health of a democratic order consists in the beliefs, standards, and competence of those who constitute the influentials, the opinion-leaders, the political activists in the order.... If a democracy tends toward indecision, decay, and disaster, the responsibility rests here, not in the mass of the people. (1967, p. 558)[10]

In the final analysis, on a day to day working level, media owners and their immediate representatives—publishers and editors—understand the concepts of social responsibility and public trust better than anyone else does, as they practise these concepts each day in putting together newspapers that serve different communities. They are also the people who feel the readers' wrath when there are perceived violations of social responsibility and public trust. They also know better than anyone else does the very real economic pressures of running large media organizations. As argued by Gordon Fisher (CanWest's president of news), "owners, generally, are smart people. They understand the public duty and they also understand it is good business to deliver on the time-honored traditions of the craft. They know our business case rests on our credibility" (2003, Feb. 13–15).[11] If this is true (and we sincerely believe that it is), let our media owners state so publicly—for who is better positioned than the publisher and the editor to make the necessary ongoing decisions regarding the proper balance between social responsibility and economic viability, without which newspapers would fail?[12]

We agree with the concept of elite responsibility, specifically owner responsibility, and on this dimension we conclude sadly that the Aspers and CanWest Global have shown themselves woefully inadequate in their ability to treat their new-found newspaper ownership as a public trust as well as a business. Having said this, we also need to take care not to catastrophize over the situation. Canadian democracy has proved remarkably resilient to a number of challenges, some of them far more serious than concentration of media ownership. After all, even in communities where CanWest owns both newspaper and broadcast properties, other media outlets are available; the CanWest national editorials were not very well done and were therefore often easy to dismiss; and, perhaps most importantly from a business point of view, the disadvantages of the national editorials were seen to outweigh their advantages. In short, the national editorial policy is unlikely to be emulated.

The world has not turned out to be the kinder and gentler place that many hoped it would become after the cold war ended, especially with the events of September 11, 2001. Canada is struggling to find its proper role in this world. The assumptions that governed Canada's defence and other aspects of foreign policy from the end of World War II to the end of the cold war may no longer be valid. In this context, as we grapple as a nation to identify and articulate current and future issues and to outline possible resolutions, our need for a diversity of voices is even more pressing than would be the case in more settled times. As Michael Binyon has commented, "Mass media are the voices of mass democracy. They must be as robustly healthy as the ideals that they claim to defend" (2002, p. 465). In these times of change and stress, we do not believe that increased government regulation will produce an outcome that is to the country's overall benefit. That said, our national media ownership elite needs, more than ever, to place the public responsibility function of media on a plane that is at least equal to the business side of the industry. We see editorial autonomy with respect to content as fundamental to achieving this balance.

Postscript

In just over a month during the fall of 2003, the two media giants whose companies provided the primary focus of this book passed from the scene. On October 7, 2003, Israel (Izzy) Asper died unexpectedly of a heart attack at the age of 71, and on November 21 Conrad Black resigned from his position as CEO of Hollinger International due to the allegations of financial impropriety discussed in Chapter 4 of this book. In that Lord Black had already sold his major Canadian newspaper holdings, his resignation had little impact on the country's current ownership scene. In any event, it will take some time to evaluate the enduring consequences of Lord Black's financial and legal difficulties on Canada's newspaper industry.

However, the impact Mr. Aspers' passing will have on CanWest Global and its corporate policies is both unclear and of immediate concern. While Mr. Asper had formally transferred direct control of CanWest Global to his sons, prior to his death he was still "behind the scenes exercising strategic control" (Damsell, 2003, Oct. 8, p. B1). His passing has opened possibilities for change, some of which may work out well, some of which may not (see Pitts, 2002, pp. 249–269). Whatever the business outcome may be, there are certainly no signs of hesitancy on the part of the new management team to continue on the path toward convergence begun by the elder Mr. Asper in 2000.

At the time of Mr. Asper's death, tributes poured in from friends and adversaries alike. There is no question that he made extraordinary contributions to his city, province, and country as a lawyer, politician, business entrepreneur, philanthropist, and patriot. In addition, he was dedicated to his family and to his religion.

In criticizing CanWest Global, we have focused on the policies introduced by Mr. Asper that affected the content of his newspapers, not on the character of the man himself. Whether in time Mr. Aspers' commitment to social responsibility, obvious in so many of his undertakings (the establishment of a Human Rights Museum being only the latest), would also have been seen in the operation of his newspaper empire remains sadly unanswered. The positive legacy Mr. Asper left to Canada is huge—we would hope that his heirs will extend it to this one further, important dimension.

Notes

Preface

1. To say that the structure of Hollinger is exceedingly complex is to significantly understate the case. In fact, there appear to be five distinct business entities using the Hollinger name, all involved in the ownership of newspapers and all associated with Lord Black. Toronto–based Hollinger Inc. (78% of which is owned by Ravelston, a partnership consisting of Conrad Black, David Radler, Peter Atkinson, David Colson, and John Boultbee) owns 30.2% of Chicago-based Hollinger International Inc., which owns 100% of Hollinger International Publishing Inc., which in turn owns 100% of (1) The Community Group, publisher of *The Jerusalem Post*; (2) the Chicago Group, publisher of the *Chicago Sun–Times*; (3) the UK Newspaper Group, publisher of *The Daily Telegraph*; and (4) Hollinger Canadian Publishing, which owns 87% of Hollinger Canadian Newspapers Ltd. Partnership (Toronto Star Wire Services, 2003, p. A6). If this is not confusing enough, also involved in the mix is Horizon Publications, headed by David Radler.

   Peter Newman describes Black's corporate structure as "a convoluted pretzel, designed to make the internal money trail virtually impossible to follow. The trail ultimately led to Ravelston Corp. Ltd., Black's personal holding company, which took in most of his earnings, while exercising stock control over the entire maze" (2003, pp. 36–37). Tim Bell (Lord Bell), the public relations specialist hired by Hollinger International to deal with the crisis, reported that he had "spent the last two days reading the most complicated filings I've ever seen in my life" (as quoted in Blackwell, 2003, Dec.5, p. B6). It was the movement of money and assets among these Hollinger entities that led to the resignation of Lord Black as CEO of Hollinger International in November 2003 (see Postscript to Chapter 4, this volume).

   Very often in the reports on Lord Black's business ventures, it was unclear exactly which of the various companies bearing the Hollinger name was doing what, and to whom. References were often made simply to "Black" or "Hollinger," used almost interchangeably. Given the intricacies of the Hollinger structure, we have chosen to use the term "Hollinger" to refer to companies using that name that were controlled in one way or another by Lord Black. The one exception to this use is in Chapter 4, where we describe the November 2003 crisis, which resulted in Lord Black's resignation from Hollinger International Inc. but his refusal to resign from Hollinger Inc.

Introduction

1. The Hutchins Commission did not offer social responsibility as an explicit formulation for press behaviour. In fact, as far as we can determine, the precise term was used only once, in an appendix to the report in the following context: "An over-all social responsibility for the quality of press services to the citizen

cannot be escaped: the community cannot wholly delegate to any other agency the ultimate responsibility for a function in which its own existence as a free society may be at stake" (1947, p. 126). Social responsibility, as a formal theory, appears to have been developed by Theodore Peterson, in his chapter in *Four Theories of the Press* (1956).

One

1. The *Chronicle-Herald*, which is owned by the Halifax Herald Company, is not counted as independent by the Canadian Newspaper Association. In that we anticipate that our readers will want to update these ownership statistics as new data become available from the Canadian Newspapers Association's Web site (http://cna-acj.ca), we have followed the CNA classification despite the fact that the *Chronicle-Herald* is family owned.

   Newspaper ownership in Canada is a moving target. Of the 108 English and French language dailies identified by Chris Dornan (1996, pp. 73–78), by 2004 over 80% had changed ownership.

2. The years 1996 to 2000, after Conrad Black's buying spree of Canadian newspapers, marked the apex of individual control of the country's print media. Since the purchase of Mr. Black's newspaper holdings by CanWest Global Communications (owner of a major television network), the concept of media convergence, as we discuss in Chapter 5, brings the scenario of one-owner control closer to reality than the Davey Committee probably ever imagined.

3. In terms of legislation, the Davey Committee's major contribution was no doubt its recognition of the plight of the nation's magazine industry in the face of American competition, specifically from the domination of advertising revenues by *Time* and *Reader's Digest*. The committee's concerns were enacted into law in 1977 in Bill C-58, which imposed Canadian ownership requirements on Canadian media for advertisers intending to claim advertising costs as a business expense (Romanow and Soderlund, 1996, pp. 102–103; also see Litvak and Maule, 1974).

4. In his presentation to the Standing Senate Committee on Transport and Communication, Patrick Watson reiterated a thirty-year old proposal to deal with the problem of ownership concentration that does not fit Eaman's four categories—that of "a national public newspaper.... a print equivalent of CBC News, beholden to no commercial interest—produced, driven and governed by journalists, not investors or advertisers" (Watson, 2003, May 5); also see the critical discussion of Watson's idea of a national newspaper in the committee's *Interim Report* (Canada, 2004, pp. 77–78).

Two

1. For more on these terms, see White (1950) on gatekeeping; McCombs and Shaw (1972) on agenda setting; Iyengar & Kinder (1987) and Mendelsohn (1994) on priming; Entman (1993), Iorio and Huxman (1996), and Iyengar (1991) on framing.
2. In December 2001, CanWest Global initiated a national editorial policy, under which editorials written at the corporation's head office in Winnipeg were to run in the chain's major papers. A corollary to the policy forbade individual newspapers from running editorials taking positions counter to the "core positions" expressed in the national editorials. This policy, combined with the firing of *Ottawa Citizen* publisher Russell Mills in June 2002, for failing to pre-clear an editorial calling for the resignation of the prime minister, raised the issue of ownership impact on news content and its implications for Canadian democracy to new heights (see Chapters 6 and 7, this volume).
3. Several American studies have been done on the issue of ownership control. See Akhavan-Majid, Rife, and Gopinath, 1991; Becker, Beam, and Russial, 1978; Coulson, 1994; Coulson and Hansen, 1995; Demers, 1996a, 1999; Donohue, Olien, and Tichenor, 1985; Entman, 1985; Gaziano, 1989; Hale, 1988; Lacy, 1991; Lacy and Picard, 1990; Lasorsa, 1991; McCombs, 1987; Nixon and Jones, 1956; Pasadeos and Renfro, 1997; Plopper, 1991; Rystrom, 1986; Schweitzer and Goldman, 1975; St. Dizier, 1986; Stone, 1987; Thrift, 1977; Wackman, Gilmour, Gaziano, and Dennis, 1975.
4. Canadian studies include Candussi and Winter, 1988; Charette, Brown-John, Romanow, and Soderlund, 1984; Clow, 1989; Romanow and Soderlund, 1978, 1988; Soderlund, Romanow, Briggs, and Wagenberg, 1984; Steuter, 1999; Trim, Pizante, and Yaraskavitch, 1983; Wagenberg and Soderlund, 1975, 1976.
5. The most puzzling finding was a non-statistically-significant increase in local and provincial, and a decrease in national and international, front page lead stories under Southam ownership, leading the authors to comment that "despite who owns a newspaper, a journalist is likely to make professional decisions about content according to the events that take place in his own and in the world societies" (Romanow and Soderlund, 1978, p. 268; also see Miljan and Cooper, 2003). It should be noted that this change appears to have accelerated a long-term trend in Canadian newspapers by which chain newspapers may have been more affected than independent papers (see Romanow and Love, 1985).
6. This information was offered by the paper's publisher, A. Roy Megarry, in an interview with the authors in 1986.
7. The findings of the study, forwarded to Fred Fletcher for his report to the Kent Commission, "Correlates of newspaper coverage of the 1979 Canadian election: Ownership, competitiveness of market, and circulation" (Romanow, Soderlund,

Wagenberg, and Briggs, 1981), focused specifically on the impact of chain ownership and found that there was no clear indication of impact. Fletcher also reported that a study on the effects of chain ownership in Quebec newspapers done for the Kent Commission (Blais and Crête, 1981) "produced similar findings" (Fletcher, 1981, p. 36).

Three

1. In a speech to Hollinger shareholders in May 2001, Mr. Black revealed that "it was never our ambition to own 55% of the newspapers in [Canada]. It was an unforeseeable accident." Likewise, he reported that in 2000 Hollinger sold more of its assets to CanWest Global "than we had originally intended" (Black, 2001, May 17).

2. Early in 2001, David Asper, Chairman of Publications Committee of CanWest Global Communications, made it clear that Conrad Black was not the only owner with a political agenda. He sent "an opinion article accompanied by a 'must run' directive to recently purchased Southam newspapers indicating it was time to back off on the prime minister with respect to charges of conflict of interest regarding the Shawinigan hotel loan" (Winsor, 2001, p. A5; see also Bryden, 2001, A9). As well, while here we have no direct evidence of a chain-wide "must run" directive, at least *The Windsor Star* and the *Calgary Herald* ran excerpts from a speech on Israel, Palestine, and Canadian foreign policy given in Toronto by Israel Asper, Executive Chairman of CanWest Global, to the Canadian Friends of Hebrew University in Jerusalem; the stories ran under different titles in the papers on June 23, 2001 (see Asper, 2001a, 2001b). An incomplete search revealed that the *National Post* and eight other Southam newspapers also ran excerpts from or stories on Mr. Asper's address (see Chapters 6 and 7, this volume).

3. There is indeed evidence that during the six-year period of the study the newspaper industry underwent substantial change due to challenges stemming from the Internet (see McChesney, 2000, pp. 119–185).

4. Our list of those to whom we wish to extend thanks includes coders Kevin Dowler, Paul Gecelovsky, Lorelle Polano, Joseph Restoule, and Lorraine Thomas; and data enterers Zoya Davidson, Melissa Elek, Timothy Lawrence, Michael McNeil, Mamatha Mutyala, and Fitzroy Smith. We are indebted to the Leddy Library for ordering endless reels of microfilm and for lending us a microfilm reader.

5. An attempt to code editorial cartoons was abandoned early in the project due to unresolvable problems with intercoder reliability. With respect to the evaluation of political partisanship, inter-coder reliability difficulties only arose in deciding whether an article reached the minimum threshold of partisan commentary; when partisan evaluations were present, coders usually agreed on whether the evaluations were positive or negative.

6. We cannot tell whether these increases in paper sizes were due to increases in news or editorial space or both. A fuller examination of the question would have to analyze the connection between the growth in size of newspapers with economic cycles, as the economy emerged from the slump of the early 1990s.

7. Coders made subjective decisions about the overall idealogical orientation of each entire article based on language and the general stance of the item. Coders were instructed that the idealogical direction had to be clear and obvious to be coded: there was to be no "reading between the lines." Following training sessions and a pre-test, the coding decisions made conformed to the consistency standards measured by the Inter-coder Reliability Coefficients.

Four

1. The Radler Formula has been defined as counting the number of chairs in the newsroom of an acquired newspaper "to figure out how many people can be laid off" (Carlin, 1998, p.102). David Radler's name is also associated with the so-called "three-person newsroom"— two of whom sell ads (Olive, 2003, p. E1; see also Theobald, 2003, p A6).

2. Over the summer of 2002, in-person interviews were conducted with executives from newspapers representing all three chains studied, including some working for small, medium, and large circulation newspapers and some working for control papers. The interviews began a month after the firing of *Ottawa Citizen* publisher Russell Mills, and this was definitely not the best time to interview newspaper executives regarding their views on ownership influence. Some refused to talk to us under any conditions, while a significant percentage of those who consented talk to us requested that their comments be treated as confidential. Given the relatively small number (11) of executives interviewed, we have decided to cite none of them by name.

3. Personnel on Southam newspapers had particular reason to be nervous of acquisition by Conrad Black. As early as 1985, as revealed in his autobiography, Mr. Black had not held Southam management or their newspapers in high regard. "The [Southam] Canadian properties were accordingly awash with money; in almost every Southam town, the newspaper building loomed up on the horizon like a Taj Mahal, a monument to the feckless lack of imagination of its owners in the art of reinvesting earnings. Nor were earnings adequate, never more than 12 per cent pre-tax cash flow on daily newspaper revenues, less than half what we wrung from very mediocre franchises such as Sherbrooke, Quebec, and Prince Rupert British Columbia. Nor, contrary to fervently propagated mythology, were they very distinguished newspapers. With the rarest exceptions, Southam newspapers tended to be illustrative of the bland worthiness, inhibitedness, and derivative impersonality of much of Canadian life." (Black, 1993, p. 332)

4. Such observations support the finding of Lydia Miljan and Barry Cooper regarding the attenuating effects of journalists on the power of owners to determine content.

5. However, in his autobiography, Mr. Black reveals at least one instance of overt editorial direction: in his newly acquired *Daily Telegraph* when, in 1985, the Reagan administration bombed Libya. "The American raid on Libya occurred on the day I arrived in London, and I made one of my rare interventions in the *Daily Telegraph's* editorial policy by telling Max [editor Max Hastings] not to take up a policy that would give aid and comfort to Gadaffi and that would strain the Anglo-American alliance.... Max promised 'not to be gratuitously beastly to the Americans' and in fact executed a subtle course correction on the issue." (Black, 1993, pp. 365–366)

Five

1. It may be presumptuous to suggest that we can define what Marshall McLuhan meant when he used the term "global village" but, as we study communication theory at the beginning of the twenty-first century, we are aware that information generated by media, despite being culture laden, truly knows no national boundaries. Thus, the urge to take McLuhan's concept of a global village literally becomes very compelling.

2. For an overview of convergence as it played out in the United States, see Taras, 2001, pp. 69–83.

3. BCE has since sold YellowPages.ca. While Quebecor does own two French-language newspapers, its large Sun newspaper chain consists mainly of English-language papers; this would likely preclude any large-scale merging of editorial functions with the French-language TVA network.

4. Gordon Pitts points out that Monty's problems were not related to the creation of Bell Globemedia, but rather to the earlier purchase of Teleglobe, "an extension of its core telecommunications business" at "an inflated price" (2002, pp. 324–325).

5. Toward the end of 2002, Michael Sabia stated "that the underlying premise, the underlying hope or dream of a convergence view of the world is probably something that is not intrinsically in the genes...of a connectivity company and a content company.... When we look at these two businesses the opportunity to create value by using capabilities of one to drive value in the other seems to us to be relatively limited" (as quoted in Damsell, 2002, p. B4).

   Writing on the second anniversary of Mr. Sabia's reign as CEO of BCE, Steve Maich points out that, compared to its competitors Telus Corp and Manitoba Telecom, which registered stock share gains of 39% and 47% respectively, "BCE stock has gone nowhere." According to Maich, the market is waiting for BCE "to sell [its] 70% in Bell Globemedia, the unit that includes the *Globe and Mail* and

CTV television network." Maich argues that "Globemedia already qualifies as a misadventure for BCE," pointing to a billion-dollar writedown on CTV assets and an expected loss at *The Globe and Mail* of "close to $20-million." Regarding the future of Bell Globemedia, he quotes the opinion offered by industry analyst Paul Holman: "I don't see any argument that those businesses are long-term holds" (as quoted in Maich, 2004, p. FP3).

6. The decision to drop "AOL" from the Time Warner name was described as "acknowledging the failure of the largest merger in U.S. history...[which had been] billed as a way to jump-start a media revolution by combining old and new media companies.... The pioneering Internet company America Online was once seen as a catalyst to breathe new life into the various media properties of Time Warner, including HBO, Time Magazine, and the number two U.S. cable company, Time Warner Cable" (Associated Press, 2003, p. B7).

   On the positive side of the convergence ledger, Rupert Murdoch's News Corp. appears to be outdoing even the Aspers. In late December 2003, it was reported that Murdoch had been successful in adding Hughes Electronics Corp. and its DirectTV satellite services to his stable of media properties which, in addition to newspapers, includes the Fox TV network (Kirkpatrick, 2003).

7. One such positive development, with significance for convergence in Canada (although not specifically for CanWest Global), has been identified by Brahm Eiley as "bundling"—providing customers with phone, TV, and Internet services from a single source. In a background to the piece, Eiley explains the short-term failure of convergence as follows: "On the way to making and losing trillions, the purveyors of hype forgot to mention that, at least where the Internet was concerned, it had to beat out established industries such as TV, newspapers and retailers to survive. Without going into the sordid history, the challengers lost. What is left is what the prize has always been about, the TV and telephone markets.... [Moreover,] in Canada, because most Canadian telcos have a TV offering, they are a step ahead of their U.S. counterparts" (2003, p. FP15).

   Not surprisingly, cable system operators are not enamoured with the bundling concept. For example, in the summer of 2003, Rogers Communications petitioned the CRTC to ban the practice, claiming that "it would be unfair to allow the phone companies to package local with other services because other companies—such as Rogers—can't match it" (Ebner, 2003, p. B7). The war between Rogers and BCE appears to be far from over (see Evan, 2003).

8. "Reaggregating fragments in order to maintain economies of scale" continues to form the basis of CanWest Global's arguments for convergence (Baxter, 2002, November, 27, p. B6; see also Baxter, 2002, Dec. 18; Goldstein, 2003, 2004).

9. For an assessment of the impact of the Internet on Canadian society, see Pannekoek, 2003.

Six

1. As part of a broad defensive strategy to protect Canadian culture, various restrictions have been placed on foreign ownership of Canadian broadcasting and publication assets, including newspapers. For broadcasting, at present foreign control is limited "to 20 per cent of an operating company and 33 per cent of a holding company...for an effective foreign ownership limit of 47 per cent" (Jack, 2003, p. F3). Foreign control of print media is "discouraged" by means of the *Income Tax Act*, as, in order for advertising to be tax deductible for Canadian businesses, 75% of the publication's ownership must be in Canadian hands (see Canada, 2004, pp. 32–33; Romanow and Soderlund, 1996, pp. 102–103).

2. On Aug. 11, 2001, well before the announcement of the national editorial policy, an editorial headlined "Canada must lead," appeared in the Montreal *Gazette*. It dealt with Canada's role in the Palestinian–Israeli conflict. While it was identified as a "Southam News Editorial," the Southam torch logo did not appear (Southam News, 2001, Aug. 11).

   In October 2003, a Quebec labour tribunal ruled that *Gazette* journalists had the right to withhold their bylines, as they did in December 2001, in protest over the national editorial policy (Canadian Press, 2003, Oct. 27).

   Interestingly, the *National Post*, CanWest's national competitor to *The Globe and Mail*, did not run the national editorials in spite of the Aspers' having gained full control of the paper from Conrad Black prior to the initiation of the policy. All 31 national editorials, run under various headlines in different papers, are included in the References section.

3. The Canadian Journalists for Free Expression quoted the following September 10, 2001 submission of CanWest Global to the Federal Heritage Committee: "Each of our metropolitan and local newspapers is a strong player it its own community. Each is relentlessly local in its coverage and fiercely independent in its editorial policy.... Consistent with our undertakings to the CRTC, CanWest will maintain policies of individual editorial integrity in the operation of our television and newspaper properties." (Canadian Journalists for Free Expression, 2002, June 17)

4. Mr. Mills had written an editorial calling for the resignation of the prime minister. Because a Southam News national editorial calling for a ban on such commentary came *after* the editorial appeared, violation of that ban cannot be cited as grounds for his termination. The firing of Mr. Mills will be further discussed in Chapter 7.

5. Most would argue that *The Globe and Mail* (a Thomson paper) was the premier newspaper in the country. While the authors tend to agree, *The Globe and Mail* had been, from the time of its purchase by the chain, treated quite differently

than other Thomson papers, which in the main served smaller communities. Thus, at the level of the *chain*, Southam occupied pride of place.

6. Mr. Black subsequently sold his 50% share of the *National Post* to the Aspers and stepped down as publisher in September 2001. For a lively account of life at the *National Post*, see Cobb, 2004.

7. Exceptions include commentary on pervasive anti-Semitism in France, the case for the export of water, the importance of continued immigration, the proper role of the crown in criminal prosecutions, and reform of party leader selection procedures. In our judgement these were the most interesting editorials, in terms of bringing forward new ideas or different points of view. All of these editorials, however, could have been written as columns and signed by the author.

8. Data from surveys of Canadian daily newspaper editors between 1995 and 2000 point to a significant shift in ideological position of newspapers from centre to right of centre. Specifically, in 1995, 67% of editors reported their papers' ideological position to be centre, while 25% reported them to be right of centre. By 2000, 45% of positions were reported to be centre, while 45% were reported as right of centre (Soderlund, Lee, and Gecelovsky, 2002, p. 81; for confirming views, see Martin, 2003; Taras, 2001).

9. For a recent view of Canadian regionalism and its implications, see the discussion by Andrew Nurse (2003).

Seven

1. This was not the first time the Aspers had come to the defence of the prime minister over his dealings in Shawinigan (see Winsor, 2001, Mar. 7).

   CanWest Global and Mr. Mills settled their differences over the dismissal in December 2002. The terms of the financial settlement were not released (Galloway, 2002; Winsor, 2002, Dec 18).

2. Unlike the inauguration of the first round of editorials, in September 2002 there was no accompanying statement of the editorial policy; thus we are unsure whether there is a continuing obligation on the part of CanWest papers to carry the editorials and identify them as national editorials, and whether the no-contradiction policy remains in effect.

3. While it was clearly identified as a "Southam Editorial" in the *Edmonton Journal*, to the best of our knowledge this editorial was not published in *The Windsor Star.*

4. Keith Damsell reported that, as part of corporate restructuring undertaken in early 2003, "CanWest has dropped the Southam name from its newspaper group" (Damsell, 2003, Jan. 31, p. B5).

5. At least one Liberal MP, Carolyn Parrish, missed the point. In a comment on a Canadian initiative at the United Nations to delay U. S. military action against Saddam Hussein, she was overheard by reporters to say, "Damn Americans—I hate those bastards" (CBC News, 2003, Feb. 27). Her continuing unflattering references to the United States and its president led to her removal from the Liberal Caucus in November 2004.

6. As the writing of this book is completed, in early December 2004, as far as we can determine no national editorial has appeared since April 22, 2003. In light of the statement regarding increased scrutiny of Liberal candidates contained in the first editorial of the second round, we see it as significant that no "national endorsement" editorial appeared in CanWest papers during the June 2004 federal election.

7. A year's notice is required before withdrawing from the CP co-operative; hence the timing of the announcement.

8. An empirical study of the impact of ownership convergence on content diversity in Canada with respect to CanWest Global and Bell Globemedia is in its early planning stages. The study will involve an examination of news coverage in the *National Post*, in the five major CanWest papers and on "Global National" news, and in *The Globe and Mail* and "CTV News" for a sample of a specified number of days over a one-year period. Data obtained will be combined with a comparison of news coverage on the CBC's "The National" and in a group of control papers on the same days.

   An example of what the study would look for is taken from October 15, 2003. On that day a story reporting on an OEDC 42-nation survey comparing rates of high school truancy, "Canada's teens among truancy leaders: study, written by Heather Sokoloff, whose e-mail address at the end of the article is hsokoloff@nationalpost.com, appeared on the front page of the *National Post* (Sokoloff, 2003a, Oct. 15). On the same day, an abbreviated version of the article, "One in four teens skipping school," by Ms. Sokoloff identified with the CanWest News Service, appeared as the front-page lead story in *The Windsor Star* (Sokoloff, 2003g, Oct. 15). Another edited version of the story, "Canadian teens like to skip class, study finds" appeared on the front pages of the Saskatoon *Star Phoenix* (Sokoloff, 2003b, Oct. 15) and, with the title "Many teens are skipping school," in the Regina *Leader-Post*, (2003d, Oct. 15), both under Ms. Sokoloff's byline with the author again identified with the CanWest News Service. In the *Calgary Herald*, the same basic story also appeared on the front page, as "Canada's teens in truant mood," with Ms. Sokoloff identified with the CanWest News Service; this time the article appeared as co-written by Shelly Knapp, who added material relevant to the situation in Calgary (Sokoloff and Knapp, 2003, Oct. 15).

   The story, as it appeared in the *National Post*, *The Star Phoenix*, and the *Leader-Post*, referred to an Ontario policy requiring every school to have at least one attendance counsellor and mentioned that the province's second largest school board has nine counsellors employed to deal with truancy. Interestingly, the article in the *Calgary Herald*, while mentioning that the Calgary Board of Education has two truancy officers to monitor its 90,000 students, omitted the material dealing with Ontario's policy.

Not all versions of the story ran on the front page of CanWest papers. The *Vancouver Sun* ran the Sokoloff story with the head "A quarter of teens cut school classes" on page A3, (Sokoloff, 2003h, Oct. 15) with the author identified with the *National Post* at the end of the article, and in the Montreal *Gazette* the story ran under the title "Canadian teens among worst truants: study" (Sokoloff, 2003c, Oct.15) on page A17, with the author this time identified with CanWest News Service. The *Edmonton Journal* ran the article "One in four teens skip school regularly—study" on page A13, (2003f, Oct. 15), while the *Ottawa Citizen* also ran a version of the article "1 in 4 teens regularly skips class, report finds," on page A6 (2003e, Oct. 15), with a one-paragraph summary on page 1. In both these cases, Ms. Sokoloff was identified with the *National Post*.

Following the basic Canadian story in the *Ottawa Citizen*, there was a six-paragraph sidebar, "U.S. high school considers paying students to attend," which described a plan devised by a school in Norcross, Georgia to pay "students up to $200.00 in special school currency which could be used at school sporting events and at stores willing to participate." The truancy rate at the high school was reported at 7% (a failing percentage); administrators wanted to reduce the rate to 5% (*Ottawa Citizen*, 2003, Oct. 15, p. A6).

As a control measure, four non-CanWest papers were checked: in *The Globe and Mail* a story dealing with the same survey, "Canada lags in school attendance test" (Alphonso, 2003, Oct. 15), written by the paper's Education Reporter also appeared on the front page. The story did not appear in *The Toronto Star*, the Halifax *Chronicle-Herald* , or the *Winnipeg Free Press*. Unfortunately we were not able to view Global's nightly national television newscast on October 15, or the newscasts of the other two national networks, to see if and how the story was presented. Such a search and comparison would of course be included in the design for the proposed study.

Canada ranked as fourteenth worst among the forty-two countries included in the study, with 26% of students reporting that they missed classes regularly. No breakdown by province was included. The truancy figure reported for New Zealand was 27%, for the United States 20%, for Great Britain 15%, and for Israel 45%, which placed that country at the top of those surveyed. China, with a 3% truancy rate, ranked lowest, followed by Japan at 4%. In the absence of the CanWest News Service (and perhaps without a gentle nudge from Winnipeg), one may ask whether nine newspaper editors, operating autonomously, would have chosen to run the story on this survey—five of these gave it prime space on the front page of their newspapers. Not explained clearly in any of the stories was whether "skipping classes" on a regular basis constituted "skipping school" (story headlines used both terms), or which of these terms was used in computing reported "truancy" rates. The 26% Canadian rate was determined by asking students "how many times over a two-week students report they missed school, skipped classes or arrived late" (Alphonso, 2003, Oct. 15, p. A8). This most likely explains why the 20% of U.S. students reported "skipping class" is so far in excess of the 5% "truancy" rate demanded of the school in Norcross, Georgia.

9. The most interesting comment on the Mills firing took the form of a question posed by a respondent as to why the Aspers chose to fire the publisher rather than the editor—the person normally responsible for decisions regarding newspaper content.

Conclusion

1. One aspect of the trend towards globalization of particular concern to Canada is that a possible relaxation of foreign ownership restrictions for newspapers would result in a greater degree of foreign cultural domination. This is likewise a problem with proposals for ownership divestment, in that consideration must be given to who in Canada has sufficient capital to buy expensive media properties. Also, for a number of financial reasons, Canadian media owners tend to favour an increase in foreign ownership, pointing as well to the advantages of a larger ownership pool in fostering greater diversity (Canada, 2004; Jack, 2003; Tuck, 2003). Again, the feared outcome of forced sales of media properties is that the properties will be controlled by American-based media conglomerates that have little interest in promoting Canadian culture. A recent discussion of these issues is available in the House of Commons Standing Committee on Canadian Heritage's Report, *Our Cultural Sovereignty: The Second Century of Canadian Heritage* (Canada, 2003).

2. The *Interim Report on the Canadian News Media* issued by the Standing Senate Committee on Transport and Communications in April 2004 contained the results of a survey of 125 journalists working for the CBC, CP, and selected newspapers. The survey was conducted by the National Guild of Canadian Media, Manufacturing, Professional and Service Workers/Communications Workers of America. While percentages of respondents expressing concern over ownership concentration tended not to be as high as those reported in the Soroka and Fournier study, they do confirm the existence of a problem: "44% of the respondents said that 'a loss of local independence in editorial policy' was a 'very serious problem' in newspapers owned by large chains, and 79.8% said they had noticed a change in the editorial content of their newspaper since it had last changed ownership. Of those who noticed a change, 71.3% said the newspaper's overall quality had declined.... [89.6% believed] that it was 'somewhat' or 'very likely' that increased media concentration would place programming in too few hands, ...[83.2% believed that it would] lead to fewer

points of view offered by the local media, ...[82.4% believed that it would] reduce the quality of news coverage, ...[66.4% believed that it would lead to a decrease in] the number of local stories covered by newspapers (Canada, 2004, p. 59). Part of the survey "dealt with the effects of recent ownership changes in the Canadian media." In this context, "on 'a loss of local independence in editorial policy,' 75.2% of respondents believed it was a 'very serious' or a 'somewhat serious' problem, 76.2% thought 'a reduction in the diversity of opinion published' a similarly serious problem, and 68.2% thought a 'decrease in the overall quality of journalism' a similarly serious problem" (p. 64).

3. Israel (Izzy) Asper, CanWest Global founder, served as leader of the Manitoba Liberal party in the early 1970s. His reported friendship with Mr. Chrétien gave rise to charges in the House of Commons (which were denied by the prime minister) that Chrétien had pressured Asper into firing Russell Mills over the editorial calling for the prime minister's resignation (Southam News, 2002, June 18; see also Chapter 7).

4. While regulation of CanWest Global's newspapers remains an elusive goal, the CRTC clearly can regulate CanWest's broadcasting properties (if it so chooses) to maintain a diversity of voices in markets where cross-ownership of newspapers exist. In the spring of 2001, CanWest Global's TV licences were up for renewal and in CRTC hearings a compromise was made calling for "voluntary codes...[to maintain separate] management structures" for TV and newspaper operations. "However, the codes were silent about whether there would be any separation of news gathering or reporting, leaving open the possibility that reporters might be assigned to work for both TV and newspapers on the same story" (Adams, 2001, p. A11). Enforcement of such a separation would nullify one of the financial advantages of convergence; that is, the treatment of information as a generic commodity, acquired one time by one reporter, then edited for delivery in multiple channels (see McChesney, 2000; Goldstein, 2004; Wilson, 2004).

   It must be noted as well that, in July 2004, the CRTC made a decision to revoke the licence of Quebec City radio station CHOI *on the basis of its content*. In a column on the issue, Andrew Coyne makes the following point with respect to ownership convergence: "So when the regulator elects to crack the whip more visibly, there is no one in a position to raise much of a fuss over it. Oh sure, the newspapers might editorialize against it, but who listens to them? And in any event, *they are themselves increasingly coming under the CRTC's shadow: their broadcaster owners would rather take shots at each other than concentrate their fire on their lord and master.*" (Coyne, 2004, p. A22; italics added)

   Our guess is that, if CHOI's appeal of this decision is denied, we have the stage set for a Supreme Court ruling regarding what the *Charter of Rights and Freedoms* actually guarantees with respect to "freedom of the press and other media of communication."

5. Kim Fridkin Khan and Patrick Kenney (2002) have convincingly documented the impact of editorial decisions on news content in the context of coverage of U.S. Senate races.

6. Given the supposed barrier between the media's editorial and news functions, it is no less than astounding that 70% of CanWest journalists believe that "owner's views and interests are regularly reflected" in newspaper content.

7. Chris Dornan and Heather Pyman identified The *National Post* as having "championed a movement to 'unite the right' under a single political banner. Again this was done not simply via editorial harangues and the opinionated commentary of columnists, but through *the choice of news stories the paper pursued and the play accorded to the issue*" (2001, p. 194; italics added).

8. Rules against cross-ownership of media in the United States have been under attack for some time by the Federal Communications Commission (FCC), the very body responsible for enforcing those rules (Shapiro, Clift, Starr, and Abbott, 1988). Over the summer of 2003, the FCC voted to lift "the ban on companies or individuals owning both a newspaper and a television or radio station in the same city" (Benjamin, 2003, p. 29). The FCC also voted to allow companies "to own outlets that in total can reach up to 45 percent of the national audience, up from 35 percent now" (Morton, 2003). This prompted a public debate over the appropriate extent of corporate media ownership, the result of which was an attempt by Congress to overturn the new FCC rules. Mortimer Zuckerman, owner and Editor-In-Chief of *U.S. News & World Report*, took a strong stand on the issue, arguing that regardless of "political ideology, we cannot risk nonelected media bosses having inappropriate local, regional, or national power. The FCC was created to ensure that the public interest is served by the media companies that use our airwaves. Everyone is entitled to a mistake sometime, but the FCC is abusing the privilege. Congress must act now and reverse the FCC's irresponsible new rules" (2003, p. 52).

   Congress did indeed "roar" on the issue, threatening to reverse the FCC decision. Senator Byron Dorgan (Democrat, North Dakota) commented: "Obviously, the administration completely misjudged the reaction of the American people to this move.... If they were out there talking to people, they would know about all the trash that people feel is coming over their transom through television sets and radios. People sense there isn't much they can do about it because of the lack of localism in broadcasting" (as quoted in Firestone, 2003, p. C4). However, in the face of a threatened presidential veto of an appropriations bill, a deal was cut, and in the compromise, the increase in "national reach" to 45% of the national audience passed by the FCC was reduced to 39% (Stolberg, 2003).

9. In this book, we have used the term "public trust" in the general sense of an owner's responsibility to society at large. However, in his presentation to the Standing Senate Committee on Transport and Communications, Tom Kent gave the term a far more specific meaning, namely "a trust arrangement between the owner of a newspaper and the editor [leading to a situation] whereby the editorial direction of a newspaper is controlled under a trust agreement [setting up an advisory board] and is not dominated by proprietorship as such" (Canada, 2004, p. 83).

10. In spite of some insensitivity to the gender issue, V.O. Key's final footnote to this paragraph, also marking the end of the book, merits repetition: "This analysis and its implications should be pondered well by those young gentlemen in whose education the Republic has invested considerable sums" (1967 p. 558, footnote 8).

11. The idea that publishers and editors have the knowledge needed to run a newspaper is not new. In 1941, George Seldes argued that the next step in producing a better press was to invite "newspapermen to run the newspapers.... Newspapermen can challenge the publishers. They can say: Prove you mean freedom of the press by letting the editorial staff run the newspaper. Here we have men of many different political, economic, and perhaps religious viewpoints, but all of them know just what a free newspaper should be. If you put them on the editorial board—as some great newspapers have done in the past—you will produce a free newspaper against which no honest man can raise a word of protest" (Seldes, 1941, pp. 381–382).

12. Given studies showing that newspapers are declining both in household penetration and in the share of advertising revenues, scenarios of newspaper failure are not to be dismissed lightly (Maxwell and Wanta, 2001).

Reference List

Adams, P. (2001, April 26). CTV, Global reject idea of separated news units. *The Globe and Mail*, p. A11.

Akhavan-Majid, R., Rife, A., & Gopinath, S. (1991). Chain ownership and editorial independence: A case study of Gannett Newspapers. *Journalism Quarterly*, 68, 59–66.

Allmand, W., Atwood, M., Berton, P., Branscombe, K., Broadbent, E., et al., (2002, April 19). Let's press for press freedom. *The Globe and Mail*, p. A13.

Alphonso, C. (2003, October 15). Canada lags in school-attendance test. *The Globe and Mail*, pp. A1, A8.

Altschull, J.H. (1984). *Agents of power: The role of the news media in human affairs*. NY: Longman.

Anderson, S., & Fisher, G. (2002, July 13). The Citizen's voice remains independent. *The Ottawa Citizen*, p. A2.

Ansolabehere, S., & Iyengar, S. (1995). *Going negative: How political advertisements shrink and polarize the electorate*. New York: The Free Press.

Asper, D. (2001, December 14). The case for national editorials. Montreal *Gazette*, p. B3.

Asper, I. (2001a, June 23). Business school to encourage Israeli prosperity. *Calgary Herald*, p. OS8.

———. (2001b, June 23). Mideast policy: Canada's stand on Israel is shameful. *The Windsor Star*, p. A7.

Associated Press. (2003, September 19). Time Warner drops AOL. *The Windsor Star*, p. B7.

Atkinson, P. (1997, May). Big chains essential to survival of quality Canadian newspapers. *Canadian Speeches*, 11, 22–28.

Bagdikian, B. (1977, March/April). Newspaper mergers—The final phase. *Columbia Journalism Review*, 15, 17–22.

Bain, G. (1996, June 24). Conrad Black and the benefit of the doubt. *Maclean's*, 109, 48.

Baldwin, T., McVoy, D.S., & Steinfield, C. (1996). *Convergence: Integrating media, information and communication*. Thousand Oaks, CA: Sage Publications.

Barlow, M., & Winter, J. (1997). *The big black book: The essential views of Conrad and Barbara Amiel Black*. Toronto: Stoddart Publishing.

Baxter, J. (2001, December 22). Liberal MP calls for new body to regulate newspaper industry. *Edmonton Journal*, p. A15.

———. (2002, November 27). CanWest execs defend strategy on consolidation. *The Windsor Star*, p. B6.

———. (2002, December 18). More broadcasters means less money: Asper. *Edmonton Journal*, p. A8.

Becker, L., Beam, R., & Russial, J. (1978). Correlates of daily newspapers performance in New England. *Journalism Quarterly*, 55, 100–108.

Benjamin, M. (2003, June 9). Fewer voices, fewer choices? Debate rages over FCC plan to relax ownership rules on big media. *U.S. News & World Report*, 134, 29.

Reference List

Bennett, W.L. (1990). Toward a theory of press–state relations in the United States. *Journal of Communication*, 40, 103–125.

———. (2001). *News: The politics of illusion* (4th ed.). New York: Addison Wesley Longman.

Binyon, M. (2002). Media in the Commonwealth: Guest editorial. *The Round Table*, 366, 461–465.

Black, C. (1993). *A life in progress*. Toronto: Key Porter Books.

———. (1998). The proliferation of choice guarantees stronger newspapers. In D. Logan (Ed.), *Journalism in the new millennium: Essays in celebration of the Sing Tao School of Journalism* (pp. 91–98). Vancouver: Sing Tao School of Journalism, University of British Columbia.

———. (2001, May 17). Speech. Retrieved Aug. 3, 2002 from http://www.Hollinger.com/chairman_speech.htm (no longer available).

Blackwell, R. (2003, November 18). Black's darkest day: Hollinger scandal forces him out as CEO. *The Globe and Mail*, p. A1.

———. (2003, December 5). Hollinger International hires PR guru. *The Globe and Mail*, p. B6.

Blaise, A., & Crête, J. (1981). La presse et les affaires publiques au Québec. Appendix I to F. Fletcher (Ed.), *The newspaper and public affairs: Vol.7. Research studies on the newspaper industry*. Ottawa: Supply and Services.

Blevens, F. (1997, April). A new weapon: Buyout, then closing emerge. *The Quill*, 85, 39–40.

Brent, P. (2004, November 17). CanWest buys 50% of Jerusalem Post. *Financial Post*, p. FP1.

Briarpatch. (1997, June). Press freedom day: Raising concerns about media ownership in Canada, p. 26.

Brown, D. (2002, January 27). Canadian publisher raises hackles: Family is accused of trying to restrict local newspapers' autonomy. *The Washington Post*, p. A25.

Browne, C. (2003, December 13). Hold Hollinger directors to account. *Financial Post*, p. FP11.

Bryden, J. (2001, March 15). Panel to study media owners: Concentration raises concerns. *The Windsor Star*, p. A9.

Burt, M., & Ingram, D. (2002). Media in the Commonwealth 2002: Setbacks, and Some Advances, on the Road to Freedom of Expression. *The Round Table*, 366, 467–492.

Canada News Wire. (2002, June 17). CAJ calls Mills firing latest chill for CanWest journalists. Retrieved Aug. 17, 2003 from http://www.newswire.ca/releases/June2002/17/c7228.html (no longer available).

Canada, House of Commons, Standing Committee on Canadian Heritage. (2003). *Our cultural sovereignty: The second century of Canadian broadcasting*. Retrieved November 1, 2004 from http://www.parl.gc.ca/InfoComDoc/37/2/HERI/Studies/Reports/heriep02-e.htm

Canada, Royal Commission on Newspapers. (1981). *Report of the Royal Commission on Newspapers*. Ottawa: Supply and Services.

Reference List

Canada, Senate. (1970). *Report of the Special Senate Committee on Mass Media: Vol. 1. The uncertain mirror.* Ottawa: Information Canada.

Canada, Standing Senate Committee on Transport and Communications. (2004). *Interim Report on the Canadian News Media.* Retrieved November 2, 2004 from http://www.parl.gc.ca/37/3/parlbus/commbus/senate/com-e/tran-e/rep-e/rep04apr04-e.htm

Canadian Dimension. (1996, November–December). This publication is not owned by Conrad Black. (Editorial), 4.

Canadian Journalists for Free Expression. (2002, June 17). CJFE calls on CanWest to rehire Mills. Retrieved November 1, 2004 from http://www.cjfe.org/releases/2002/mills.html

Canadian Newspaper Association. (2003, March 31). Canadian circulation data. Retrieved November 3, 2004 from http://www.cna-acj.ca

———. (2004, October 15.). Ownership of Canadian daily newspapers. Retrieved November 3, 2004 from http://www.cna-acj.ca

Canadian Press. (2001, December 20). Chain rebuked for nationwide editorials. *The Edmonton Sun*, p. 29.

———. (2002, June 19). CanWest roasted. *The Edmonton Sun*, p. 18.

———. (2003, October 27). Tribunal: Gazette reporters can withhold bylines. Retrieved November 26, 2004 from http://cnews.canoe.ca/CNEWS/MediaNews/2003/10/27/238742-cp.html

———. (2003, November 21). Black prospers despite collapse of news empire. *The Windsor Star*, p. B6.

———. (2003, November 26). Hollinger stock falls. *The Windsor Star*, p. D6.

———. (2003, December 29). Publishing mogul gets top award. *The Windsor Star*, p. A11.

Candussi, D., & Winter, J. (1988). Monopoly and content in Winnipeg. In R. Picard, J. Winter, M. McCombs, & S. Lacy (Eds.), *Press concentration and monopoly: New perspectives on newspaper ownership and operation* (pp. 139–145). Norwood, NJ: Ablex Publishing.

CanWest Global. (2002). Vision. Retrieved July 13, 2003 from http://www.canwestglobal/vision.html (no longer available).

CanWest News Service. (2003, October 30). CanWest offers new look. *The Windsor Star*, p. C2.

———. (2004, June 4). Newspapers playing key role, CEO says. *The Windsor Star*, p. B7.

CanWest Publications. (2003, March 11). Clear choice on Iraq. *Edmonton Journal*, p. A12.

———. (2003, April 22). Quebec albatross off PM's back. *The Windsor Star*, p. A6.

———. (2002, November 28). Strong relations with the U.S. essential. *The Windsor Star*, pp. A1, A8.

Carlin, V. (1988). The good, the bad and the ugly of corporate newspaper control. In D. Logan, (Ed.), *Journalism in the New Millennium: Essays in Celebration of the Sing Tao School of Journalism.* (pp. 101–110). Vancouver: Sing Tao School of Journalism.

Carlin, V. (2003). No clear channel: The rise and possible fall of media convergence. In D. Taras, F. Pannekoek, & M. Bakardjieva (Eds.), *How Canadians communicate* (pp. 51–69). Calgary, AB: University of Calgary Press.

CBC News. (2002, June 17). Citizen publisher fired after critical coverage of PM. Retrieved November 4, 2004 from http://www.cbc.ca/story/canada/national/2002/06/17/mills_fired020617.html

———. (2003, February 27). MP apologies for calling Americans "bastards." Retrieved November 3, 2004 from http://www.cbc.ca/stories/2003/02/26/bastards030226

Chaffee, S., & Metzger, M. (2001). The end of mass communication? *Mass Communication & Society*, 4, 365–379.

Charette, M., Brown-John, L., Soderlund, W., & Romanow, W. (1984). Acquisition et fermeture de journaux par des chaînes de journaux: effets sur les tarifs de publicité. *Communication Information*, 6, 46–62.

Chew, F. (1994). The relationship of information needs to issue relevance and media use. *Journalism Quarterly*, 71, 676–688.

Chomsky, D. (1999). The mechanisms of management control at the *New York Times*. *Media, Culture & Society*, 21, 579–599.

Clarkson, A. (2003, February13–15). Speech on the occasion of the annual conference of the McGill Institute for the Study of Canada. In *McGill Conference: Who Controls Canada's Media?* Montreal, Quebec. Retrieved November 1, 2004 from http://www.misc-iecm.mcgill.ca/media/clarkson.pdf

Clow, M. (1989). *The limits to debate: Canadian newspapers and nuclear power.* Unpublished doctoral dissertation, York University, Toronto.

Cobb, C. (2004). *Ink and egos: The inside story of Canada's newspaper war.* Toronto: McClelland and Stewart.

Cohen-Almagor, R. (2002). Responsibility and ethics in the Canadian media: Some basic concerns. *Journal of Mass Media Ethics*, 17, 35–52.

Commission on Freedom of the Press. (1947). *A free and responsible press. A general report on mass communication: Newspapers, radio, motion picture, magazines and books.* Chicago: University of Chicago Press, 1947.

Compaine, B. (2000). The newspaper industry. In B. Compaine and D. Gomery, *Who owns the media? Competition and concentration in the mass media industry* (pp. 1–59). Mahwah, NJ: L. Erlbaum Associates.

Corcoran, T. (2003, February 13–15). What are the limits of government control? In *McGill Conference: Who Controls Canada's Media?* Montreal, Quebec. Retrieved November 1, 2004 from http://www.misc-iecm.mcgill.ca/media/corcoran.pdf

———. (2004, October 9). Black beats RICO: What's next? *Financial Post*, p. FP11.

Coulson, D. (1994). The impact of ownership on newspaper quality. *Journalism Quarterly*, 71, 403–410.

Coulson, D., & Hansen, A. (1995). *The Louisville Courier-Journal's* news content after purchase by Gannett. *Journalism Quarterly*, 72, 205–215.

Coyne, A. (2004, July 17). CHOI's lonely battle. *National Post*, p. A22.

Craig, S. (2000, May 2). Ottawa to review newspaper ownership. *The Globe and Mail*, p. A1.

Curry, J., & Dassin, J., Eds. (1982). *Press control around the world*. New York: Praeger Publishers.

DaCruz, M. (2004, March 25). CanWest reaffirms convergence plans. *Financial Post*, p. FP7.

Dahl, R. (1991). *Modern political analysis* (5th ed.). Englewood Cliffs, NJ: Prentice-Hall.

Damsell, K. (2002, December 19). Sabia questions convergence. *The Globe and Mail*, p. B4.

———. (2003, January 20). CanWest set to launch news hub. *The Globe and Mail*, p. B2.

———. (2003, January 31). Whyte stepping aside as Post editor. *The Globe and Mail*, p.B5.

———. (2003, March 20). CanWest's entertainment plan draws fire. *The Globe and Mail*, p. R5.

———. (2003, October 8). CanWest head's death sends media giant into uncertainty. *The Globe and Mail*, p. B1.

DeCloet, D. (2003, November 18). Small-town papers, but large payments, *The Globe and Mail*, pp. B1, B8.

Demers, D. (1996a). Corporate newspaper structure, editorial page vigor and social change. *Journalism and Mass Communication Quarterly*, 73, 857–877.

———. (1996b). *The menace of the corporate newspaper: Fact or fiction?* Ames, Iowa: Iowa State University Press.

———. (1999). Corporate newspaper bashing: Is it justified? *Newspaper Research Journal*, 20, 83–97.

Desbarats, P. (1996). *Guide to Canadian news media*. Toronto: Harcourt Brace and Co.

Donohue, G., Olien, C., & Tichenor, P. (1985). Reporting conflict by pluralism, newspaper type and ownership. *Journalism Quarterly*, 62, 489–499, 507.

Dornan, C. (1996). Newspaper publishing. In M. Dorland, (Ed.), *The cultural industries in Canada: Problems, policies and prospects* (pp. 60–92). Toronto: James Lorimer.

———. (2003a, February 13–15). Closing remarks. In *McGill Conference: Who Controls Canada's Media?* Montreal, Quebec. Retrieved November 1, 2004 from http://www.misc-iecm.mcgill.ca/media/dornan.pdf

———. (2003b). Printed Matter: Canadian newspapers. In D. Taras, F. Pannekoek & Maria Bakardjieva (Eds.), *How Canadians Communicate* (pp. 97–120). Calgary, AB: University of Calgary Press.

Dornan. C., & Pyman, H. (2001). Facts and arguments: Newspaper coverage of the campaign. In J. Pammett & C. Dornan (Eds.), *The Canadian General Election of 2000* (pp. 191–213). Toronto: Dundurn Press.

Reference List

Driedger, D. (1996, May 13). Black all over: As others exit, one media mogul bets heavily on print. *Maclean's*, 109, 42–43.

Eaman, R. (1987). *The media society: Basic issues and controversies.* Toronto: Butterworths.

Ebner, D. (2003, July 3). Rogers asks CRTC to ban local bundling. *The Globe and Mail*, p. B7.

Eckstein, H. (1974). Case study and theory in political science. In F. Greenstein & N. Polsby (Eds.), *Handbook of political science: Vol. 7. Strategies of inquiry* (pp. 3–137). Reading, MA: Addison-Wesley.

Eiley, B. (2003, October 9). Convergence is no longer a dirty word. *Financial Post*, p. FP15.

Entman, R. (1985). Newspaper competition and first amendment ideas: Does monopoly matter? *Journal of Communication*, 35, 147–165.

. (1991). Framing U.S. coverage of international news: Contrasts in narrative of the KAL and Iran air incidents. *Journal of Communication*, 41, 6–28.

———. (1993). Framing: Towards a clarification of a fractured paradigm. *Journal of Communication*, 43, 51–58.

Estok, D. (2002, October 2). Aspers' views won't disappear, but just take on subtle guise. *The Globe and Mail*, p. B11.

Evan, M. (2003, December 10). Rogers edges toward telephony war v. BCE. *Financial Post*, p. FP1.

Firestone, D. (2003, November 1). Congress appears set to reverse F.C.C. *The New York Times*, p. C4.

Fisher, G. (2003, January 29). Russell Mills, rest assured there is no CanWest bogeyman. *The Globe and Mail*, p. B16.

———. (2003, February 13–15). To what extent can or should media owners intervene in their own commercial or ideological interest with respect to content? In *McGill Conference: Who Controls Canada's Media?* Montreal, Quebec. Retrieved November 1, 2004 from http://www.misc-iecm.mcgill.ca/media/fisher.pdf

Flavelle, D. (1996, May 11). Fade to Black? *Toronto Star*, pp. E1, E8.

Fletcher, F. (1981). *The newspaper and public affairs: Vol. 7. Research studies on the newspaper industry.* Ottawa: Supply and Services.

Fletcher, F., & Taras, D. (1995). The mass media: Private ownership, public responsibilities. In M. Whittington & G. Williams (Eds.), *Canadian politics in the 1990s* (pp. 292–319). Scarborough, ON: Nelson Canada.

Fox, J. (1988). Social influences on decision-making in *The Toronto Star* newsroom. Unpublished master's thesis, University of Windsor.

Francis, D. (1986). *Controlling interest: Who owns Canada?* Toronto: Macmillan of Canada.

Fraser, J., Webster, N., & Harrison, M. (2001, December 15). National editorial line will curtail public debate. *The Gazette*, p. B6.

Fridkin Kahn, K., & Kenney, P. (2002). The slant of the news: How editorial endorsements influence campaign coverage and citizens' views of candidates. *American Political Science Review*, 96(2), 381–394.

Galloway, G. (2002, December 14). Ex-publisher settles lawsuit against Asper and CanWest. *The Globe and Mail*, p. A16.

Gamson, W. (1989). News as framing. *American Behavioral Scientist*, 33, 157–161.

Gans, H. (1979). *Deciding what's news: A study of CBS Evening News, NBC Nightly News, Newsweek and Time*. New York: Pantheon Books.

Gazette (Montreal). (2001, December 6). National editorials in Gazette, pp. A1, A2.

Gaziano, C. (1989). Chain newspaper homogeneity and presidential endorsements. *Journalism Quarterly*, 66, 836–845.

Gerbner, G., Mowlana, H., & Schiller, H., Eds. (1996). *Invisible crisis: What conglomerate control of media means for America and the world*. Boulder, CO: Westview Press.

Gigliotti, K. (2003, May 12). Pipped at the Post, fiscal realities intrude. *Maclean's*, 16.

Goldberg, K. (1998, December). Newswatch Canada questions *The Sun*. *Canadian Dimension*, 32, 6.

Goldstein, K. (2002, January). *Fragmentation, consolidation, and the Canadian consumer: An overview of the Canadian media market in 1950, 1975 and 2000*. Winnipeg: Communications Management Inc.

———. (2002, June 14). Leaving the eye of the hurricane: The news media and convergence. Address to the Canadian Conference of Press Councils, Winnipeg, MN.

———. (2003, February 13–15). Text of remarks. In *McGill Conference: Who Controls Canada's Media?* Montreal, Quebec. Retrieved November 1, 2004 from http://www.misc-iecm.mcgill.ca/media/goldstein.pdf

———. (2004, March 5). *From assumptions of scarcity to the facts of fragmentation: The impact on public policies and private business models for the media*. Presentation to the University of Calgary Conference: How Canadians Communicate.

Great Britain. (1949). *Report of the Royal Commission on the Press, 1947–1949*. London: His Majesty's Stationery.

Green, G. (2002, June 1). Double standard. *The Ottawa Citizen*, pp. B1–B4.

Green, M. (1998, July). Fear of a Black planet. *The Democrat*, 38, p. 28.

Greenspon, E. (1986, April 2). Southam's tenets cited in defense of swap, *The Globe and Mail*, p. B4.

Grenier, M. (1992). *Critical studies of Canadian mass media*. Toronto: Butterworths.

Gumbel, P. (2003, December 1). Conrad's Black eye. *Time*, p. 64.

Ha, T. (2001, December 21). Sparks fly in Quebec over changes at Gazette. *The Globe and Mail*, p. A7.

Hackett, R., & Zhao, Y. (1998). *Sustaining democracy? Journalism and the politics of objectivity*. Toronto: Garamond Press.

Hale, F.D. (1988). Editorial diversity and concentration. In R. Picard, J. Winter, M. McCombs, & S. Lacy (Eds.), *Press concentration and monopoly: New perspectives on newspaper ownership and operation* (pp. 161–176). Norwood, NJ: Ablex Publishing.

Hallman, E., Oliphant, P., & White, R. (1981). *The newspaper as a business: Vol. 4. Research publications, Royal Commission on Newspapers*. Ottawa: Minister of Supply and Services.

Hannigan, J. (2002). The global entertainment economy. In D. Cameron & J. Stein, (Eds.), *Street protests and fantasy parks: Globalization, culture, and the state*. (pp. 20–48). Vancouver: UBC Press.

Hartley, T., & Mazzuca, J. (2002, February 19). *Local, network and specialty television news sources most popular*. Toronto: Gallup Canada Inc.

Hatchen, W. (1992). *The world news prism: Changing media of international communication*. Ames, Iowa: Iowa States University Press.

Herman, E., & Chomsky, N. (1988). *Manufacturing consent: the political economy of the mass media*. New York: Pantheon Books.

Hildebrandt, K., & Soderlund, W. (2002). International reporting in Canadian newspapers at the end of the 20th century. Paper presented at the 10th Biennial Conference of the Midwest Association for Canadian Studies, East Lansing, MI.

Hill, R. (1968). A note on newspaper patronage in Canada during the late 1850s and early 1860s. *Canadian Historical Review*, 49, 44–59.

Hodgson, J. (2004, November 17). Black announces bid to take Hollinger private. *Financial Post*, p. FP5.

Holsti, O. (1969). *Content analysis for the social sciences and humanities*. Reading, MA: Addison-Wesley.

Innis, H. (1972). *Empire and communications*. Toronto: University of Toronto Press.

Iorio, S., & Huxman, S. (1996). Media coverage of political issues and the framing of personal concerns. *Journal of Communication*, 46, 97–115.

Iyengar, S. (1991). *Who Is responsible? How television frames political issues*. Chicago: University of Chicago Press.

Iyengar, S., & Kinder, D. (1987). *News that matters: Agenda-setting and priming in a television age*. Chicago: University of Chicago Press.

Jack, I. (2003, February 28). Ownership rules must be the same for all, Asper says. *Edmonton Journal*, p. F3.

Jedwab, J. (2003, February 10). Canadian Media: Trust, Bias and Control. Poll conducted by Environics Research. In *McGill Conference: Who Controls Canada's Media?* Montreal, Quebec. Retrieved November 4, 2004 from httm://www.misc-iecm.mcgill.ca/media/acs%20survey%20results.doc

Jones, T. (1998, March/April). That old black magic. *Columbia Journalism Review*, 36, 40–43.

Kesterton, W. (1967). *A history of journalism in Canada*. Toronto: McClelland and Stewart.

Key, V.O., Jr. (1967). *Public opinion and American democracy*. New York: Knopf.

Kim, P. (1999). Deconstructing interactive TV networks. *The Public*, 6, 87–99.

Kimber, S. (2003). A global warning against national media monopolies. Retrieved October 16, 2003 from http://www.adbusters.org/magazine (no longer available)

Reference List

Kingston, A. (2004, May 15). Last straw: tipping the doorman. *National Post*, p. SP1.

Kirchgaessner, S., & Burt, T. (2003, December 16). Hollinger in talks with hicks muse on financing woes. *Financial Post*, p. FP3.

Kirkpatrick, D. (2003, December 29). Will it be Lachlan, James, or Elizabeth? *Financial Post*, p. FP1.

Lacy, S. (1991). Effects of group ownership on daily newspaper content. *Journal of Media Economics*, 3, 35–47.

Lacy, S., & Picard, R. (1990). Interactive monopoly power in the daily newspaper industry. *Journal of Media Economics*, 3, 27–38.

Lamey, M. (2003, November 22). Bell's TV arm not aiming for profit. *The Windsor Star*, p. A21.

Lasorsa, D. (1991). Effect of newspaper competition on public opinion diversity. *Journalism Quarterly*, 68, 38–47.

Lorimer, R., & Gasher, M. (2001). *Mass communication in Canada*. (4th ed.). Don Mills, ON: Oxford University Press.

Lorinc, J. (2002, Spring). National Affairs Committee Chair's letter. *PEN Canada Newsletter*, 13.

Lowenstein, R., & Merrill, J.(1990). *Macromedia: Mission, message and morality*. New York, Longman.

Lunman, K., & McCarthy, S. (2002, June 19). Sacking of Ottawa publisher draws international criticism. *The Globe and Mail*, p. A1.

Maich, S. (2003, November 25). Four Hollinger directors quit after report rejected. *The Windsor Star*, p. A21.

———. (2003, November 27). Hollinger lawsuit in the works, says Denton. *Financial Post*, p. FP1.

———. (2004, April 23). Can Sabia learn to play offence? *Financial Post*, pp. FP1, FP3.

Maich, S., & Shecter, B. (2003, November 20). SEC OSC to Probe Hollinger. *Financial Post*, p. FP1.

Marotte, B., & Peritz, I. (2001, September 1). Differences with new owners, CanWest Global, cited for October 1 resignation. *The Globe and Mail*, p. A8.

Martin, L. (2003, January 23). Its not Canadians who've gone to the right, just their media. *The Globe and Mail*, p. A19.

Maxwell, A., & Wanta, W. (2001). Advertising agencies reduce reliance on newspaper ads. *Newspaper Research Journal*, 22, pp. 51–65.

McCarthy, G. (1997, November/December). Conrad Black and media monopolies: The bad news boy. *Our Times*, 16, pp. 24–29.

McChesney, R. (2000). *Rich media, poor democracy: Communication politics in dubious times*. New York: The New Press.

McCombs, M. (1987). Effect of monopoly in Cleveland on diversity of newspapers content. *Journalism Quarterly*, 64, 740–744, 792.

McCombs, M., & Shaw, D. (1972). The agenda-setting function of mass media. *Public Opinion Quarterly*, 36, 176–187.

McDonald, D. (2004, July). The Black watch. *National Post Business*, 36–46.
McFarland, J., & Damsell, K. (2003, January 29). CanWest unveils management shuffle. *The Globe and Mail*, p. B3.
McKenna, B., & Stewart, S. (2003, December 23). Black refuses to testify before SEC. *The Globe and Mail*, pp. A1, A8.
McNish, J., & Waldie, P. (2003, November 18). Black's darkest day: Improper payments led to mogul's demise. *The Globe and Mail*, p. A1.
McPhail, T., & McPhail, B. (1990). *Communication: The Canadian Experience*. Mississauga, ON: Copp Clark Pitman.
McQuaig, L. (1995). *Shooting the hippo: Death by deficit and other Canadian myths*. Toronto: Viking Press.
———. (2003, November 23). Canada come of age with its first world-class corporate scandal. *Edmonton Journal*, p. A12.
Mendelsohn, M. (1994). The media's persuasive effects: The priming of leadership in the 1988 Canadian election. *Canadian Journal of Political Science*, 27, 81–97.
Merrill, J. (1974). *The imperative of freedom: A philosophy of journalistic autonomy*. New York: Hastings House.
Miljan, L., & Cooper, B. (2003). *Hidden agendas: How journalists influence the news*. Vancouver: UBC Press.
Miller, J. (1998). *Yesterday's News: Why Canada's daily newspapers are failing us*. Halifax, NS: Fernwood Publishing.
Mills, R. (2002, July 1). Pressing for freedom. *Time*, 47.
———. (2003, January 21). CanWest plan a threat to local independence. *The Globe and Mail*, p. B11.
———. (2003, February 13–15). To what extent can or should media owners intervene in content? In *McGill Conference: Who Controls Canada's Media?* Montreal, Quebec. Retrieved November 1, 2004 from http://www.misc-mcgill.ca/media/mills.pdf
Morton, P. with Schecter B. (2003, June 3). US media gets freer rein. *Financial Post*, p. FP3.
Mowlana, H. (1986). *Global information and world communication: New frontiers in international relations*. New York: Longman.
National Newspaper Guild. (2002, June 14). Former Southam execs blast CanWest. Retrieved Nov, 4, 2004 from http://www.newsguild.org/Gr/gr_display.php?StoryID=820
Nesbitt-Larking, P. (2001). *Politics, society and the media: Canadian perspectives*. Peterborough, ON: Broadview Press.
Newman, P. (1996, June 17). Conrad Black's private agenda. *Maclean's*, 109, 25, 34.
———. (2003, December 1). The Black perils of greed. *Maclean's*, 116, 6–37.
Nimmo, D., & Combs, J. (1990). *Mediated political realities* (2nd ed.). New York: Longmans.
Nixon, R., & Jones, R. (1956). The content of non-competitive vs. competitive newspapers. *Journalism Quarterly*, 33, 299–314.
Nurse, A. (2003). A profile of Canadian regionalism. In K. Pryke & W. Soderlund (Eds.), *Profiles of Canada* (3rd ed., pp. 35–61). Toronto: Canadian Scholars' Press.

Olive, David. (2003, November 18). Black always laid the blame elsewhere. *Toronto Star*, p. E1.

Ottawa Citizen. (2002, June 1). Time to go. (Editorial), p. B6.

———. (2003, October 15). U.S. high school considers paying students to attend. p. A6.

Ottawa Citizen Staff. (2002, June 21). We simply have strong principles. *The Windsor Star*, p. D11.

Paddon, D. (2003, June 4). National Post's Ottawa bureau to be more integrated with CanWest New Service. Retrieved November 4, 2004 from http://www.cnews.canoe.ca/CNEWS/MediaNews/2003/06/04/103503-cp.html

Pannekoek, F. (2003). Canadian memory institutions and the digital revolution: The last five years. In D. Taras, F. Pannekoek, & M. Bakaardjieva (Eds.), *How Canadians Communicate* (pp.71–94). Calgary, AB: University of Calgary Press.

Parenti, M. (1997). Methods of media manipulation. *The Humanist*, 57, 5–7.

Pasadeos, Y., & Renfro, P. (1997). An appraisal of Murdoch and the U.S. daily press. *Newspaper Research Journal*, 18, 33–50.

Picard, R. (1985). *The press and the decline of democracy: The democratic socialist response in social policy*. Westport, CT: Greenwood Press.

Picard, R., & Brody, J. (1997). *The newspaper publishing industry*. Boston: Allyn and Bacon.

Pitts, G. (2002). *Kings of convergence: The fight for control of Canada's media*. Toronto: Doubleday Canada.

———. (2003, November 18). The plutocrat we love to hate. *The Globe and Mail*, p. B9.

Plopper, B. (1991). Gannett and the *Gazette*. *Newspaper Research Journal*, 12, 58–71.

Robb, P. (2001, December 14). Asper defends national editorial policy. *The Windsor Star*, p. A2.

Rogers, E., & Dearing, J. (1988). Agenda setting research: Where has it been and where is it going? In J. Anderson, (Ed.), *Communication Yearbook: Vol. 11* (pp. 555–594). Beverly Hills, CA: Sage Publications.

Romanow, W., de Repentigny, M., Cunningham, S., Soderlund, W., & Hildebrandt, K. (1999). *Television advertising in Canadian elections: The attack mode, 1993*. Waterloo, ON: Wilfrid Laurier University Press.

Romanow, W., & Love, J. (1989). Canadian newspaper front pages: A study of change. Paper presented at the Annual Meeting of the Canadian Communication Association, Université Laval.

Romanow, W., & Soderlund, W. (1978). The Southam Press acquisition of *The Windsor Star*: A Canadian case study of change. *Gazette*, 24, 255–270.

———. (1988). Thomson newspapers' acquisition of *The Globe and Mail*: A case study of content change. *Gazette*, 41, 5–17.

———. (1996). *Media Canada: An introductory analysis*. (2nd ed.). Toronto: Copp Clark.

Romanow, W., Soderlund, W., Wagenberg, R., & Briggs, E.D. (1981). Correlates of newspaper coverage of the 1979 Canadian election. In F. Fletcher (Ed.), *The newspaper and public affairs: Vol. 7. Research studies on the newspaper industry* (Appendix III). Ottawa: Supply and Services.

Russell, F. (2002, July 12). Feudal news has long tradition. *Winnipeg Free Press*, p. A14.

Rystrom, K. (1986). The impact of newspaper endorsements. *Newspaper Research Journal*, 7, 19–28.

Saunders, J., Mahood, C., & Waldie, P. (1996, June 1). Black reigns. *The Globe and Mail*, pp. B1, B3.

Schweitzer, J., & Goldman, E. (1975). Does newspaper competition make a difference to readers? *Journalism Quarterly*, 52, 706–710.

Scotton, G. (2002, April 25). Convergence opens doors for success: Media head. *The Windsor Star*, p. A9.

Seldes, G. (1941). *Lords of the press*. New York: Twentieth Century Fund.

Shapiro, L., Clift, E., Starr, M., & Abbott, N. (1988, January 18). No absence of malice. *Newsweek*, 25.

Shecter, B. (2002, January 31). Editorial policy "mischaracterized." *Financial Post*, p. FP5.

———. (2003, October 18). Bain to help Hollinger with debt, report says. *Financial Post*, p. FP3.

———. (2003, November 18). Black quits among furor. *The Windsor Star*, p. A1.

———. (2003, December 18). CanWest suing Hollinger for $25M. *Financial Post*, p. FP1.

———. (2003, December 23). Conrad Black refuses to testify to SEC. *Financial Post*, p. FP1.

———. (2004, May 8). Hollinger accuses Black of "racketeering" activities. *Financial Post*, p. FP1.

———. (2004, May 28). Black says he's still a "Darwinian capitalist." *National Post*, p. A1.

———. (2004, June 23). Barclays win Telegraph in US$1.33B deal with Hollinger. *Financial Post*, p. FP1.

———. (2004, October 2). Black threatens to raise libel suit to $1.1 billion. *Financial Post*, p. FP5.

Shecter, B., & Dabrowski, W. (2004, September 1). A corporate kleptocracy. *National Post*, p. A1.

Shecter, B., & Tedesco, T. (2003, December 9). Hollinger documents sought in U.S. *Financial Post*, p. FP5.

Shields, N., & Soderlund, W. (2001). The digitization of conflict: U.S. network TV News framing of the 1994 Zapatista rebellion in Chiapas, Mexico. Paper presented at the Conference, The Intercultural World and the Digital Connection, Rochester, NY.

Shoemaker, P., & Reese, S. (1996). *Mediating the message: Theories of influence on mass media content* (2nd ed). White Plains, NY: Longman.

Siebert, F., Peterson, T., & Schramm, W. (1956). *Four theories of the press: The authoritarian, libertarian, social responsibility and Soviet Communist concepts of what the press should be and do*. Urbana, IL: University of Illinois Press.

Siegel, A. (1983). *Politics and the media in Canada*. Toronto: McGraw-Hill Ryerson.

Silcoff, S. (2004, January 30). CanWest keen to join media buying spree. *Financial Post*, p. FP6.

Smith, A. (1990). Media globalism in the age of consumer sovereignty. *Garnett Center Journal*, 4, 1–16.

Smith, D. (2002, July/Aug.). The war of the windbags. *Canadian Dimension*, 48.

Smith, G. (2003, July 2). National Post warns it may withdraw from Canadian Press. *The Globe and Mail*, p. A14.

Soderlund, W. (1994). The impact of the Aquino assassination on the press image of Ferdinand Marcos: Transformation or amplification? *Communication Reports*, 7, 36–42.

Soderlund, W., Lee, M., & Gecelovsky, P. (2002). Trends in Canadian newspaper coverage of international news, 1988–2000: Editors' assessments. *Canadian Journal of Communication*, 27, 73–87.

Soderlund, W., Romanow, W., Briggs, E.D., & Wagenberg, R. (1984). *Media and elections in Canada*. Toronto: Holt, Rinehart and Winston.

Sokoloff, H. (2003a, October 15). Canada teens among truancy leaders: study. *National Post*, p. A1.

———. (2003b, October 15). Canadian teens like to skip class, study finds. Saskatoon *StarPhoenix*, p. A1.

———. (2003c, October 15). Canadian teens among worst truants: study. Montreal *Gazette*, p. A17.

———. (2003d, October 15). Many teens are skipping school. Regina *Leader-Post*, p. A1.

———. (2003e, October 15). 1 in 4 teens regularly skips class, report finds. *The Ottawa Citizen*, p. A6.

———. (2003f, Oct, 15). One in four teens skip school regularly—study. *Edmonton Journal*, p. A23.

———. (2003g, October 15). One in four teens skipping school. *The Windsor Star*, p. A1.

———. (2003h, October 15). A quarter of teens cut school classes. *Vancouver Sun*, p. A3.

Sokoloff, H., & Knapp, S. (2003, October 15). Canada's teens in truant mood. *Calgary Herald*, p. A1.

Soroka, S., & Fournier, P. (2003, February 11). Survey results: Newspapers in Canada pilot study. In *McGill Conference: Who Controls Canada's Media?* Montreal, Quebec. Retrieved November 4, 2004 from http://www.misc-iecm.mcgill.ca/media/results.html

Soupcoff, M. (2003, October). Could less be more? The truth about media consolidation and concentration. *Fraser Forum*, 8–10.

Southam News. (2001, April 26). Media giants pledge diverse "voices." *The Windsor Star*, p. A9.

———. (2001, Aug. 11). Canada must lead. Montreal *Gazette*, p. B6.

———. (2001, December 6). The challenge for Ottawa. Montreal *Gazette*, p. B2.

———. (2001, December 13). Private care has its place. Montreal *Gazette*, p. B2.

———. (2001, December 20). Crush the terrorists. *Edmonton Journal*, p. A14.

Southam News. (2001, December 27). Unchain our MPs. *Edmonton Journal*, p. A16.
———. (2002, January 3). Getting used to giving. Montreal *Gazette*, p. B2.
———. (2002, January 10). A right we need. *Edmonton Journal*, p. A14.
———. (2002, January 17). So much from so little. *Edmonton Journal*, p. A16.
———. (2002, January 18). Why the Alliance can't shake its redneck stereotype. *Edmonton Journal*, p. A16.
———. (2002, January 24). More than money. *Edmonton Journal*, p. A14.
———. (2002, January 29). Let the readers decide. *Edmonton Journal*, p. A10.
———. (2002, January 31). UN must change. *Edmonton Journal*, p. A18.
———. (2002, February 8). Joe's reform falls short. *Edmonton Journal*, p. A18.
———. (2002, February 14). History is our heritage. *Edmonton Journal*, p. A18.
———. (2002, February 21). National regulations. *Edmonton Journal*, p. A18.
———. (2002, February 28). Water worth exporting. *Edmonton Journal*, p. A18.
———. (2002, March 7). Serious citizens please. *Edmonton Journal*, p. A14.
———. (2002, March14). Immigration vital. *Edmonton Journal*, p. A18.
———. (2002, March 21). Just one taxpayer. *Edmonton Journal*, p. A18.
———. (2002, March 28). A worrisome ruling. *Edmonton Journal*, p. A18.
———. (2002, April 2). Apocalyptic creed. *Edmonton Journal*, p. A12.
———. (2002, April 4). Time for a long shot. *Edmonton Journal*, p. A14.
———. (2002, April 18). Our downward slide. *Edmonton Journal*, p. A18.
———. (2002, April 25). The flatter the better. *Edmonton Journal*, p. A18.
———. (2002, April 29). Tower of tax babble. *Edmonton Journal*, p. A14.
———. (2002, May 2). Protest script written. *Edmonton Journal*, p. A14.
———. (2002, May 16). France's "judéophobie." *Edmonton Journal*, p. A18.
———. (2002, May 23). A prudent move. *Edmonton Journal*, p. A18.
———. (2002, May 30). The cult of Arafat. Montreal *Gazette*, p. B2.
———. (2002, June 3). Overheated rhetoric. *Edmonton Journal*, p. A12.
———. (2002, June 4). The leadership issue. *Edmonton Journal*, p. A14.
———. (2002, June 17). Firm control on cabal. *Edmonton Journal*, p. A10.
———. (2002, June 18). Chrétien gov't denies role in Ottawa publisher's firing. *Edmonton Journal*, p. A5.
———. (2002, September 30). Liberal party needs real leadership race. *The Windsor Star*, p. A6.
———. (2002, October 26). Rate hikes risky. *Edmonton Journal*, p. A18.
St. Dizier, B. (1986). Editorial page editors and endorsements: Chain-owned vs. independent newspapers. *Newspaper Research Journal*, 8, 63–68.
Stairs, D. (1977–78). Public opinion and external affairs: Reflections on the domestication of Canadian foreign policy. *International Journal*, 33, 128–149.
Steuter, E. (1999). The Irvings cover themselves: Media representations of the Irving Oil Refinery strike, 1994–96. *Canadian Journal of Communication*, 24, 629–647.
Stolberg, S. (2003, November 25). Congress bows to veto threat on spending bill. *The New York Times*, p. A18.

Reference List

Stone, G. (1987). *Examining newspapers: What research reveals about America's newspapers*. Newbury Park, CA: Sage Publications.

Taras, D. (2001). *Power and betrayal in the Canadian media*. Updated edition. Peterborough, ON: Broadview Press.

———. (2003). Introduction: The new world of communications in Canada. In D. Taras, F. Pannekoek, & M. Baakardjieva (Eds.), *How Canadians Communicate* (pp. 9–23). Calgary, AB: University of Calgary Press.

Tedesco, T., & Shecter, B. (2004, November 16). Black hit with fraud charges. *Financial Post*, p. FP1–2.

Theobald, S. (2003, November18). Radler know as corporate slasher. *Toronto Star*, p. A6.

Thrift, R. Jr. (1977). How chain ownership affects editorial vigor of newspapers. *Journalism Quarterly*, 54, 327–331.

Toronto Star Wire Services. (2003, November 18). Media empire expected to be sold off in pieces. *Toronto Star*, p. A6.

Trim, K., Pizante, G., & Yaraskavitch, J. (1983). The effect of monopoly on the news: A before and after study of two Canadian one newspaper towns. *Canadian Journal of Communication*, 9, 33–56.

Tuck, S. (2003, Feb, 28). CanWest urges removal of ownership limits. *The Globe and Mail*, p. B4.

Twentieth Century Fund. (1972). *Press freedoms under pressure: Report of the Twentieth Century Fund Task Force on the Government and the Press*. New York: Author.

Underwood, D. (1998, January/February). It's not just in LA. *Columbia Journalism Review*, 36, 24–26.

Wackman, D., Gilmour, D., Gaziano, C., & Dennis, E. (1975). Chain newspaper autonomy as reflected in presidential campaign endorsements. *Journalism Quarterly*, 52, 411–420.

Wagenberg R., & Soderlund, W. (1975). The influence of chain-ownership on editorial content in Canada. *Journalism Quarterly*, 52, 93–98.

———. (1976). The effects of chain ownership on editorial coverage: The case of the 1974 Canadian federal election. *Canadian Journal of Political Science*, 9, 682–689.

Wagenberg, R., Soderlund, W., Romanow, W., & Briggs, E.D. (1988). Campaigns, images and polls: Mass media coverage of the 1984 Canadian election. *Canadian Journal of Political Science*, 21, 117–129.

Waite, P. (1962). *The life and times of confederation 1864–1867: Politics, newspapers and the union of British North America*. Toronto: University of Toronto Press.

Watson, P. (2003, May 5). Why we need a public newspaper. *The Globe and Mail*, p. A15.

Wells, J. (1996, November 11). Prince of papers. *MacLean's*, 109, 56–61.

———. (2003, November 18). How a peer fell from grace. *Toronto Star*, p. A1.

Wendland, M. (2001, February 21). Newspapers, TV stations and Web sites converge to create a new media entity—A news factory. *Detroit Free Press*, p. E1.

Weston, G. (2001, December 22). Memo tells *Gazette* reporters to shut up. *Edmonton Sun*, p. 4.

White, D. (1950). The "Gatekeeper": A case study on the selection of news. *Journalism Quarterly*, 27, 383–390.

Wilson, P. (2004, March 12). Consumers rule in digital age: Asper. *Financial Post*, p. FP5.

Winseck, D. (2002). Netscapes of power: Convergence, consolidation and power in the Canadian mediascape. *Media, Culture & Society*, 24, 795–819.

Winsor, H. (2001, March 7). Journalism 101: Currying favour in the new world of convergence. *The Globe and Mail*, p. A5.

———. (2002, June 19). Aspers may feel heat of backfiring after Mills firing. *The Globe and Mail*, p. A4.

———. (2002, December 18). We'd like to hear Russell Mills do the talking. *The Globe and Mail*, p. A6.

Winter, J. (1995, November). A paper king: Conrad Black ascends the throne. *Canadian Forum*, 74, p. 9.

———. (1997). *Democracy's oxygen: How corporations control the news*. Montreal: Black Rose Books.

———. (2002, May/June). Canada's media monopoly. *Extra!* Retrieved November 4, 2004 from http://www.fair.org//extra/0205/canwest/html

Zerbisias, A. (2003, November 18). Formidable news mogul fades to Black. *Toronto Star*, p. A9.

Zuckerman, M. (2003, June 23). A sure-fire recipe for trouble. *U.S. News & World Report*, p. 52.

Name Index

Amiel, Barbara (Black), 78, 85
Arafat, Yasser, 116, 119
Asper, David, 126, 135, 154 n.2
Asper, Israel (Izzy), 96
 career of, 150, 163 n.3
 commitment to social responsibility, 150
 friendship with Jean Chrétien, 163 n.3
Asper, Leonard
 acquisitions by, 104–5
 on CanWest's convergence strategy, 104–5
 on executive changes at CanWest, 99
Atkinson, Peter, 151 n.1

Babick, Donald, 98–99, 121
Bagdikian, Ben, 17
Bain, George, 123
Barclay brothers (bidders on *Daily Telegraph*, UK), 84
Bell, Lord Tim, 151 n.1
Binyon, Michael, 149
Bird, Roger, 131–32
Black, Barbara Amiel, 85
Black, Conrad. *See also* Hollinger chain (subject index)
 attitudes of
  on acquisitions, 154 n.1
  on editorial influence, 45, 47, 86, 89, 109, 112
  on newspapers as businesses, 79
  on ownership, 35, 145
 career
  Canadian Press business newsmaker, 2003, 84
  chairman and CEO of Hollinger, 45
  resignation, 82–85, 150
 divestments, xiv, 46
 downsizing, 46, 78
 editorial autonomy under, 35, 77, 81–82, 109
 editorial influence, attitudes on
  in Armadale newspapers, 45, 47
  of Hollinger newspaper holdings, 86, 89, 109, 112
 editorial influence of, xiv, 37, 45, 76, 137, 145, 156 n.6
  in Big Five newspapers, 81
  of *Daily Telegraph* (UK) 156 ch. Four n. 6
  on Regina *Leader-Post*, 47
  on Saskatoon *StarPhoenix*, 47
  in smaller newspapers, 81
 ownership, 80–82, 126, 151 n.1
  acquisitions, 45, 47, 112
  divestments, xiv, 13, 154 n.1
  Horizon Publications Inc., 84
  1995-96 major expansion, 45, 112, 123
  1999 peak, 13
  reactions to takeover by, 80–82
 and Radler, David, 81
 Winter, James on, 46
Boultbee, John, 151 n.1
Browne, Christopher, 83
Brown-John, Lloyd, 37
Bryden, John, Liberal MP, 127
Burt, Murray, 123

Calamai, Peter, 78
Camilleri, Rick, 99, 104–5,
Carlin, Vince, 43, 77–78, 93–94, 148
Chaffee, Stephen, 94
Charette, Michael, 37
Chrétien, Jean, xv
 Asper, Israel, friendship with, 163 n.3
 coverage of, 125–26
 editorial about, 36
 in national editorials
  directive to be easy on, 116
  focus on, 119
  praising, 131
  re leadership campaign, 129–30
  on retirement issue, 36, 114
Clark, Joe, 41–42, 118–19, 128
Clarkson, Adrienne, Governor General of Canada, xv
Clow, Michael, 42
Colson, David, 151 n.1
Cooper, Barry, 75–76
Copps, Sheila, Heritage Minister, 109
Corcoran, Terence, 21, 27, 143
Coyne, Andrew, 78, 163 n.4

Name Index

Dahl, Robert, 119
Dalfen, Charles, 92
Damsell, Keith, 132, 159 n.4
Desmarais, Paul, 45, 112
Dore, Kathleen, 105
Dorgan, Senator Byron, 164 n.8
Dornan, Christopher
  on circulation, 13–14
  on cross-media ownership, 96
  on Kent Commission, 112
  on local content, 121
  on *National Post*, 164 n.7
  on newspaper data, 152 n.1
  on on-line advertising, 100
  on ownership concentration, 11
  on regulation, xvi
Dryburgh, Heather, 95
Ducros, Francois, 130

Eaman, Ross, 2, 18, 25
Eckstein, Harry, 42
Estok, David, 129

Fecan, Ivan, 106
Fisher, Gordon, 132–34, 143, 149
Fletcher, Fred, 43, 153–54 n.7
Fournier, Patrick, 138
Francis, Diane, 12
Fraser, Blair, 77
Fraser, Joan, 77, 78
Fridkin Khan, Kim, 164 n.5
Fritz, Johann, 127

Gherson, Giles, 78
Goldstein, Kenneth, 91–92, 94, 95, 99, 148
Graham, Bill, Minister of Foreign Affairs, 118
Green, Graham N., 125

Hackett, Robert, xv, xvi, 11
Haddrall, Lynn, 34
Harper, Stephen, 115, 119
Harris, Mike, 68
Holman, Paul, 157 n.5

Ingram, Derek, 123

Kenney, Patrick, 164 n.5
Kent, Tom, 21, 112, 165 n.9
Key, V.O., Jr., 146, 148
Kimber, Stephen, 132
Kingston, Anne, 85
Klein, Ralph, 68
Lapointe, Kirk, 106
Luce, Henry, 2

Maich, Steve, 156–57 ch. Five n.5
Mangione, Joseph, 105
Manley, John, 119
Manning, Preston, 118
Martin, Paul, 114, 119, 130
McChesney, Robert, 9, 11, 92–93, 141
McDonough, Alexa, NDP leader, 127
McQuaig, Linda, on power of the elite, 32
Merrill, John, 5–8
Metzger, Miriam, 94
Miljan, Lydia, 75–76
Miller, John, 11, 25, 77, 78, 126
Mills, Russell
  firing of, 111, 121–22, 125, 142
    Aspers on, 126, 128
    effects of, 128, 129
    public enquiry into, 129
    reasons for, 126–27
    responses to, xv, 123, 127–29, 142
  honourary degree of, 126
  and Jean Chrétien, 128, 163 n.3
  views of
    on diversity, 132
    on editorial influence, 133, 144, 146
    on importance of local voices, 133
    on public right to information, 135
Monty, Jean, 96, 98, 156–57 ch. Five n.4
Mulroney, Brian, xv, 25, 118
Murdoch, Peter, 132
Murdoch, Rupert, 77, 157 n.6

Nesbitt-Larking, Paul, 146–47
Newman, Peter, 123
Nobel, Gerry, 99

Pasadeos, Yorgo, 77
Peladeau, Pierre-Karl, 96
Peterson, Theodore, 1, 4, 5, 152 n.1
Picard, Robert, 6, 8–9
Pitts, Gordon, 89, 96, 156 ch. Five n.4
Pizante, Gary, 37
Pyman, Heather, 164 n.7

Radler, David
  on controlling papers' content, 35
  exercising control for Black, Conrad, 81
  as head of Horizon Publications, 151 n.1

and Horizon Publications Inc., 84
ownership of Ravelston Corp., 151 n.1
Renfro, Paula, 77
Reynolds, Neil, 36
Rock, Alan, 119
Rogers, Ted, 96

Sabia, Michael, 98, 156–57 ch. Five n.5
Schramm, Wilbur, 1
Seldes, George, 165 n.11
Shaw family, 96
Siebert, Fred, 1
Siegel, Arthur, 25–26
Sifton family, 45
Smith, Anthony, 89
Soroka, Stuart, 138
Soupcoff, Marni, 92–93, 95–96, 123–24
Southam, William, 112
Stanfield, Robert, 41
Steuter, Erin, 42–43

Taras, David, 90–91, 93, 96, 103, 147
Thomson, Kenneth, 40
Travers, James, 78, 126
Trim, Katherine, 37
Trudeau, Pierre, 18, 41–42

Watson, Patrick, 152 n.4
Whyte, Kenneth, 78–79
Williams, Michael, 105
Winsor, Hugh, 135
Winter, James, 31, 46

Yaraskavich, James, 37
Young, Christopher, 77

Zhao Yuezhi, xv, xvi
Zuckerman, Mortimer, 164 n.8

Subject Index

abuse of power. *See also* power
  by corporations, 20
  by governments, 4, 148
  potential for
    of chain ownership, 43, 128, 141
    through technology, 144
  threats to diversity of voices by, 106–7
  through convergence, 103, 128, 144
accountability, 4, 19
advertising
  and convergence, 102
  and monopoly, 38–39
  and newspaper profitability, 8
  on-line, 100–101
  revenue, and the magazine industry, 152 n.3
Alliance/Reform party, 118–19
AOL/Time Warner, 90–91, 98, 157 n.6
Armadale chain, 23, 45, 47
Asper family. *See also Asper entries* (name index); CanWest conglomerate; national editorial policy
  Asper Foundation, 116
  convergence, faith in, 104
  editorial control taken by, 109, 119, 129, 138
  editorial influence by, 36, 133, 142
  on Mills, Russell, firing of, 126, 128
Atlantic Canada, 14, 41, 57
audience, 91–92, 94–95, 103

BCE (Bell Canada Enterprises), xiv, 96
  and CanWest Global Communications, xiv, 96–97
  and cross-media ownership, 97, 156 ch. Five n.3
  and francophone newspapers, 98
  holdings
    Bell ExpressVu, 98
    Bell Globemedia, 96, 97, 156–57 ch. Five n.5
    CTV, 96, 106, 156–57 ch. Five n.5
    ExpressVu satellite TV, 96
    Sympatico-Lycos Internet portal, 96
    Telesat, 96
    VMP.com, 96
    YellowPages.ca, 96, 156 n.3
Bill C-58 (Income Tax Act), xvi, 152 n.3, 158 Six n.1
Black, Conrad (name index). *See also* Hollinger chain
Bloc Quebecois, 119
Boston Globe, 133
branding, 120–21, 130
British Royal Commission on the Press, 18
bundling, 157 n.7

Calgary Herald, 47, 51, 112, 120, 154 n.2
Canada.com, 89, 96
Canada Newspaper Act, 22
Canadian Alliance Party, 115, 119
Canadian Association of Journalists, 128
Canadian Community Newspaper Association, 91
Canadian Dimension, 45
Canadian Journalists for Free Expression, 128, 158 n.3
Canadian Newspaper Association, 17, 98, 121, 152 n.1
Canadian Press, 84, 132–33
CanWest conglomerate. *See also* Asper family; national editorial policy
  acquisitions by, 86, 89, 109, 112
  audience, 91–92
  and Canadian Press news co-operative, 132–33
  convergence
    as conglomerate, 46, 89, 97
    cross-media ownership, xiv, 96, 97
    motivations, 157 n.8
    strategy, 104–5
  cost-cutting measures, 133
  editorial autonomy under, 109, 110, 131–34, 158 n.3
  editorial control by, 138, 141–42
    firing of Russell Mills, xv, 142
    on-line tracking of journalists, 132
    retirement of "publisher" position, 133
  editorial influence of, 117–18, 120, 147
  holdings
    CanWest Global Communications, xiv, 46
    CanWest MediaWorks, 104–5

CanWest News Service, xv, 131, 133–34, 142
CanWest Publications, 130
Global TV, 96, 99
Southam, 98–99
and Hollinger, xiv, 83, 86, 89, 109, 112
restructuring, 105
Cardinal Capital Management, 83
Carleton University, 126
censorship, 123
Charlottetown *Guardian*, 47, 50–51
Charter of Rights and Freedoms, xvi, 147, 148, 163 n.4
Chicago Group, 151 n.1
Chicago Sun-Times, 84, 86, 151 n.1
circulation, 13–14, 92, 97, 128
Clarity Act, 131
Clow, Michael, 42
collusion, 21
Combines Investigations Act, 1980, 112
Commission on Freedom of the Press, xv, 2–4, 9, 18,
common good. *See* public good
Community Group, 151 n.1
concentration, ownership. *See also* convergence, ownership
Davey Committee on, 13
Dornan, Christopher on, 11
effects of, 25, 32, 34
Kent Commission on, 22
level in Canada, 4, 8, 11, 13, 16–17, 45
as newspaper chains, xiv
strategies to deal with, 25
content, 35, 93–94. *See also* national editorial policy; *individual newspapers*
factors influencing, 43, 80, 81, 120
costs, 95
cross-media sharing, 99
editorial control, 35, 91, 119, 144
personnel decisions, 78
region, 40
technology, 144
convergence, ownership. *See also* Asper family; BCE; Black, Conrad (name index); CanWest conglomerate; cross-media
and AOL/Time Warner, 90–91
consequences of, xiv, 89, 103, 106
and diversity, 109, 144
and fragmentation of communications, 157 n.8
future of, 103–4
and Kent Commission, 23
key figures in, 96
motivations for, xiv, 89, 91, 94, 95, 157 n.8
types
functional, 99
horizontal, 104–5
of news and entertainment, 91
vertical, 104–5
variation across Canada, 98
corporate branding, 120–21
Corporate Kleptocracy, A, 85
costs, media, 19, 24, 95, 106–7, 133
coverage
business, 58–59
economic, 47, 53–55
free trade, 47, 56–58
labour, 47, 59–62, 137
political, 39, 40–41, 47, 63
in Atlantic Canada, 41
in ex-Armadale papers, 53
in ex-Southam papers, 55
in ex-Thomson papers, 52–53
by independents, 41
in individual newspapers, 39, 40, 53, 55
negative, effect on democratic system, 73
shifts in, 40–41, 71, 73, 159 n.8
of political parties, 56, 63–65, 67, 70
social, 54–55
cross-media. *See also* convergence, ownership
advertising, 46, 99, 102–4
content sharing, 99, 102, 104
culture differences, 102
integration, 96, 104–5, 106, 132, 163 n.4
monitoring, 101
ownership, xiv, xvi, 97–99
staffing, 99
CRTC (Canadian Radio-television and Telecommunications Commission)
on access to Internet, 92
against bundling, 157 n.7
on Canadian content, xv-xvi
on license renewals, 106
on ownership, xv-xvi, 89, 163 n.4
CTV, 96, 106, 156–57 ch. Five n.5

Daily Telegraph (UK), 84, 151 n.1, 156 ch. Four n.6
Davey Committee, xiv, 13, 18–20, 25, 152 n.3
  reactions to, 25
demassification of the media, 94
democracy, 8, 31
  and citizens' need for information, 9, 12, 31
  convergence as threat to, 32, 34, 45
  critical elements for, 148
  and national editorial policy, 111
  negative political coverage, effect of, 73
  newspapers' essential role in, 8–9, 24, 31
  Standing Senate Committee on Transport and Communication on, 12
Democracy's Oxygen, 31
deregulation, xv–xvi, 109, 147, 162 n.1. *See also* regulation
Le Devoir, Montreal, 17, 138

diversity
  need for, 103, 132, 135, 149
  paucity of, 8, 93–94
  perspectives on, 82, 132
  protecting, 109, 141
  reduction of, 162–63 n.2
  restrictions on, 32
  and social responsibility, 144, 147
  threats to, 106–7, 127

editorial advisory committees, 24
editorial autonomy. *See also* freedom of the press
  under Black, Conrad, 81, 109
  under CanWest, 109–10, 131–34, 158 n.3
  under chain ownership, 34
  erosion of, 162–63 n.2
  at *Globe and Mail*, 40
  journalists' views on, 139
  protecting, 148
  public views on, 140
editorial control
  by Black, Conrad, 156 ch. Four n.6
  under CanWest, 138, 141, 142
  by setting expectations, 142
  through budgets, 142
  through personnel changes, 142
editorial influence, xiii, 34, 80
  in Armadale newspapers, 45, 47
  by Aspers, 36, 133, 142, 154 n.2
  by Black, Conrad, 45, 76, 137, 145
  and Kent Commission, 23
  news, need for exemption from, 138
  on newspaper content
    Globe and Mail, 138
    Montreal, Le Journal de, 138
    Montreal *Gazette*, 138
    Montreal *La Presse*, 138
    Saint John *Telegraph-Journal*, 35–36
    Vancouver Sun, 138
  potential for, 119
Edmonton Journal, 112, 130
elections, federal, xiii, 25, 40, 41, 120
elite, power of, 2, 7–8, 12, 32, 93
Environics, 139–40
ExpressVu satellite TV, 96

Financial Post, 21–22, 132
Four Theories of the Press, xiv, 1–2, 5, 152 n.1
fragmentation
  audience, 103
  of communications, 94, 143
  convergence as a response to, 94, 157 n.8
framing, xiii, 32, 153 n.1
Fredericton *Daily Gleaner*, 42
freedom of the press
  and *Charter of Rights and Freedoms*, xvi, 147, 163 n.4
  Commission on Freedom of the Press on, 2
  dangers facing, xv, 3, 4, 20, 129
  and democracy, 3, 9
  and editorial autonomy, 110–11, 122, 127, 165 n.11
  and owner responsibility, 5
  perspectives on, 21–24, 148
  protecting, xv, 24
Free Press (FP) chain, 17, 40, 42
Free Trade Agreement (FTA), xv

Gallup, 1992, 95
gatekeeping, xv, 32, 142, 153 n.1
Global TV, 96, 99
Globe and Mail, xiii–xiv
  coverage
    of Black's resignation, 84–85
    business, 59
    of CanWest restructuring, 105
    political, 40
    social, 55
  difficulties at, 156–57 ch. Five n.5
  editorial autonomy at, 40, 158–59 n.5

editorial influence at, 138
and Kent Commission, 12, 23
ownership of, 12, 42, 96
Thomson, Kenneth on, 40
Groupe Videotron, Le, 96

Halifax *Chronicle-Herald*, 48, 53, 57, 70, 152 n.1
Halifax Herald Company, 152 n.1
Hamilton Spectator, 112
Hollinger chain. *See also* Black, Conrad (name index)
acquisitions, 45, 47, 112, 154 n.1, 155 n.3
divestments, 13, 46
Hollinger Board of Directors Committee, 83, 85
Hollinger Inc., 83–84, 86, 151 n.1
Hollinger International, 83, 85–86, 151 n.1
Hollinger ownership, xiv
ownership, 35, 45
structure of, 151 n.1
House of Commons Standing Committee on Canadian Heritage, 162 n.1
Hutchins Commission. *See* Commission on Freedom of the Press
hypotheses, 46–47
Imperative of Freedom, 5–6
independent newspapers, 13, 17, 41
indexing, xv
Interim Report on the Canadian News Media. *See* Standing Senate Committee...
International Press Institute (IPI), 127
Internet
Canadians' access to, 92, 95–96
and convergence, 89, 97, 132, 157 n.6
editorial control through, 132, 144
effects on newspaper industry, 95, 154 n.3
effect on revenues, 100–101
newspapers on-line, 91, 99–100
media presence on, 89, 96
Irving chain, 23, 36, 42

Jerusalem Post, 84, 86, 105–6, 151 n.1
Le Journal de Montreal, 138
journalists
characteristics of, 81, 135, 153 Two n.5
and national editorial policy, 111, 129, 158 n.2
self-censorship of, 35–36, 110, 127, 128, 139
as shapers of coverage, 75, 144
and television, 102
tracking of, under CanWest, 132
views of
on editorial autonomy, 139
importance of, 75–76
on owner influence on content, 138
surveys of, 138–40, 162–63 n.2

Kent Commission, xiv, 21–25
creation of, 18, 112
effect on media companies, 112
key statements of, 12, 21–24
perspectives on, 21, 25–26, 27, 112
reactions to, 25
recommendations of
divestment strategy of, 23
editorial advisory committees, 24
freezing of chain size, 12
National Press Rights Panel, 24
proposal for a Canada Newspaper Act, 18
refusal of license renewal, 12
for regulation, 25
value of, 18
and regions, 23
report to, 43
Kings of Convergence, 103
Kingston Whig-Standard, 34

Libel and Slander Act of Ontario, 85
Liberal government, xv, 24–25
Liberal Party
coverage of, 42
in ex-Armadale papers, 63–64
in ex-Southam papers, 65–66
in ex-Thompson papers, 63
in the Prairies, 63–64
in Free Press (FP) chain, 40
in national editorials, 116, 118, 119, 129–30
libertarian approach, 1–2, 5
local content, 50–52, 121
local coverage
decreasing, 46–47
importance of, 158 n.3
importance of community to, 51–52, 81, 120
lack of, 164 n.8
in Southam newspapers, 153 n.5
local news imperative, 76, 133
local staff, 46–47, 52, 77, 81

Maclean's, 99
magazine industry, 152 n.3
Manitoba Telecom, 156–57 ch. Five n.5
market share, 97
Marxist theory, 7, 27
mass media
  and democracy, xiii, xv, 149
  and public service, 9
  role of, in shaping news, 32
  and society, xvi, 3
McGill Institute for the Study of Canada, 138–39, 143
Media and Elections in Canada, 41
Media Canada: An Introductory Analysis, xiii, 19
Médias Transcontinental, 14
Mirkaei Tikshoret Group (MTL), 105
monopolies
  breaking up of, 23
  Davey Committee on, 13
  inevitability of, 8, 19, 23, 32
  and power, 1
  regional, 17–18, 98
  study of, 37–39
Montreal, *Le Devoir*, 17, 138
Montreal, Le Journal de, 138
Montreal, *La Presse*, 138
Montreal *Gazette*, 47, 51, 78, 110, 138, 158 n.2

national editorial policy. *See also under Asper family; under* CanWest conglomerate; Mills, Russell (name index)
  defence of, 110–11
  editorials, 113
    on Arafat, Yasser, 116, 119
    on Chrétien, Jean, 36, 114, 116, 119, 121–22, 129–31
    on Clark, Joe, 118–19
    intent of, 113, 121
    personal views in, 117
    on political parties, 118–19
  effects of, 111, 123, 135
  responses to, 122
    Black, Conrad on, 123
    crystallization of opposition, 127
    from the press, 110, 134–35
    Soupcoff, Marni on, 123–24
  and Southam, 109
  timing of, 111, 129, 131, 137–38, 160 n.6
national editorial policy study
  research methods, 113
  research questions, 111
National Guild of Canadian Media, 162–63 n.2
National Post
  Aspers, under, 99–100, 132, 158 n.2, 159 n.6
  Black, Conrad, under, 78, 84, 99, 112, 133
  Dornan, Christopher on, 164 n.7
  editorial influence at, 138, 154 n.2
  on-line, 99–100
Netgraphe, 96
New Democratic Party (NDP), 18, 47, 56, 63–64, 66–70, 119
newspapers
  as businesses, 33, 45, 79, 123, 149, 150
  as drivers of other media, xiv
  French-language, ownership of, 156 ch. Five n.3
  as local institutions, 121
  on-line, 99–100
  as public service, 33
  size of, 51
newspapers (Canadian)
  Big Five, 81, 112
  Calgary Herald, 47, 51, 112, 154 n.2
  Charlottetown *Guardian*, 47, 50–51
  Edmonton Journal, 112, 130
  Financial Post, 21–22, 132
  Fredericton Daily Gleaner, 42
  Globe and Mail (see individual listing)
newspapers (Canadian) *(continued)*
  Halifax *Chronicle-Herald*, 48, 53, 57, 152 n.1
  Hamilton Spectator, 112
  Kingston Whig-Standard, 34
  Montreal, *Le Devoir*, 17, 138
  Montreal, Le Journal de, 138
  Montreal, *La Presse*, 138
  Montreal *Gazette*, 47, 51, 78, 110, 138, 158 n.2
  National Post (see individual listing)
  Ottawa Citizen (see individual listing)
  Ottawa *Journal*, 21, 112
  Ottawa Tribune, 17–18, 21, 112
  Saskatoon *StarPhoenix*, 47, 51, 120
  Toronto Star, 42, 48, 51, 55, 59, 138
  Windsor Star (see individual listing)
  Winnipeg Free Press (see individual listing)
  Winnipeg Tribune, 17–18, 21, 112
newspapers (foreign)
  Boston Globe, 133
  Chicago Sun-Times, 84, 86, 151 n.1
  Daily Telegraph (UK), 84, 151 n.1, 156 ch. Four n.6

Jerusalem Post, 84, 86, 105–6, 151 n.1
New York Times, 133
no contradiction policy. See national editorial policy
North American Free Trade Agreement (NAFTA), xv–xvi

Osprey Media Group, 14, 83
Ottawa, 17–18, 21, 81
Ottawa Citizen, 51
Chrétien, Jean, 125–26, coverage of
content of, 120, 142
editorial influence, 138, 146
Mills, Russell, firing of, 111, 121–22, 125, 128, 142
on-line, 99–100
ownership of, 37–39, 47, 112, 126
Ottawa Journal, 21, 112
Ottawa Tribune, 17–18, 21, 112
ownership. See also concentration, ownership; convergence, ownership
Canadian, xv–xvi, 11, 109, 152 n.3
chain, xiv, 13, 17, 34, 78, 153–54 n.7
changes in, 13, 152 n.1
editorial influence, xiii, 25–26, 45
desire for, 138
on news, 32–35, 134, 140, 145
through personnel decisions, 35
ethical issues of, 123
guidelines for, 23, 145, 146
motivation, 45, 95
obligations of, 2, 146
Commission on Freedom of the Press on, 2, 145
freedom of the press, 5
to maximize diversity of voices, 144
public good, 10, 26, 149
and social responsibility, 145, 146, 148
regional, 14
regulation of, 89, 152 n.3
rules of, 22

Parti Quebecois, 68
Politics and the Media in Canada, 25
power. See also abuse of power
centre of, 1
of the elite, 2, 7–8, 32, 93
and monopoly, 1
Press and the Decline of Democracy, 8–9
press councils, 19, 26
La Presse, Montreal, 138
press ownership review board, 19–20
Press Rights Panel, National, 24
press systems
authoritarian, 1
democratic, 1–2
democratic socialist, 9
developmental, 6
libertarianism, 5
revolutionary, 6
social responsibility (see individual listing)
Soviet Communist, 1
priming, 32, 153 n.1, xv
Progressive Conservative government, 25, xv
Progressive Conservative party
coverage of, 41–42, 47, 56, 63–64, 66–70
in national editorials, 118–19
response to firing of Russell Mills, 128
in Winnipeg Free Press, 67
protection
of Canada's magazine industry, 19
of Canadian culture, xv, 158 n.1
of Canadian ownership, 109, 162 n.1
of diversity of voices, 109, 141
of editorial autonomy, 148
of freedom of the press, xv, 24
publications development loan fund, 19
public good, xv, 2, 8, 9, 12, 22, 24, 31, 145, 149
balance with business interests, 150
and Davey Committee, 19, 20
right to information, 135
public trust, 149, 165 n.9

quality of journalism
and chain ownership, 23, 25–26, 34
and convergence, 106–7, 139
and costs, 24
erosion of, 162–63 n.2
perspectives on
Black, Conrad, 82
Carlin, Vince, 78
Haddrall, Lynn, 34
Kent Commission, 22, 24
Soupcoff, Marni, 93
at Southam, 112
and tax incentives, 24
Quebecor, xiv, 96, 97, 98, 156 n.3

Radler formula, 78, 155 n.1
Ravelston Corp., 83, 86, 151 n.1

Subject Index

Reform party
coverage of, 47, 56, 63–66
in national editorials, 118
Regina *Leader-Post*, 47, 51
regulation, 163 n.4. *See also* CRTC; deregulation
failure of commissions to stimulate, 18
freedom of the press, interfering with, 20, 26–27, 32, 141
and government, 25
need for, 3, 8
and newspapers, xvi, 24–25
on ownership, 22, 89, 144, 152 n.3, 163 n.4
perspectives on, xv, 5, 90, 139–45
Carlin, Vince on, 148
Corcoran, Terence, 143
Dornan, Christopher, xvi
Fisher, Gordon, 143
Key, V.O., Jr., 146
Taras, David, 93
Report of the Commission on Freedom of the Press, xiv, 145
Report of the Special Senate Committee on Mass Media. *See* Davey Committee
Revelston Corp., 85
Rich Media, Poor Democracy, 11
rights, moral, 5
rights, natural, 2
rights of media owners
to control content, 122, 135, 141–42
to control their property, xiii, xvi, 9, 140
Kent Commission on, 21
rights of the public
to access mass communications, xiii, 9
to control mass communications, xiii
to information, xvi, 21, 135, 141, 145
Rogers Communications, 97, 157 n.7
Royal Commission on Newspapers. *See* Kent Commission
rule of five, 22–23

Saint John *Telegraph-Journal*, 35–36, 42
Saskatoon *StarPhoenix*, 47, 51, 120
Saturday Night, 78
self-regulation, 148
Senate, Canadian, 128–29. *See also* Standing Senate Committee on Transport and Communication
social responsibility, 22, 148
Asper, Israel (Izzy), commitment to, 150
Commission on Freedom of the Press on, xv, 2, 4
in democratic mass media systems, 1, 2
development of term, 152 n.1
and diversity, 147
in *Four Theories of the Press*, xiv
Hutchins Commission on, 151–52 n.1
Kent Commission on, 22–24
libertarianism, as opposed to, 5
owner self-regulation for, 148
in *Report of the Commission on Freedom of the Press*, xiv
validity of, 147
violations of, 149
Southam chain, 98–99, 159 n.4, xiii
as business, 121, 130, 133, 155 n.3
and Combines Investigations Act, 1980, 112
history of, 112, 131–33, 159 n.4
local news in, 153 n.5
and national editorial policy, 109, 129
newspapers, 40–41
Big Five under, 112
Kingston Whig-Standard, 34
Ottawa Citizen, 21
Windsor Star, 39
ownership, 46
by CanWest Global Communications, 46
decreasing holdings, 13
by Hollinger, 45, 47, 112
monopoly, 17–18, 21
quality of journalism at, 112
Soviet Communist press system, 1
Special Senate Committee on Mass Media. *See* Davey Committee
St. John's *Evening Telegram*, 47, 50–51
Standing Senate Committee on Transport and Communication, xiv, 12
on Canadian access to Internet, 92, 96
on democracy, 12
on evolution of ownership, 13
on Mills, Russell, firing of, 128–29
presentations to, 43, 152 n.4
and public trust, 165 n.9
surveys of journalists, 162–63 n.2
Statistics Canada, 95
Sun chain, 72, 96, 156 n.3

tax, Income Tax Act (Bill C-58), xvi, 24, 152 n.3, 158 Six n.1

Teleglobe, 156 ch. Five n.4
Telus Corp, 156–57 ch. Five n.5
Thomson chain, xiii
  and Combines Investigations Act, 112
  and Kent Commission, 23
  newspapers
    Charlottetown *Guardian*, 47
    Globe and Mail, 17, 39–40, 158–59 n.5
    St. John's *Evening Telegram*, 47
    Winnipeg Free Press, 21
  ownership
    decreasing, 13
    domination, 12
    of Free Press (FP) chain, 17
    by Hollinger, 45, 47
    Kent Commission recommendations for, 12
    monopoly, 17–18, 21
Time Inc., 2
Time Warner, 157 n.6
top-down rule, 1
Toronto Star, 42, 48, 51, 55, 59, 138
Torstar, 97, 112
transnational media empires, 89
TVA network, 96, 156 n.3
Tweedy, Browne, 82–83

UK Newspaper Group, 151 n.1
University of Windsor, 72
U.S. Federal Communications Commission (FCC), 164 n.8
U.S. News & World Report, 164 n.8
U.S. Twentieth Century Fund Task Force on the Government and the Media, 141

Vancouver *Province*, 112
Vancouver Sun, 47, 51, 106, 138
VMP.com, 96

Washington Post, 110
Western International Communications, 96
Who Controls Canada's Media? conference, 138–39, 143
Windsor group, xiii
Windsor Star, xiii, xiv
  national editorials in, 130, 131
  owner influence on, 154 n.2
  under Southam, 39
Winnipeg, xv, 17–18, 21. *See also* Asper family; CanWest conglomerate
Winnipeg Free Press
  coverage by, 55, 57, 67
  as monopoly, 21, 37–39, 112
  right-left shift in, 71
Winnipeg Tribune, 17–18, 21, 112

YellowPages.ca, 96, 156 n.3